Placing herself in the avid reader's chair, Linda Wagner-Martin writes about women's biography from George Eliot and Virginia Woolf to Eleanor Roosevelt and Margaret Mead, and even to Cher and Elizabeth Taylor. Along the way, she looks at dozens of other life stories, probing at the differences between biographies of men and women, prevailing stereotypes about women's lives and roles, questions about what is public and private, and the hazy margins between autobiography, biography, and other genres. In quick-paced and wide-ranging discussions, she looks at issues of authorial stance (who controls the narrative? who chooses which story to tell?), voice (is this story told in the traditional objective tone? and if it is, what effect does that telling have on our reading?), and the politics of publishing (why aren't more books about women's lives published? and when they are, what happens to their advertising budgets?). She discusses the problems of writing biography of achieving women who were also wives (how does the biographer balance the two?), of daughters who attempt to write about their mothers, and of husbands trying to portray their wives. Amid the current controversy over biography

(continued on back flap)

Telling Women's Lives

Telling Women's Lives

The New Biography

Linda Wagner-Martin

Rutgers University Press
New Brunswick, New Jersey

Excerpts from "Why We Tell Stories" by Lisel Mueller reprinted by permission of Louisiana State University Press from *The Need to Hold Still* by Lisel Mueller. Copyright © 1980 by Lisel Mueller.

Library of Congress Cataloging-in-Publication Data
Wagner-Martin, Linda.
    Telling women's lives : the new biography / Linda Wagner-Martin.
      p.   cm.
    Includes bibliographical references and index.
    ISBN 0-8135-2092-4
    1. Biography as a literary form. 2. Women—Biography—
Methodology.   I. Title.
CT22.W34   1994
808′ .06692—dc20   93-42403
                                                    CIP

British Cataloging-in-Publication information available

This book is intended for all readers who tell stories as a way of negotiating their way through life. Its focus is writing by women—all kinds of writing—but its particular emphasis is the work being done in women's biography, a most undervalued and largely unstudied form of writing. Because the images and stereotypes that dominate any study of women and their writing in today's culture have—for the most part—originated in literature, my discussion draws on much women's writing besides biography.

It is dedicated with love to two of my favorite storytellers, Andrea Wagner and Cathy N. Davidson.

Contents

Preface

Like most books, this one began with a personal experience. In the early 1980s, when I decided to write a new biography of Sylvia Plath, the American poet and fiction writer whose *Ariel* and *The Bell Jar* have had a lasting impact on both American literature and American women's lives, I never dreamed I was about to undergo what would appear to be a personality change. From being a moderate university professor and the author of many quietly respectable academic books about American literature, I became an "unethical" commercial writer who was supposedly willing to malign Plath's husband and family in the effort to write her biography—and a radical women's libber, as some British critics liked to say, to boot.

Battered from dealings with the hostile estate, which remains under the control of Plath's then-estranged husband, Ted Hughes—now the poet laureate of England—because their divorce at the time of her suicide was not final, I was first bewildered and then amazed at the lambasting some British reviewers attempted to give *Sylvia Plath, A Biography.* I had written as careful, as accurate, as interesting a biography as I could. I had corresponded or talked with nearly two hundred people who had known Plath during her thirty years. I had had the cooperation of her mother and close family friends. I had read thousands of letters, written to Plath or by her, and thousands more pages of her manuscripts. How could such a book be either unscholarly or unscrupulous?

And, the corollary question, who was this woman who was under siege by the British critics? I asked my husband and children, students and friends: was I the same Linda Wagner-Martin they had always known? Their answers reassured me. I had not changed, but my life had *been* changed in the process of writing Sylvia Plath's life. Telling a woman's life had become a dangerous cultural and literary project. That was in 1987. In 1988 Carolyn Heilbrun's *Writing a Woman's Life* asked key questions about ways

of portraying the life experiences of women and started the dialogue that led to Blanche Wiesen Cook's 1991 comment in *Ms.*
that "feminist women have revolutionized biography. We ask different questions, perceive different issues, look for secrets, and
take seriously issues of lust or passion." What Cook saw as positive growth was itself challenged, and in 1993 Janet Malcolm's
highly subjective exploration of the various Plath biographies—
and biographers—recast a number of issues about biography in
general. Her sixty-three-thousand-word essay capped a series of
reviews and commentaries by various writers questioning both the
place of biography in the literary world and the boundaries of
its genre (consider Joe McGinniss's fictionalized telling of Edward
Kennedy's life).

By 1994 much of the literary world has realized that telling
certain women's lives has become so dangerous that writers must
think twice before undertaking the task. From publishers' decisions about what works to print, to reviewers' decisions about
which books to notice, to bookstores' decisions about which biographies to stock, the process of any manuscript's becoming a book
and finding readers is complex in both economic and political
terms.

Telling Women's Lives tries to put the writing of biography, and
the criticism of women's writing, into the wider context of all kinds
of writing by women. At issue is the way literary history has sometimes prevented women from telling stories—their own, those of
their female friends and relatives, and those narratives of women's
lives that they have created from their rich imaginations. In chapters about women's fiction and autobiography, I discuss the work
of Kate Chopin, Lillian Hellman, Sandra Cisneros, Virginia Woolf,
Alice Walker, Edith Wharton, and others, hoping to meld the
forms of autobiography, biography, short story, novel, drama, and
poem into the larger category of writing by women. Genre divisions collapse under the weight of pervasive themes in women's
writing. The problem of being recognized as someone's daughter,
someone's wife, or someone's mother rather than as oneself, is a
recurrent motif; another is society's reaction to a woman's ambition—whether she is denigrated or applauded for it. A third is a
woman's struggle both to fit into her family and her community
and to avoid the restrictions that those entities might create for

her. Still another is a woman's attempt to balance the demands of loved ones against her individual needs.

Telling Women's Lives is intended to be a modest contribution to the reassessment of the work of the hundreds of women writers who have made such a difference in our conception of what women's stories—and women's lives—have been and are becoming.

Acknowledgments

Friendships with other women biographers—especially Emily Toth and Shari Benstock—made my thinking about all these matters more fruitful. I owe them a debt, as I do my editor Leslie Mitchner, whose advice and encouragement was essential throughout the project. For many kinds of help, thanks also to Melva Boyd, Sharon O'Brien, E. M. Broner, Susan Fromberg Schaeffer, Thadious Davis, Diane Wood Middlebrook, Kelly Cannon, and Sally Greene.

One section of this work appeared in different form in *Narrative* 1 (Fall 1993), and I thank James Phelan for his permission to reprint it.

I wish to thank the National Endowment for the Humanities for the senior fellowship that allowed me to finish other projects and have time for this one, as well as the Rockefeller Study Center in Bellagio, Italy, and its wonderful staff, where this work took shape. And thanks as always to my supportive family, who pretend not to notice when books have invaded all our living space.

Because the story of our life
becomes our life

because each of us tells
the same story
but tells it differently

and none of us tells it
the same way twice. . . .

Lisel Mueller,
"Why We Tell Stories"

Telling Women's Lives

Introduction

Throughout literate history and even before it, people have written, or told, biographies. The lives of real people have always been more interesting than stories about fictional characters; we may temporarily believe in the exploits of imaginary human beings, but biography wears better. From the time of the 1579 translations of Plutarch's *Parallel Lives* through Izaak Walton's *Life of John Donne* (1640) and, in this country, Cotton Mather's 1702 *Magnalia Christi Americana*, his studies of famous New Englanders, readers have found in biography both entertainment and moral instruction.

Modern biography in the English-speaking world began with James Boswell's *Life of Samuel Johnson* in 1791. Diligent as he was about copying down Dr. Johnson's witty conversations, Boswell became a metaphor for the dedicated biographer—one who lives to make the record of another's life an art. He also learned at the source, as he studied Johnson's ideas about literature and art, for the great Johnson himself began writing his own *Lives of the Poets* in 1779. But while Boswell was creating Dr. Johnson, in 1771 in the States, Benjamin Franklin was creating himself: *The Autobiography of Benjamin Franklin*, unfinished at the time of his death, appeared in 1818. Throughout American literary history, autobiography has been a more appealing form than biography, and innumerable narratives of religious conversion, slavery, travel, captivity, and other exploits were written and published. Some of these were written by women; more often, the writer was a man.

While Americans wrote autobiography with relish, biography in the States grew slowly and continued to imitate the genre as it was written in England. *Biography* meant stories about the lives of prominent male subjects, written with an emphasis on the external and usually historical events of their lives, praising the subjects rather than questioning their characters. Biographers were often men, and their subjects were nearly always male. When American women did write biography, as Lydia Maria Child did during the 1830s and Elizabeth Ellet did twenty years after that, their work was often considered inferior. When Julia Ward Howe published *Margaret Fuller* (1889), Ednah D. Cheny, *Louisa May Alcott, Her Life, Letters and Journals* (1889), Alice Brown, *Mercy Warren* (1896), or Annie Fields, *Life and Letters of Harriet Beecher Stowe* (1897), reviews of their biographies were mixed. Women writing about women were somehow suspect. Even later, when Laura E. Richards and Maude Howe Elliott won the 1917 Pulitzer Prize in biography for *Julia Ward Howe*, their biography of their mother, male critics did not take the writing of women biographers seriously. Yet these biographers often presented vivid accounts of their subjects' characters, motivations, and inner lives. Readers felt that the biographers cared about their subjects.

Had critics noticed what women biographers wrote about their subjects—even during the nineteenth century—the so-called revolution in biography might have come earlier. As it was, literary history claims the modernization of the form for a male, British biographer Lytton Strachey. In his *Eminent Victorians* (1918) and *Queen Victoria* (1921), Strachey moved from writing hagiography of the famous and great to showing his subjects as human beings, flawed, lusty, and susceptible to flattery. In the States, Gamaliel Bradford's attempts to build what he called a "psychograph" of the subject, through prodigious research, paralleled Strachey's inclusive method. Among Bradford's works were such collections of biographies of women as *Portraits of Women*, *Portraits of American Women*, and *Daughters of Eve*, published between 1916 and 1930; in 1931 *Jenny Lind*, a biography by his student Edward C. Wagenknecht, showed the psychograph method in a longer format. These works helped to create a more welcoming climate for the reception of women's biographies as well.

This change to more psychoanalytic biography attracted women writers, as well as women readers, and during the 1920s, with Freud's theories of repressed sexuality underlying most discussions of character, women were writing biographies of women subjects with élan. In 1920 Katharine Anthony published *Margaret Fuller: A Psychological Biography*, using psychology to show the writer's motivation that would otherwise have been ignored. Anthony's *Catherine the Great* in 1925, *Queen Elizabeth* in 1929, and *Marie Antoinette* in 1932 continued to emphasize the inner lives—and often the sexual behavior—of the subjects. Obviously, however, these women were chosen as subjects of biography because their lives were, in some way, manlike (i.e., these women did things that history recognized as meaningful; they were not exclusively domestic). Their narratives were dependent on historical events; they could be framed as quest or adventure plots. Rheta L. Dorr's 1928 biography of Susan B. Anthony, Alice S. Blackwell's *Lucy Stone* in 1930, Ruth Finley's 1931 *Lady of Godey's: Sarah Josepha Hale*, and Fleta C. Springer's biography of Mary Baker Eddy dealt in nonformulaic ways with women subjects, but their subjects still had name recognition. Even in the twentieth century, then, a biography of a woman differed little from that of a man.

The kind of biography that validated and valued women's inner lives—domestic and private—did not yet exist, although in 1928 Constance Rourke wrote about the actress Lotta Crabtree and in 1931 Dorothie Bobbe wrote about Fanny Kemble, women who were famous but not historically important figures. Change was imminent. Freed from the necessity of writing about only public figures, a few women wrote biographies that emphasized domestic lives over the historical.

Capable women biographers also retold the stories of earlier women writers: in 1930 both Josephine Pollitt and poet Genevieve Taggard wrote new biographies of Emily Dickinson, and Agnes Repplier, Emanie L. Sachs, Edith Curtis, Helen Augur, Winifred K. Rugg, and others also wrote about women subjects. Unfortunately, the Great Depression of the 1930s, followed by the paper shortages of World War II, suspended the publication of many books, including women's biographies, and—except for an occasional good study, such as Mary Gray Peck's *Carrie Chapman Catt* in 1944—the form did not fully recover popularity until Nancy Milford's 1970 *Zelda*. In her sympathetic and well-researched biography of F. Scott Fitzgerald's problematic wife, Milford told the couple's story from the woman's perspective and thereby led several generations of readers to reassess the better-known male writer's history. She drew Zelda not as just one of a pair but rather as a sentient and talented woman caught in a habit of patriarchal protection that continued into her marriage. Readers came to care about this woman who had previously been only a companion to the more famous Fitzgerald.

If curiosity is the motive for a reader's beginning a biography, caring quickly takes over as the dominant reason for continuing to read. Identification with the subject is the attraction of the form, which continues to sell even in today's lukewarm literary market-place, as biographies of women become more and more insightful. Women readers are demanding narratives of women's lives told with one focus on the subject's interior life and another on the external values and conflicts they, as women, recognize.

What changed in biography during the 1960s and the 1970s was that readers developed a new consciousness about both the facts of women's lives and the many possible ways stories about those lives might be told. Admittedly, they reasoned, women's lives were different from men's: that difference deserved to be visible. An increasing number of readers of biography were women, so their ideas of what facts were interesting also brought changes to the form. Years before ground-breaking work in women's psychology by Jean Baker Miller, Carol Gilligan, Alice Miller, and others, women readers of biography knew that they wanted to read contextualized lives: they knew that women's lives seldom developed, or existed, in vacuums. They wanted to understand the woman's position as a child within her family, her relationship with parents and siblings, her school experiences, her physical prowess (or lack of it), her sexual history.

Too, modern consciousness about the personal, bodily self questioned the rules of writing conventional biography. Readers wanted to know whether the subject, like them, had spent hours in front of bathroom mirrors, playing dress up in her mother's clothes, experimenting with lipstick and mascara. They wanted to know about her battle to maintain a consistent weight, about her sexual and psychological health. Women readers of women's biographies demanded different kinds of information, and, as a result, the role of the biographer changed dramatically.

1
Biography:
The Old and the New

Nothing happens while you live . . . but everything
changes when you tell about life.
Jean-Paul Sartre, *Nausea*

The differences between biography of men and biography of
women have been described frequently in the past twenty-five
years of theoretical attention to the genre. Men's lives are usually
focused outward, and the important "facts" of their existences are
external and public. For example, early biographies of American
writer and historian Henry Adams scarcely mentioned the suicide
of his talented, beloved wife Marian (Clover) Hooper—in this, following the lead of his own famous memoir, *The Education of Henry
Adams*. What was important about Henry Adams, the historical
and biographical worlds believed, was his participation in the
events of his time and his own writings. That his never-ending
grief over his wife's death in 1885 might have led to the most moving of his works, *Mont-Saint-Michel and Chartres* and *The Education*,
has been immaterial to his biographers. They devote more attention to his college education than to his thirteen-year marriage—
or to his marital infidelity, which may have prompted his wife's
suicide.

Part of the explanation for omitting Clover Adams's suicide is
that traditional biography tells a success story. Its narrative is built
through rising action, recounting the subject's accomplishments
and accolades, to a comfortable denouement that parallels the
physical winding down of old age. American biography has long
attempted to inscribe moral norms through its narratives. The stories of Thomas Jefferson, or Patrick Henry, or Tom Paine, for

example, run few risks—at least as told in traditional biography. Complex issues that might interfere with the reader's response to the intended effect of the narrative can be softened or, as in the case of Clover Adams's suicide, entirely omitted.

Biography of a male subject, then, has usually been a relatively uncomplicated presentation of the persona, shaped in the pattern of the personal success story. That narrative pleases readers, who probably chose to read the book in the first place because of what they already knew about the man. Telling a woman's life, however, is less formulaic. For one thing, most women's lives are a tightly woven mesh of public and private events. The primary definition of a woman's selfhood is likely to be this combined public-private identity. So, to write the story of these interconnected parts of a woman's life, in order to tell her complete story, means creating different structures for women's biography. Comparing biographies of Franklin Delano Roosevelt and his wife, Eleanor—who might have been said to have led the same life—shows that all the biographies of FDR feature his life marked by external event, political incident, and association with other leaders of state. In contrast, Eleanor's life is more frequently described through quiet domestic events, social happenings, and friendships (Blanche Wiesen Cook's 1992 biography begins redressing that imbalance).

While writing biography of men means concentrating on the subject's accomplishments, one of the main questions in writing women's biography is, What *are* the accomplishments in a woman's life? What motivation has driven the subject's choices? What led the subject to do more than lead a traditional woman's life? Historically, most women lived within family households; even in this century, women who have gained public recognition have also run homes. Creating drama from these women's lives is a challenge to any biographer. For all our supposed interest in the way people develop, in the psychological evolution of competence and strength, the subject of a best-selling biography today is not ordinary life, not dailiness, but *exceptional* life. The fact that women may have had to overcome great obstacles for even moderate success does not put the woman subject on a par with a Donald Trump or a Nelson Rockefeller. People read biographies in the 1990s for the same reason they read them fifty years ago: to learn about someone other than themselves. The allure of lives of great success, great acclaim, or great personal satisfaction depends on reader expectations—and on contemporary culture's definitions of *success, acclaim,* and *satisfaction.*

The writing of women's lives is problematic in part because so few women have had the kind of success that attracts notice. Women's biography is more often based on private events because few women—even women like Eleanor Roosevelt—live public lives. Harder to discover, private events may be ones purposely kept secret by the subject (such as sexual abuse, dislike for parents, dislike by parents, or other unfortunate childhood or adolescent happenings) or those regarded as unimportant by society. When a woman spends much of her life doing housework, driven by economic need as well as societal expectation, does the biographer simply discount those hours/days/years because the activity is boring? How dramatic can shopping and taking children to dance lessons be? In writing the Plath biography, I knew that her choices of menu were important; given her limited means and the fact that she herself prepared the food, there was a code to what she served. Yet when I included details about her cooking, my editor cut them because he assumed they were trivial.

In the 1990s it is a given that biography attempts to find explanations for a subject's acts. Biography is the ultimate use of psychoanalytic knowledge: it takes insights about the figure's behavior and shapes a life story from those fragments. Traditional biography completes the narrative of the subject's life. Yet, as postmodern readers reject oversimplification, the form of biography must become more open to inquiry. What has been considered good biography leaves few questions in the reader's mind, yet it may be those unanswered questions that bring a reader to some fulfilling involvement in the narrative. In the case of a subject who committed suicide, for example (Plath, John Berryman, Virginia Woolf, Vachel Lindsay, Anne Sexton, Sara Teasdale, Ernest Hemingway, Hart Crane), a biography that does not try to answer every question can still provide explanations that will both satisfy readers and lead them past the death to the writer's legacy.

For the subjects of most biographies, the life curve is less dramatic—and less abrupt. The subject develops, accomplishes, and ages into death. Sometimes biographers will rearrange chronology in their telling, particularly if the period of old age and death is comparatively uninteresting, as Justin Kaplan did in his life of Walt Whitman, which began with the poet's old age and death. Because biography has its factual base as scaffolding for whatever narrative is to be told, the biographer's choices come largely in writing the narrative. Finding the ideal shape, texture, and pace for the story is the way the biographer puts his or her mark on it. Formal, balanced sentences and page-long paragraphs may be appropriate for a biography of Mahatma Gandhi, but a biography of a child dying of leukemia might better be told without pretention.

The most difficult problems in writing biography are not those of organization, sentence variety, or language choice, however; they are, rather, to do with conceptualization. Biography forces the writer to put real-life problems into place, which means allowing the reader to understand complexity rather than forcing the subject's experiences into an oversimplified pattern. Most life events and their motivations are not simple; making them sound as if they were, or as if they were the subject's obvious (or only) choice, is falsification. Just as the human subject orchestrates actions to construct the appearance of a unified or consistent identity, so must that person's biography present that self with integrity. In this regard, then, biography is the enactment of cultural performance.

If all life activity is defined as one kind of performance and the way the subject has viewed his or her life as another kind, the biographer must work from both matrices of performative identities. The biographer is forced by the results of factual research either to accept or to reject the subject's self-definition. If the biographer sees that self-definition as inaccurate, then he or she must find ways of building a different story from the same facts the subject had at hand. If the biographer sees the self-definition as true, then his or her role is to enhance the subject's account—to put it in a wider context, to relate it to other histories, to find new threads in events, and then to connect them in one compelling portrait.

The performative self is often the external self, and describing it may be the easiest phase in writing the biography. While biography draws on material about that self, good biography also attempts to unearth the hidden, more interior self. As it does this, it creates a somewhat different narrative. The story told by biography is, in some respects, as much fiction as the narrative created by the fiction writer: though biography is based on the subject's external and internal characteristics, it is also based on the experience, or lack of experience, of the biographer doing the work. When a biographer emphasizes the death of a parent in the subject's life, for example, it might be surmised that the biographer has either experienced that loss or known intimately someone who has.

Yet despite today's greater cultural awareness of how complicated the shaping of identity is, biography is still thought to be an art dependent on fact. The premise is that if enough letters and manuscript materials are available, if enough photos are scrutinized, if enough people are interviewed, somehow objective truth about the subject will surface. Through the years, this definition of biography has been proven a fantasy, yet the reading public still prefers to think of biography as factual, something based in those facts that are sometimes missing in fiction. The market for biography continues while the market for fiction diminishes; how close the two forms really are is a secret all biographers hold dear.

Finding facts, unearthing information, is the easy part of writing biography. As I have suggested, the real art of the form is that of selection: the biographer has the responsibility to determine what life events have been most important to the subject. Even if the subject does not reveal or write about an experience, the biographer has the authority to place that event within the narrative. The biographer's art is that of refashioning and revising the life narrative, bringing to it more background and, it is hoped, more insight than the subject may ever have had.

The biographer, sorting through the events of the subject's life and creating explanations for the subject's choices, also becomes a cultural historian. Part of the writing of any biography involves letting readers decide whether or not the subject's choices made sense, given the cultural norms of the times. Defiance on a woman's part in the nineteenth century need not have been the murder of a parent, a lover, or a minister; it might well have been her decision not to marry or not to become a part of her community, as it was in the case of Emily Dickinson, who chose seclusion within her father's home rather than the life of community service of most unmarried women. It took Adrienne Rich's empathetic essay on Dickinson, explaining her choice to withdraw as a reasonable means of giving herself time and space to be the poet she was, to change years of censure of the "strange" poet. Once Dickinson was seen as being a hard-working, ambitious writer, as serious about her art as her peer Whitman or her followers in the twentieth century, the factual biography of her life became credible.

Professional biographers agree that they write about subjects that have value for themselves and, they hope, for their readers. Either the subject is great in some way, or his or her life shows some greatness of spirit or endeavor. The notion sounds old-fashioned, but in this age of fluid moral positioning, when a subject can be praised by one group of readers and reviled by another, it is finally the biographer's conviction that directs the narrative.

2

Telling Women's Lives

> History is too much about wars;
> biography too much about great men.
> Virginia Woolf, *A Room of One's Own*

Writing the biography of a woman, then, has many things in common with writing traditional biography, which was often of male subjects. But it is the differences that are more interesting, and because of them, the biographer of a woman subject feels somehow separate from the profession. If biographies of men are dominated by external events, most biographies of women are a blend of external and interior, and it is often the inclusion of women's private lives that creates the biographer's problems—aesthetic, legal, and ethical as well as literary. If the reader expects only certain kinds of materials in good biography, then to find attention paid to biological processes (menstruation, pregnancy, and menopause, as well as general sexual experience) may be troublesome. Readers, and some biographers, wonder, Does this material belong in a biography? Yet for women, whose lives often fuse public and private, a biography of less than the complex whole would be inaccurate.

Controversial Material

Life processes can be both unliterary and embarrassing, though they may be necessary to understand the subject's development. Sylvia Plath's description of a woman's vaginal tear in *The Bell Jar* replicated her own frightening sexual experience, yet such details as the extensive bleeding—the blood pooling in the character's shoes and soaking through layers of towels—are considered in poor taste. Plath's insistence that she breast-feed her children (in the early 1960s) was atypical for that generation of mothers and becomes important to show how intensely concerned she was about every detail of her children's lives. If what a woman does within her household, in her domestic life, on a daily basis, is considered to be of no value to women's biography, then the representation of women's lives will be badly skewed.

Portraying women's lives has the added complexity of skirting sometimes negative judgments of the reading public. (While men's lives have the same problem, somehow social censure of their behavior seems muted in comparison with reactions to women's histories.) If a woman is promiscuous, what kind of response will readers have to this aspect of her existence? If Isak Dinesen had contracted her syphilis—which brought her decades of physical agony and debilitation—from intercourse not with her husband but with a casual lover, the now-universal sympathy for her might instead be suspicion or denigration. Reactions to women's choices tend to be as complex as the choices themselves. To acknowledge that Gertrude Stein and Alice Toklas had a lesbian "marriage" for nearly forty years (from 1907 until Stein's death in 1946) is to satisfy some readers while alienating others. Like most forms of art, biography can be a double-edged sword; portraying a woman's life faithfully and explicitly is sometimes dangerous—for as many reasons as there are readers of biography.

The psychological development of creative or otherwise achieving women who are likely subjects for biographies is another problematic focus for the study of the form. Louise DeSalvo's recent *Virginia Woolf: The Impact of Childhood Sexual Abuse on Her Life and Work*, emphasizing her sexual victimization by her stepbrothers, has received mixed response. Even though DeSalvo shows carefully, and with astute readings of Woolf's fiction, how Woolf used disguising strategies in her work (one hallmark of the psyche struggling to hide past experience), the biographer's attention to sexual matters has been criticized. When Sharon O'Brien, in the first volume of her biography *Willa Cather: The Emerging Voice*, contended that Cather was a lesbian, in the sense of the word as she defines it, disapproval again was the response. Unfortunately, many of the tragedies that mark women's lives—rape, incest, emotional victimization as well as physical—fall into the category of "women's issues." Although the male subject who has been traumatized by war injuries, poverty, or parental abuse or neglect has been written about for decades, somehow to name the trauma in women's lives is controversial. When a biographer names the woman subject's injuries, he or she may be accused of being political. Disclosing certain kinds of details about a woman's life is sometimes described as an arbitrary choice the biographer makes, rather than the duty of any biographer searching for truth. The long-standing suspicion within literary circles of things psychoanalytic also colors readers' reactions to the use of such material, particularly in biographies of women.

Ethical Issues

When women's life experiences involve other people, other kinds of ethical and legal questions develop. When biographers interview partners in extramarital affairs, therapists, doctors, and friends privy to intimate details of subjects' lives, they come into possession of information that could harm other people. To omit such material would leave gaps in the narrative, yet using it demands prudence.

One of my problems in writing the Plath biography was treating the fact of her sexual activity before marriage with sympathy and understanding. I saw her promiscuity as a rebellion against the edicts of her mother, and her 1950s culture, about a woman's need to preserve her virginity until marriage. I worried in part that readers would respond negatively to Plath but also that the men who had been her sexual partners would be identified. It turned out, however, that one of those men had already written at length about his liaison with Plath and that several others were eager to prove that they had been the first to consummate a sexual relationship with her. At one time, correspondence got so heated that I sent Lover A's letters to Lover B, and the reverse, so they could carry on their argument in person. In this instance, less commentary in the biography seemed the wiser choice, so the book includes only one sentence about Plath's being sexually active before marriage, and no partners are named.

Corresponding with both the Boston therapist Plath trusted and loved and the London physician who cared for her at the end of her life posed a different set of ethical issues. How much could a biographer ask from people who were obviously still grieving over her suicide? Though both responded to questions, neither would be actively involved in the biography. The therapist had changed both her name and her professional field; she graciously read my manuscript and made corrections. My ethical decision here was how much to ask of her.

In the case of the physician who saw the treatment he had prescribed lead directly to Plath's death, when he asked me not to describe that treatment in the biography—because he did not want his choice of medication criticized—I did as he requested. Unfortunately, a later biographer, who received the same information from him, used it all. (It was some of the "new" information her publishers touted in publicizing the book.)

Plath's therapy—both in the States and in England—was also a family matter; she had worked through a number of family conflicts as well as marital ones. Her mother, whose strength of will had posed a number of problems for her daughter, was still alive; I wanted neither to hurt nor to offend her. Some Plath papers in the Smith College collection, labeled "psychiatric records," are sealed until the deaths of both Plath's mother and her younger brother; eventually, her journals about her therapy will be open to scholars. These restricted papers are those Plath wrote about her therapy; her therapist also has records.

Today, a biographer cannot mention medical or psychiatric treatment as an ethical issue without reference to Diane Wood Middlebrook's experience in writing the biography of American poet Anne Sexton, who killed herself in 1975. When one of Sexton's therapists gave the biographer tapes of therapy sessions that included information about Sexton's sexual abuse by another (still practicing) therapist, a number of ethical problems surfaced. The most visible was that of the confidentiality of the doctor-patient relationship: if nothing is confidential, then all patients are likely to find the details of their lives in print. Although the therapist who provided the tapes said he wanted to help Diane Middle-brook, he also released damaging information about a colleague. Middlebrook's having access to these highly confidential materials gave new meaning to the concept of public-versus-private issues in biography.

The media explosion that accompanied the publication of *Anne Sexton, A Biography* showed the fascination the forbidden has for readers. While Middlebrook's book made comparatively little use of Sexton's therapy sessions per se (although they served as valu-able undergirding for her understanding of the poet), most of the reviews, editorials, and letters to the press about the book focused exclusively on the problem of patient-therapist confidentiality. Here, ethical issues came close to obscuring biographical ones.

The privacy issue of the Sexton biography made national head-lines, but all too often such personal information is labeled "trivial" and dismissed. In Plath's development, an important detail about her living space was ignored—or repeatedly considered insignifi-cant. Until she left for England shortly before her twenty-third birthday, she shared a bedroom with her mother, and after her ma-ternal grandparents moved into the house when she was ten, Syl-via had no space of her own. Already angry about the arrange-ment, Plath was also jealous of her younger brother: no one asked him to share his room. It seemed clear that her self-sacrificing mother expected her to play the martyr as well. All this resentment surely led to Plath's writing the scene in *The Bell Jar* where Esther wishes her mother dead as she sleeps and snores within arm's reach.

Issues of Sentiment

Another kind of dismissal of information about women's lives may occur because an event supposedly leads to a "sentimental" reac-tion. Negatively charged from years of condemnation in literary history, the word *sentimental* suggests the melodramatic evocation of feeling, something contrived to make readers respond predict-ably. The negative connotations of the word, and the fact that it is often applied to women's lives or writings, should be balanced with the reminder that not everything that evokes emotion is bad. In the case of Gertrude Stein's life, my handling of two "sentimental" situations during her adolescence—the deaths of her parents—became a source of disagreement with my first editor.

Amelia, Gertrude's mother, developed abdominal (or ovarian) cancer when Gertrude was eleven. Milly Stein had for many years kept a diary about the children's activities and the Stein family life. When she became ill, her diary changed, focusing entirely on her health. It seemed to me that quoting from the diary was a truthful, moving way to show the abrupt change in the parent and, accordingly, in the household. My editor disagreed, claiming that this use of the diary played too obviously on the reader's emotions. In retrospect, I tend in part to agree with his objection, but at the time I chose to quote Milly's terse comments—"am not well yet," "At home. Everything going on as usual"—and to describe the daily routine of her visits to Dr. Fine, her "electric" treatments and salt baths, and the effects of her illness on the five children. Here are the passages that were in question:

> By December 21, after weeks of almost daily visits to Dr. Fine's office, Milly admitted how much she relied on her older daughter: Bertha "always goes with me to the Dr. I do not trust to walk alone." Throughout the holidays, Milly's visits continued to dominate her days. On Dec. 25, Daniel took her to see Dr. Fine at 8:30 a.m. and then "Bertha prepared dinner." At scarcely fifteen, Bertha was running the household. The rest of December, Milly and Daniel went to the doctor's and then walked in the afternoon. December 28 Milly recorded, "in the afternoon we walked to Leasts. I had not walked so far for more than three months." On New Year's Day she was well enough to write that the day, with everyone at home, had been "glorious." Even though she was weak enough to spend most of her time in bed, and did little, Milly's spirit remained calm.
>
> Once 1886 began, however, Milly's diary entries changed. Uncomplaining in its tersely objective statements, Milly's voice now left out all other members of her family. Except for naming who was taking her to the doctor's, she mentioned no one; it was as if the Stein family life had stopped abruptly. And Milly's diaries also mention nothing about her illness except those doctor's visits—she never voices fear, or records pain or

other physical symptoms. What became the only content of her diary, from late in 1885 through the March 13, 1886, entry which was its last, was a relentless list of two-word phrases, entered day by day,

To drs.

To drs.

To drs.

To drs.

On February 21, the phrase changed to "Dr. Fine" with no verb or preposition. That note appeared each day until March 12, when the entry read "Did not go" and then resumed—"Dr. Fine"—on the last day of writing. The rest of the pages in Milly's last diary are blank.

As a biographer, I was attempting to do several things with this emphasis on Milly Stein's illness and her death two years later. The first was to show that Gertrude, the youngest and best-loved of the five children, lost not only her beloved mother but her protected place in the family. Life changed drastically for everyone, because Milly was the buffer between the children and their increasingly erratic father. But in Gertrude's case, too—and here we move back to the issue of what is thought seemly and appropriate in women's biography—her first menstrual period coincided with her mother's first treatment for cancer. The child was reassured that her pain and fear were natural and harmless, whereas she saw plainly that her mother's discomfort required daily treatments at the doctor's—until those were abandoned, and Milly was left at home to die.

Daniel Stein's death three years after his wife's was even harder to present narratively. Always a difficult and controlling man, after his wife's death Daniel shut himself up for days at a time, courted women, and said he had had financial losses that made keeping household help impossible. The hearty German-Jewish family even saw its mealtimes disappear, as the household structure collapsed. Of the five children, Leo, the second youngest, had had great emotional difficulties with his bullying father. Ironically, it fell to Leo on a morning when Daniel did not appear for breakfast to climb onto the roof and into the locked bedroom—to find his father dead in bed. The Freudian family romance so perfectly executed, with the son taking power from the dead father, underscored again the maxim that truth is stranger than fiction. One of the biographer's jobs is to use fact to create patterns that implicitly explain the biographical subject. In the cases of parents' deaths, a biographer must create a text that avoids the maudlin or sentimental, while giving the reader a sense of the orphaned children's experiences.

Avoiding Stereotypical Responses

Another problem in writing biography of women is working around the stereotypes of what is appropriate behavior for women. Joan Givner's *Katherine Anne Porter: A Life* was criticized because it drew Porter as a complicated, often unlikable woman. Instead of being a loyal friend who was circumspect about her sexual relationships, Porter imposed on her women friends, lied habitually, and had affairs with a number of men (some married, others considerably younger than she). Givner showed clearly that Porter the writer was in conflict throughout her life with the dependent role her depressive father had forced on her: she was to be his beautiful daughter and, after the early death of her mother, his chief source of happiness. Yet even while readers sympathized with Porter as she struggled to develop autonomy, her self-destructive behavior was anything but endearing. Readers felt betrayed that the author they admired turned out to be so unappealing.

While many men have led similarly objectionable lives, truthful biographies of their lives have occasioned less comment. For one thing, in the past, biographies that existed in part to establish moral norms disguised personal faults. Readers of men's biography also may come to such books with less rigid notions of acceptable behavior. Only recently have some disclosures in biographies of male subjects been as troublesome as those in biographies of women, and these have often been disclosures of sexual practices. When Scott Donaldson's biography of John Cheever admitted the writer's bisexuality, its careful discussions of Cheever's homosexual experiences disturbed readers who expected more eulogistic treatment of him. Peter Ackroyd's biography of T. S. Eliot faced the same kind of disapproval, as if homoerotic experiences were new to the literary reader. Nor is all controversy aimed at information about homosexual experience: the sexual revelations of Nigel Hamilton's *JFK: Reckless Youth* unleashed similar controversy.

One of the most difficult problems facing the biographer of women is to make what may be only moderate achievement as important to the reader as it was to the subject. The self-educated woman who made her own living may have an inspiring life story, but book buyers would rather read about astronauts or the eminently wealthy. Another is making ambitious women understandable rather than monstrous. Cultural stereotypes again force women into professional patterns that interfere with their approved life roles: the woman who worked sixty or seventy hours a week to succeed at her job probably didn't spend much time in charitable activities. Because American artist Georgia O'Keeffe knew that her life depended on her painting and that she needed certain physical and psychological conditions to do her best work, she spent lengthy periods of time away from her husband, the photographer Alfred Stieglitz. Her struggle for independence was also her means of coping with his infidelities. While O'Keeffe's recent biographers have written expert narratives of her complex bisexual life, some readers resent the fact that she treated the bond of marriage so casually, relinquishing some of the duties of wife and homemaker to devote herself to her painting. When Kathleen Jones published a new biography of British poet Christina Rossetti in 1991, she chose as its title a shorthand version of this attitude: *Learning Not to Be First*. Women's roles—whether in relation to husbands like Alfred Stieglitz or to brothers like William and Dante Gabriel Rossetti—are difficult to reimagine. And, at times, predicting readers' responses is equally difficult.

3

The Trap of the Stereotype

Since when was genius found respectable?
Elizabeth Barrett Browning, *Aurora Leigh*

The biographer must face the fact that choosing to write about a woman may not be the way to literary success: women usually lead lives that seem less interesting to readers. The issue here is the status of the subject of the biography; the more important the subject, the more readers will be attracted to the life. Publishers are in business to sell books, and they know that Edmund White's biography of Jean Genet is going to sell more copies than a book about Susan B. Anthony, despite her dynamic, controversial life. The 1992 Pulitzer Prize in biography was awarded to David McCullough's *Truman,* and other recent awards have gone to Richard Ellmann for *Oscar Wilde* and to David Herbert Donald for *Look Homeward: A Life of Thomas Wolfe.* When in 1986 Elizabeth Frank won the Pulitzer for her biography of poet Louise Bogan, she was the first woman biographer of a woman subject to be so honored in thirty-five years, and she remains the most recent woman biographer to win the award.

Marketplace surveys show that women readers buy 60 percent of the biographies and autobiographies sold and have done so since the early 1980s. Such surveys, unfortunately, do not break purchases down by gender of subject. There are comparatively few biographies of women marketed, so book buyers' choices are determined in part by availability, but informal assessment suggests that women buy all kinds of biographies, whereas men tend to buy biographies of men. For whatever reasons, however, despite the fact that women buy more books than men, publishers have not responded to this statistic by publishing larger quantities of biographies about women. And when such books appear, they are seldom exhaustively promoted. Large advertising budgets are rarely spent on biographies about, or by, women.

For all the professed interest today in women's lives, the cultural assumption remains that most women who have biographies written about them are eccentric rather than exemplary, and eccentricity is not a trait that wins admiration. On many grounds, Harry Truman could be considered an unusual politician—perhaps even an eccentric one—but his posthumous fame now rests on his far-sighted political decisions, his use of the atomic bomb being less controversial than it was forty years ago. A reader would come to a biography of Truman, however, with a very different attitude from that with which he or she would approach Anne Taylor's 1992 *Annie Besant: A Biography* or Sylvia Cranston's 1993 biography of Madame Blavatsky, both women founders of theosophy. Cranston's full title provides all the reader needs to know to choose the book: *H.P.B.: The Extraordinary Life and Influence of Helena Blavatsky, Founder of the Modern Theosophical Movement*. However inaccurate, visions of table rappings and séances slant the lives of the women portrayed toward the eccentric.

One continuing problem with women's writing biography of women is that gender stereotypes block the reader's recognition of both the character portrayed and the biographer's method of portraiture. Readers have expectations about gender that the biography of a woman must both meet and answer, all within the guise of seeming objectivity. In almost every case, the woman who is the biographer's subject is situated "within conflicting and mutually constricting roles (wife, mother, daughter, sister, lover)," to borrow Shari Benstock's phrase. For the reader, each role comes complete with its own set of stereotypes.

The first question society (still) asks of any woman is whose daughter she is. Steeped in connotations of dependency both financial and emotional, the question reifies the patriarchal pattern that the loving father first supports his daughter and then chooses (or at least approves) the man to whom he "gives" her in marriage. The traditions of both patriarchy and heterosexuality are confirmed.

Throughout history, women have complained about being

called "daughter." Antigone had reasonable objections to the role, as did Persephone, Electra, and the golden daughter of King Midas. Virginia Woolf treats women's dependent social and economic position ironically in her 1928 *A Room of One's Own,* justifying her need for both space and money in order to become a writer, and more bitterly in her later *Three Guineas.* But even in the flood of biography and critical studies published about Woolf in the past decade, she cannot escape being described as Sir Leslie Stephen's daughter—and thereby an "intellectual" and so an appropriate member of the high-modernist Bloomsbury group.

The irony of Virginia Woolf's remaining somebody's daughter, even at the height of interest in her own great writing, underscores the fragile position of women who work in fields that historically belong to men. When Woolf's *Three Guineas* appeared in *The Atlantic Monthly* in May 1938, she was described in "The Contributors' Column" as, "Chief ornament of the Bloomsbury Group, Mrs. Virginia Woolf is the daughter of Sir Leslie Stephen." Putting Woolf in a decorative female role, *The Atlantic* also slotted her into the wife role (her marriage to Leonard Woolf is discussed later in the note). The chief emphasis of the biography, however, is the role her father, and his "magnificent library," played in her becoming a writer. Years of this kind of description had taught Woolf about the social perception of women's roles, and in answer to that perception she created her metaphoric character to illustrate that women don't belong: the tragic Judith Shakespeare.

As William Shakespeare's ambitious and talented younger sister, Woolf's Judith runs away to become a writer but is scoffed at and taken advantage of every step of her short life. When she kills herself, she is pregnant with the child of a man who is influential in the theater. Culturally, biologically, economically, Woolf claims in *A Room of One's Own,* Judith Shakespeare had no chance.

Woolf's grim narrative of the fictional Renaissance woman, both somebody's daughter and somebody's sister, hovers over whatever success stories today's women attempt to tell about themselves and their female peers. And there are others. Charlotte Perkins Gilman's deranged woman protagonist in "The Yellow Wallpaper" suffers from the paternalistic care of her authoritative doctor-husband, who is supported in his erroneous diagnosis of her illness by her brother, also a physician. Anzia Yezierska's daughters must defy their Russian-Jewish fathers in order to make lives for themselves in modern America, as must the daughters in the works of Louise Erdrich, Amy Tan, Toni Cade Bambara, Terry McMillan, Marge Piercy, Grace Paley, Paule Marshall, and Anne Tyler. Escaping control of the patriarchy has long been a central theme in writing by contemporary women, though the daughter's break from fatherly control does not always end productively.

Another theme that haunts current women's fiction as well as biographies of women is part of the original inquiry: *Whose daughter are you?* is implicitly coupled with *Where is your father?* Within every book on Louisa May Alcott is a profile of her unsuccessful (but "brilliant") father, Bronson, whose education of his daughters surely led to their adult achievements. The implication is that, notable as Louisa's life was, Bronson Alcott better deserves the biography. Biography all too often works to link women with male patrons, as if responding to the unasked question, What man has been responsible for this woman's accomplishment? So Russian immigrant writer Anzia Yezierska's friendship with John Dewey is given disproportionate emphasis, as are Mary McCarthy's relationship with Edmund Wilson and Gertrude Stein's with her brother Leo, as well as with both Pablo Picasso and Ernest Hemingway (as if she somehow would not have known the things she did but for their tutelage).

In both literary criticism and biography, women writers who have lived more traditional womanly lives fare better than their troublesome sisters. One of the best examples of this tendency to reward the art of modest women is the treatment given Anne Bradstreet. Bradstreet, who was apparently handed from a loving father to an equally loving husband—both men active in public service in the colonies—remained innocent herself of unwomanly ambition because it was her brother-in-law who secretly found an English publisher for her poem collection, *The Tenth Muse Lately Sprung Up in America*. Bradstreet's productive life as daughter, wife, and mother of eight children was suitably self-abnegating: after her death, twenty-eight years after her poems first appeared, her only book was republished in Boston with additional late poems, the strongest of the collection.

Harriet Beecher Stowe, who benefited from the connections her birth name suggested, was a somewhat more dangerous case.

But even if *Uncle Tom's Cabin* unloosed a powerful antislavery sentiment, she was supposed to have calmed down in later works and focused on the more suitable subject of women's domestic lives. Her own stable role as daughter of a minister, sister (to seven ministers), wife (of a theologian), and particularly mother (of six children) no doubt helped her understand that women's fiction should affirm existing values, not challenge them. Stowe's diminished place in literary history during the past fifty years, however, seems suitable for an upstart wife in the unlikely place of Cincinnati, Ohio: she has been ridiculed for the sentimental overstatement of *Uncle Tom's Cabin* and, on stylistic grounds, evaluated as a minor writer. With a better understanding of the centrality of her fiction to later nineteenth-century writing, however, more recent criticism has found Stowe's writing of great value.

Stowe's literary reputation shared the fate of that of the troublesome (Sarah) Margaret Fuller, whose immense importance as essayist, leader of various "conversations," and editor of *The Dial* was consistently denied—first by her male peers and friends and later by literary historians. In her case, the diminishment of her achievements was even more ironic in view of her major role in the male literary movement of transcendentalism. (Because women writers often mine separate fields, they can more easily be omitted from serious critical attention.) Fuller's early death at forty might have ensured the reputation that should have been hers, except that during the last years of her life she had kicked over the traces of respectable New England village life to become involved in the Italian revolution (she went to England in 1846 as one of America's first foreign correspondents and found herself fascinated by the insurgency in Rome). Worse, in 1848 she had had a child with the Italian Giovanni Ossoli, whom she had not married until 1849. Interestingly, after all three died in a shipwreck off the New York coast, when her loving male American friends prepared a volume of tributes to her, several of them spoke of her unfortunate physical ugliness—a strange way of undermining her marital success and the importance of her writing. Some of her friends were also guilty of bowdlerizing her journals and rewriting her letters.

Many of the women writers who were marked by the daughter stereotype in literary history came from the nineteenth or early twentieth centuries, although that way of describing women is far from obsolete. A more recent trend, equally insidious, is that of categorizing women in terms of what kind of mothers they were, or are.

The now-classic text for this vexing characterization is Kate Chopin's 1899 novel, *The Awakening*. Edna Pontellier's drive to free herself from the paternal care of her husband would be entirely sympathetic to women readers today if Chopin had not made the role of woman-as-mother so central to the book. Edna trying to find herself, to decide who she has become since her protected girlhood in Kentucky with her father, is a moving and understandable characterization. But when Chopin chooses to give Edna two young children, she complicates the story immensely.

Trained from the eighteenth century to think that the treatment of children is an important index of character, writers used their presence in fiction like a Rorschach inkblot test, to make readers aware of their own moral standards. Chopin's creation of Madame Ratignolle as "mother-woman," one who truly lives in the service of her babies and their father, intentionally questions the role of the idealized mother. In becoming more than a story of a woman's self-fulfillment, *The Awakening* forces readers to face the dilemma any woman finds when her sexual awakening comes later in life, after she is a mother. For that highly charged designation has built-in expectations, and first among them is self-sacrifice: all good mothers are selfless, generous to a fault, and completely focused on their children's lives. Chopin questions each of those premises by showing that Edna *is* a good mother (her sons are independent and secure). Her impropriety in the eyes of society is that she insists on defining the role of mother for herself rather than accepting society's (and Madame Ratignolle's) definition of the mother-woman.

Edna herself comes to understand that she can never be free, so long as she has children. The key section of the denouement of *The Awakening* is Edna's happy visit to the boys during their stay at their grandmother's. Caught in the imbroglio of loving her children, seeing how quickly she will lose any right to them once her husband gives up his pose of being understanding, Edna will not back down into her earlier life as conventional wife and mother. Compared to that psychological confinement, she chooses the freedom of her death. In Chopin's hands, *The Awakening* becomes a novel less about Edna than about women's lives spitted on a single cast-iron image of a proper identity.

Much of Edith Wharton's fiction of the 1920s and 1930s also dealt with the role of woman as mother and the penalties society exacted if she played the role incorrectly. Kate Clephane in *A Mother's Recompense* (1925) abandons her young child to elope with a lover. After her husband's death years later, she returns, but just as Wharton's biting short story "Joy in the House" makes clear that the "fallen" mother cannot ever return, so her novel shows the powerlessness of the absent mother. Wharton's most devastating fiction of a woman who defined herself only as mother, relinquishing her self and what remained of her life and fortune to make up for an early abandonment, is the novella "Her Son."*

Literary life in the second half of the twentieth century suggests that changing the image of the mother role remains difficult. Some of the harshest criticism of Sylvia Plath's suicide was couched in the argument that she had willingly abandoned her young children. What male writer is judged on the basis of his children's lives? As Margaret Atwood, Erica Jong, and countless other women writers have pointed out, critics do not begin reviews of a man's work by discussing to whom—or whether—he is married or how many children he has. Yet nearly all women writers are subjected to that treatment. Anne Tyler may have been readily accepted as a writer because she was also a mother, steadily married to a Baltimore professional. Readers took comfort in the fact that her narratives about macabre families were gentle mockery, not parody. One wonders, too, whether there has been change in critics' often hostile reactions to Margaret Atwood's bleak poetry and fiction, now that she has had a child and the mother-daughter bond appears in at least some of her recent writing. Marge Piercy, Alice Walker, Toni Morrison, Joan Didion, Doris Betts, Jill Mc-Corkle, Lee Smith—is the trend to mention children when women writers are interviewed a message to the would-be woman writer that her contribution to literature might be allowed as long as she keeps her life roles in perspective?

*In the 1990s, Sue Miller's *The Good Mother* describes the crucial conflict between mothering and finding sexual joy and independence—as have novels by Gail Godwin, Marilyn French, Marge Piercy, Tama Janowitz, and others.

Tillie Olsen's rightly famous *Silences* is not exclusively about women; rather, it treats those marginalized by race, class, or gender who tried to write. Without economic support, under the demands of caring for family and children, many writers throughout history have been unable to develop their potential gifts. Even the most talented must have time and space to work. In a family with children, with no domestic help, daily emergencies make sustained intellectual or artistic work difficult, if not impossible. Much broader in intention than Virginia Woolf's *A Room of One's Own*, Olsen's *Silences* describes the economic inequities that, finally, separate the successful writer or artist or composer from the incipient. Publishing as Tillie Lerner during the 1930s, Olsen made a remarkable start as a writer. Even with one child (her model for the memorable daughter in her classic story "I Stand Here Ironing"), she was able to write. But after marriage and three more children and her own jobs outside the home to keep the family together, Tillie Lerner Olsen's writing career ended. Revived during the 1970s, she became a paradigm for the woman of modest means whose sacrifice for her family includes her own career.

For every woman who told the story and tried to live it successfully, there were dozens of others who felt trapped by the conflicts inherent in the combined lives of wife, mother, and writer and gave up some part of the conflict: they abandoned their work; they left their husbands and sometimes—though not often—their children; they became the embittered wives and mothers American culture is famous for.

A primary reason women's roles as daughters, wives, and mothers remained important to readers is that most fiction followed the "marriage novel" pattern. The woman character was slated to move from her father's house to her husband's, so readers were experienced in reading about such protagonists and saw such conventional novel structure as the proper shape for storytelling. It has been said that narrative form reifies social codes. The marriage novel came into being during the eighteenth and nineteenth centuries, when the only desirable fate for women was marriage. Within traditional narratives, there was no pattern for a woman as quest hero (Odysseus traveled, but Penelope stayed home). Neither was there—except in science fiction or fantasy—a pattern for the woman's hero novel.

What has happened during the past twenty years of women writing fiction is that authors have been forced to change traditional narrative shapes to tell what they see as necessary and accurate stories. As women's lives have changed, the stories about their lives must also change. For example, instead of a marriage novel, with either a proposal or a ceremony as the work's happy ending, Nora Ephron's *Heartburn* (1983) pictures marriage as an indigestion that demands divorce. Penelope Mortimer's *The Pumpkin Eater* (1975), Sue Kaufman's *The Diary of a Mad Housewife* (1970), and Doris Lessing's *Children of Violence* novels in the 1970s show marriage as a route to madness. Erica Jong's *Fear of Flying* (1973) announced sexual freedom to the previously virginal women characters the patriarchy preferred—although women writers had long created characters who were not doomed by out-of-wedlock sexual relations (Ellen Glasgow's Dorinda in *Barren Ground* [1925] and Willa Cather's Lena and Ántonia in *My Ántonia* [1918]).

Creating the woman's hero novel was a means of presenting strong women characters who might, if they wished, sidestep marriage. Ellen Olenska, the exotic European cousin in Edith Wharton's 1920 *The Age of Innocence*, is a forerunner of a bevy of women protagonists who both dare and survive in the writing of Margaret Atwood, Toni Morrison, Lee Smith, Josephine Humphries, and countless others.

Many of these independent women add to their self-sufficiency by existing within women's communities. As Nina Auerbach suggested in her 1976 *Communities of Women*, some women have been happiest living together, without men. In Marilyn French's *The Women's Room* (1977), for example, talented women in the Harvard community try to wrest enough power from the male establishment to support themselves as a unit. In Alice Walker's *The Color Purple* (1982) and *Possessing the Secret of Joy* (1992), women's friendships underlie whatever success women characters find. Novels and linked story collections by Amy Tan, Julia Alvarez, Helena María Viramontes, Paula Gunn Allen, Louise Erdrich, Ana Castillo, Hisaye Yamamoto, and others also describe the collective strength of women characters living in community. E. M. Broner's sometimes comic stories of Jewish women creating their own rituals in *A Weave of Women* (1978) and *The Telling* (1993) have been praised for providing answers to the questions frequently raised in women's science fiction, science fantasy, and utopian narratives.

Change—whether in characters or narrative structures—is usually controversial, and much recent women's fiction has been charged with being both depressing and difficult. Because women's fiction tries to be reasonably true to women's lives, it rejects oversimplified endings. It also has adopted some distinctive narrative structures. The most obvious is the work that collects fragments of story and juxtaposes them, mixing chronology or narrators or themes, in a design that forces readers to supply personal connections. Susan Willis refers to this as the "four-page formula," meaning that narrative units are short, and while she discusses fiction by only black women writers, the term describes many women's fictions.

Because the woman writer believes that experience is interconnected, she often chooses circular patterns for stories. There is no definite ending for a narrative, just as there is no single voice for the storyteller. Gloria Naylor's *The Women of Brewster Place* (1982) and *Bailey's Cafe* (1992) and Sandra Cisneros's *The House on Mango Street* (1989) and *Woman Hollering Creek* (1991) collect the narratives of as many characters as there are sections in the books, all speaking with distinctive voices about their common experiences. Toni Morrison borrows that structure for *Jazz*, her 1992 three-part novel. Ntozake Shange's choreopoem *for colored girls who have considered suicide when the rainbow is enuf* (1975) was an earlier use of this collective narrative—which began a hundred years ago with Sarah Orne Jewett's intricately shaped collection, *The Country of the Pointed Firs* (1896).

IT IS IMPORTANT for both women writers of fiction and women biographers who attempt to tell women's lives truthfully to recognize that they must tell the stories they want to tell with integrity, regardless of criticism about structure or genre. They must understand the way their culture views women and the patterns in their lives, women's roles, and women's narratives. And biographers of women have a further responsibility: to understand both their subjects' cultures and their own and to provide their readers with a bridge back into history, so that they understand why certain behaviors then were approved or disapproved.

4

Relinquishing Stereotypes

Only women stir my imagination.
Virginia Woolf

The writing of women's biography is also caught in a web of genre conflicts. What rules of biography exist are sporadic, but most assume that *biography* means an adulatory recounting of events in the life of a male subject. So far as structure is concerned, then, the narrative begins with a subject's ancestry and birth, follows the events of his life, and ends with his death. As the structures of recent women's fiction suggest, women's lives often break away from conventional patterns; sometimes the breaking away is, indeed, the story worth telling. Accordingly, the voices of women characters and narrators must appear in a format that lets them speak for their own emphases—their own sense of event—in a structure that may need to differ from the traditional.

The problem of applying strict rules of form and voice to women's writing of all sorts has been described by Shari Benstock in her introduction to *The Private Self*: "Women's writings are as individual as women themselves, and they often resist easy classification." Add to this suggestion of inherent richness Carolyn Heilbrun's observation that "the woman who writes herself a life beyond convention, or the woman whose biographer perceives her as living beyond conventional expectations, has usually early recognized in herself a special gift without name or definition." Whether herself living beyond or outside marriage or other approved women's life options or writing about women who live out more controversial roles, the woman writer must expect criticism. Guardians of the literary establishment will chastise her because she seems not to know the rules, and neither fiction nor biography is yet an appropriate place to write a prolegomenon about the writer's intention. (British biographer Robert Skidelsky, however, recently called for such a statement of intention to preface every biography ["Only Connect," 14].) On one hand, the very reason a woman becomes an interesting subject to treat in biography—her life's difference from the expectations of her culture—may make a standard linear narrative about external events unsuitable. On the other, too experimental a structure, or too little emphasis on external events, leaves the biography open to criticism. What should be most compelling about the woman as subject, to return to Heilbrun's comment, is her possession of "a special gift without name or definition." The explanation of that gift, and its place in the subject's life narrative, should ideally create the biography's structure.

One wishes it were possible to be more explicit about what constitutes greatness, or even specialness, in any subject. Heilbrun's vagueness is undoubtedly meant to suggest that some mystery be allowed the achieving woman and that her story be told in whatever mode seems appropriate to her own sensibility. Luckily, biography of women during the 1980s and 1990s has given readers wonderful and varied examples of effective ways the stories of women's lives might be told, building on the seminal example of Nancy Milford's 1970 *Zelda.* Among excellent recent books are Elisabeth Young-Bruehl's *Hannah Arendt* (1982), Victoria Glendinning's *Vita* (1983), Noel Riley Fitch's *Sylvia Beach and the Lost Generation* (1983), Jane Howard's *Margaret Mead* (1984), Hilary Spurling's *Secrets of a Woman's Heart (Ivy Compton-Burnett)* (1984), Elizabeth Frank's *Louise Bogan* (1985), Sharon O'Brien's *Willa Cather* (1987), Brenda Maddox's *Nora: A Biography of Nora Joyce* (1988), Louise DeSalvo's *Virginia Woolf: The Impact of Childhood Sexual Abuse on Her Life and Work* and Ina Taylor's *George Eliot, Woman of Contradictions* (1989), Emily Toth's *Kate Chopin* and Katherine Frank's *A Chainless Soul: A Life of Emily Brontë* (1990), Carole Ione's *Pride of Family: Four Generations of American Women of Color* and Sissela Bok's *Alva Myrdal: A Daughter's Memoir* (1991), Blanche Wiesen Cook's first volume of *Eleanor Roosevelt* and Ellen Chesler's *Woman of Valor: Margaret Sanger and the Birth Control Movement in America* (1992), and Kay Mills's biography of Fannie Lou Hamer, *This Little Light of Mine* (1993).

Each of these biographies is successful, yet each is very different from the others. Each subject led an intrinsically interesting life, and each biographer found a means to reflect both the substance and the tone of the life and, in the cases of Hilary Spurling and Sharon O'Brien, to educate their readers about the process of writing biography. When Spurling faced a dearth of personal information, she drew from Ivy Compton-Burnett's own writing to create a pastiche of the author's words, bringing the form of biography near that of autobiography. O'Brien included a quantity of women's history, theory, and feminist psychology in the Willa Cather story, giving readers a context for understanding some of the choices Cather made during her life.

Just as new information about possible ways of viewing women's life choices can be helpful, so some history of the relationship between cultural expectations and women's acts must also be considered in reading a woman's life—particularly the life of an unconventional woman. Conventions, like stereotypes, often exist because society enforces its rules through such uniform expectations. Biographical interpretations of women's lives, too, are also subject to change through time. The case of British novelist George Eliot—and various biographies of her—provides a fascinating example of these cycles of changes.

Versions of the George Eliot Biography

If considered from a stereotypical nineteenth-century notion of what a young woman should be, Mary Ann (Marian) Evans fell short from the start. Her physical ugliness, combined with her considerable intellect, caused a number of difficulties. But at first, born in 1819 at peaceful South Farm, Warwickshire, she had the benefit of a tranquil, proper childhood. Of the five Evans children, her favorite was Isaac; both went to a dame-school and then to separate boarding schools. When she was sixteen, her mother died; the next year, her older sister married, and Mary Ann started managing her father's home, which she did for a long fourteen years. During that time, she read widely, learned to translate from the German, left the Anglican church, and cared for her ailing parent. After his death in 1849, she traveled with friends to Europe, lived for a while in Switzerland, and eventually found work in publishing. She fell in love with John Chapman (nick-named Byron), in whose home she lived while she edited *Westmin-ster Review*. She may also have proposed to Herbert Spencer. Living modestly on income from her small estate, the thirty-four-year-old woman then fell in love with the married George Henry Lewes, and in July of 1854, when she was thirty-five, they ran away to Germany.

The marriage was intentionally childless. Living down some of the scandal, the couple returned to London, where both became successful writers. Lewes championed her fiction, and she took the name of her beloved as her own when she became George Eliot; the successes of *Scenes of Clerical Life, Adam Bede, The Mill on the Floss, Silas Marner, Romola, Felix Holt,* and *Middlemarch* seem to have vindicated her immoral life-style. When Lewes died in 1878, a dis-traught Eliot turned to the friendship of John Cross, twenty years her junior. In May 1880, at age sixty-one, Eliot married Cross; seven months later she died of pneumonia.

Immediately, the young widower wrote a three-volume ideal-ized biography of his wife. *George Eliot's Life, as Related in Her Let-ters and Journals* is the beginning point for every subsequent biography. Replete with utter praise for the woman he viewed as both mother and friend, Cross's book explored her intellectual education in tedious detail. In 1902, to further the hagiography, Eliot's friend (and Virginia Woolf's father) Sir Leslie Stephen pub-lished his monograph of Eliot in the English Men of Letters series. Stephen had also written the volumes on Pope, Johnson, and Swift, and this account—although it was the only book in the series about a woman—was little different.

According to Stephen, Eliot led a straightforward intellectual existence, somehow capitalizing on events to become a major nov-elist. Stephen credits her learning to her friendships with the Bray family after the family's move to Coventry: "Cara and Sara (Mrs. Bray and Miss Hennell) became as sisters to George Eliot, and Mr. Bray her most intimate male friend. The alliance lasted through life, and produced an important correspondence. The ef-fect upon George Eliot's mental development was immediate and remarkable. The little circle at Coventry introduced her to a new world of thought."

While Stephen found Eliot's mental evolution understandable, he did not pretend to condone her living with Lewes; about that relationship he wrote only, "I have not, and I suppose that no one now has, the knowledge which would be necessary for giving an opinion as to the proper distribution of praise and blame among the various parties concerned, nor shall I argue the ethical question raised by George Eliot's conduct." He dismisses her marriage to Cross in a paragraph, and her death in the same space, leaving the real conclusion of his study to be his pronouncement upon her success in having led life as "an industrious student." What Stephen liked best about Eliot was her knowledge, which he summarizes, concluding: "Her powers of assimilating knowledge were, in fact, extraordinary, and it may safely be said that no novelist of mark ever possessed a wider intellectual culture."

Working from the stereotypes of what a good, moral woman should be, both Cross and Stephen found ways to erase the obvious social censure in which Eliot lived by valorizing the nonsexual part of her being—her intellect. They both disliked her best novel, *Middlemarch*, which they called unpredictable and uneven. It seems clear, biographically speaking, that Eliot was being rescued from her actual role as fallen woman by two diligent male biographers—neither of whom mentioned that she was refused burial in Westminster Abbey.

Much that Cross and Stephen also chose not to mention surfaced in Rosemary Sprague's 1968 *George Eliot, A Biography*, Phyllis Rose's 1983 *Parallel Lives*, and Ina Taylor's 1989 *George Eliot: Woman of Contradictions*. These biographies present Eliot's early frustrated life: the child knew she was not pretty. They also see her taking over the family home after her mother's death as definite martyrdom. Sprague emphasizes that, once her father died and Eliot lived abroad, she felt as if her family had abandoned her, as if there was no reason to return to England. (This reading is quite different from the story of an idyllic girlhood and the travels of a young woman that Stephen created.)

Sprague also makes clear Eliot's propensity to find herself in sexual trouble. Living in Switzerland, she seems to have been involved with her host, Dr. Brabant—or so his blind wife felt. She was asked to leave the household, and Brabant did not defend her. Similarly, when she lived with John Chapman in his home—which already included both his legal wife and his mistress—she was again perceived as a threat and asked to leave. Her proposal to Spencer, her willingness to become involved with Lewes, and her later proposal to John Cross are all presented as the acts of a woman who wants to be sexually claimed. Sprague says comparatively little about Eliot's intellectual development; she instead portrays a needy woman who defies all social conventions to become a man's beloved.

This biographer points out that after Eliot eloped to Germany with Lewes, her family was outraged, and she was not reconciled with her favorite brother Isaac for twenty-five years, until her marriage to Cross. Earlier biographies suppressed these difficulties within the Evans family, just as they did many of the other kinds of difficulties Eliot experienced as a free-thinking and sexually adventurous woman. While Sprague does not condemn her, she acknowledges the disapproval Eliot's acts would have warranted.

The legends of proper women's biography die hard. Appearing the same year as Sprague's, 1968, Gordon S. Haight's authoritative *George Eliot, A Biography* was replete with stories of John Cross's romantic persistence. In Haight's account, Cross "declared that he wanted to be more than a friend to Marian [Mary Ann]. She probably dismissed it as impossible." After a third proposal, so the narrative went, Eliot finally accepted. Haight, one of the most prominent Eliot scholars, continued the emphasis on the significance of women's friendship in Eliot's life, calling it her "extraordinary attraction for women." When faced with his subject's heterosexuality, however, he apparently could not imagine her as aggressive.

In 1983, Phyllis Rose included George Lewes and Eliot in *Parallel Lives*, her study of five Victorian marriages. Emphasizing Eliot's sexual nature, Rose traces the relationship with Lewes to show Eliot's skill in manipulating him. Lewes, better known than Eliot at the start of their liaison, gradually became the mentor for Eliot's novice writing and then watched as she grew past him in fortune and reputation. Rose stresses the woman's intricate play for Lewes's encouragement, bringing to Germany her one bit of fiction, asking him if she might read it aloud, actively seeking his support for this new venture. Lewes, according to Rose, thought her writing fiction was all his idea: "He was prepared to devote himself to her, and she accepted an immense amount of devotion.

It became understood between them that without his help she could not write." As they neared sixty, both ill and pain-ridden, Lewes kept doing all the things to support Eliot that he customarily did. He died, in effect, in her service, Rose writes, so decimated by his illness that he looked as if he had been "gnawed by rats."

Despite these newer emphases of biographers Sprague and Rose, the outlines of the earliest George Eliot biography remained in place. New material appears as decoration on the earliest scaffolding, rather than as change in or departure from that narrative. The full story of Lewes's services to his common-law wife is told only in 1989 by Ina Taylor. In response to friends' shock, the sick man's haggard appearance was explained away as aging, an explanation his wife readily accepted. "To the end George put Marian [Mary Ann] first. For as long as possible he hid the severity of his own disease [cancer] from her. . . . As the frequency of his attacks increased he attempted to keep up the image of the funny man, telling his usual hilarious anecdotes or getting Marian to accompany his singing on the piano." Taylor called the weeks preceding his death "a grim charade."

The portrait of Eliot that emerges in the more recent biographies by women is that of an eminently strong-willed woman who, by playing a feminine, dependent role, manages to coerce George Lewes and, later, John Cross, into doing what she wants. Reestablishing Eliot as a woman, separating her as a sexual and sexed being from the sterile intellectual that Cross and Leslie Stephen tried so hard to create, brings an entirely different portrait into view.

Taylor's 1989 biography does the most to shatter earlier portraits of Eliot. For example, her late, short-lived marriage was usually pictured as a pleasant romantic denouement to her life. In reality, it was macabre, especially for Cross—whose painstaking biography of his wife in this light becomes an atonement for his having tried to leave her. Yet in 1983, when Phyllis Rose suggested that Cross's jump from his and Eliot's honeymoon hotel into a Venetian canal was a suicide attempt, she, too, accepted Cross's own story—that his madness was the result of a fever. He was sedated, however, and his brother came from the States to escort him back to America. Carefully watched, he stayed in the marriage. In contrast, Taylor's version of the story rejects Cross's explanation and draws from accounts of his family members. Although the public story was that Cross had proposed to Eliot, his family was sure that the reverse was true. They believed Eliot had proposed to Cross, whose mother had died at the same time as George Lewes, and that Cross was too much the gentleman to refuse. From that point, his health declined. Emaciated at the time of their marriage, he left on the honeymoon clearly aghast at finding himself in an oedipal trap, married to this motherlike figure. Hysterical in Venice, Cross "threw himself from the balcony of their room into the Grand Canal below. . . . He fought against two gondoliers who tried to rescue him, and pleaded that he should be allowed to drown."

For Sir Leslie Stephen, writing his 1902 book on Eliot in proper biographical style, such dramatic personal material had no place in the life of a great author. Rather, the content of any biography was to be factual, historical, and improving. Such anecdotes of passion—or what passed for passion—were none of these, and any biographer's reliance on letters or stories to confirm such tales discredited them. That Stephen had himself drawn heavily on the account of the young husband in question, on the man who devoted much of his life to commemorating his dead wife, perhaps as penance, somehow seemed to be objective research.

Recent women biographers find it difficult to resolve the obvious conflicting stories, and conflicting emotions, in the life of Mary Ann Evans/George Eliot, a woman who wanted it all. Not content with writing intellectual essays or with living as an old maid in a relative's home, this woman wanted sexual comfort, a home, fame, and happiness on her own terms. That the current biographies create a venturesome woman who, in the eyes of today's readers, is more admirable—though also more complex and much more sexual—than she was in Stephen's book nearly a hundred years ago is a tribute to the changing nature of biography. But such changes carry with them an implicit warning. This is probably not the last evolution of approach and style that Eliot's biography will undergo. In another decade, her character—and her ambition—may take on another cast, in the hands of yet other biographers. For example, even the portrait of Eliot as intellectual has changed. Valerie Dodd's 1990 *George Eliot: An Intellectual Life* traces Eliot's immersion in women's writing (that of George Sand, Margaret Fuller, Mary Wollstonecraft and particularly Elizabeth Barrett Browning's verse novel *Aurora Leigh*) and suggests that the real bond between George Eliot and Lewes was his knowledge of—and support for—such work.

These different versions of the George Eliot biography suggest some of the complexity that Victoria Glendinning spoke to in a recent essay when she asked, "Is the story of your life what happens to you, or what you feel happens to you, or what observers see happening to you?" Her answer was that biography is all these stories, and perhaps others, given the number of sources any single biographer might draw from. The factual "what happens," on which Cross and Stephen thought they were relying, differs greatly from "what you feel happens to you," the subject's own account, told in letters, autobiography, memoir, or—today—interviews. In the process of writing or telling her own story, the subject can create an emphasis, shape events, or fictionalize directly—as Eliot seemed to do in her fictions. (Part of the reason today's readers acclaim *Middlemarch* even though earlier critics found it inferior is the passion evident in Eliot's telling of the siblings' story.) The least credible point of view—but the one most often used today through interviews with people who were contemporaries of the subjects or descendants of those contemporaries—is the third, "what observers see happening to you." Were Eliot's story to be told through the eyes of the society that shunned her, it would be much more negative than it currently is. Eliot might then appear to be only a sexual being, out to entrap every man who crossed her path, especially the young and recognizably unstable John Cross. Kaleidoscopically, disparate images exist within the research field, and the power of biographers is that they can focus the reader's eye on the image that they have decided is most accurate.

The Stories of Emily Brontë

Some of the greatest changes in the present writing of women's lives, however, have resulted from more than the abstracted—

and timeless—problem of point of view, which Glendinning describes. In the past thirty years, the study of women's history has given biographers quantities of new information: Carroll Smith-Rosenberg's now classic research into women's friendships during the later nineteenth century, for example, in which she discovered through a quantity of private letters between women that most women had passionate relationships with other women, even while happily—or at least dutifully—married. Whether or not the women's passion was ever physically expressed, the love gave rise to erotic letters and helped establish what was often the fact—that proper women married largely because it was expected of them, but their true loves were other women. What such allegiances meant in women's lives—and the reason many men were so fearful of what came to be known as inversion/lesbianism—is only now being explored. At the very least, it questions the overarching social and gender stereotype that women lead lives intent on finding some male partner to validate their existences. (It could well be that some future research into Eliot's life will uncover an essential friendship with another woman—such as the closeness to the Bray sisters that Stephen privileged in his biography, a friendship as important as, or more important than, her liaison with George Lewes.)

Women's health, both physical and mental, is another vast area of new research. The pioneering studies of Phyllis Chesler (*Women and Madness*, 1972) and Barbara Ehrenreich and Dierdre English (*For Her Own Good: 150 Years of the Experts' Advice to Women*, 1978), combined with literary applications of the interest in women's health in Sandra Gilbert and Susan Gubar's *The Madwoman in the Attic: The Woman Writer and the Nineteenth-Century Literary Imagination* (1979), led to broader studies in 1985—Elaine Showalter's *The Female Malady: Women, Madness, and English Culture, 1830–1980* and Carroll Smith-Rosenberg's *Disorderly Conduct: Visions of Gender in Victorian America*—as well as literally hundreds of essays and books that respond to, and correct, much of the misleading work of Charcot, Freud, and Jung on women's hysteria and madness. Increasingly in the past century, the issue of madness or health plays a substantial role in the consideration of women's lives. One ramification of this interest is readers' fascination with suicide, but a more constant attention to women's social and antisocial behaviors, and the relationship of those behaviors to creativity, also gives new perspectives.

A corollary of this area of research in women's health is the work being done presently on the eating disorders that plague so many women and, under different names, men. A dramatic concern with body images, and society's view of those images, has formed a culture that doesn't even notice when its young destroy themselves through food abuse. The adolescent wrestler who gains or loses thirty or forty pounds a season (sometimes a third of his body weight) because his team needs a middle weight instead of a heavy weight differs little from the young woman who wills herself to grow down to a size four dress. Through the lens of this current research, the sometimes inexplicable lives of past biographical subjects may also grow clearer.

One of the most fascinating of writers—who until very recently was fascinating in part because she was enigmatic—is Emily Brontë. Younger sister of the better-established and more often studied Charlotte, Emily was the erratic, moody, antisocial child among the pastor Brontë's six talented offspring. For Emily, being away at school was even more torture than was her barren life in Haworth at the top of the Yorkshire moors.

The comfort readers have come to feel with the existing portraits of Charlotte Brontë, who survived the miseries of charity schools, unrequited love, and the death of nearly her entire family as she became a famous novelist, has obscured much of the pain of that isolated life. Charlotte's isolation and poverty was, in fact, shared by Emily, Anne, and Branwell, the four survivors of the Brontës' six children. Until recently, biographers romanticized the Brontës' lives to stress the positive side of both the geography of their home and their lonely adolescence in the Haworth parsonage after the early death of their beloved mother.

In 1988, however, young British journalist Rebecca Fraser published *The Brontës: Charlotte Brontë and Her Family*, an exemplar of the popular family biography that can reveal more about a person's development than can an individual study. Her stark account of minds forced to exist in a fantasy world to escape the poverty and unhappiness they knew in Yorkshire was both moving and revisionary. Her attention to Branwell's drug addiction and the way his problems—inability to study or work, addiction, manic and suicidal behavior, illness—overloaded the already-dysfunctional family, explained much of the household dynamic. But even though Fraser's work dealt with the family relationships in significant new ways, the Emily character remained a mystery.

In quoting from Charlotte's correspondence, Fraser only deepened the mystery of the sister's character. Why was Emily so angry when Charlotte referred to her as her sister rather than as Ellis Bell, her nom de plume? Why would she never care for herself or permit a doctor to be called? Why did she give up and await her death once Branwell was dead? As Charlotte wrote in Emily's obituary, "I have seen nothing like it. . . . Stronger than a man, simpler than a child, her nature stood alone. The awful point was . . . on herself she had no pity. . . . From the trembling hand, the unnerved limbs, the faded eyes, the same service was exacted as they had rendered in health." The specter of the gaunt and silent Emily never left Charlotte.

In 1990, however, Katherine Frank's study of Emily Brontë proposed a reasonable solution to her enigmatic, hostile drivenness: anorexia. Emily Brontë was one of the many women who learned to control her life by either eating or not eating. Her private rebellion first showed itself at boarding school soon after her mother's death, and the same will to die accompanied her recognition of Branwell's addiction. In *A Chainless Soul: A Life of Emily Brontë*, Frank traces the countless references in the family papers as well as the sisters' fiction to someone's refusing food. She describes Emily's behavior at Roe Head school:

> In addition to being silent and withdrawn, Emily was barely eating and growing thinner and thinner and more and more languid and unresponsive each day. The acts of speaking and eating were strangely intertwined in Emily's life. She would often substitute one for the other: words for food or food for words. Or she would withhold one for the other: silence for fasting or fasting for speech. At Roe Head, in the late summer and autumn of 1835, she refused, as far as possible, to eat or speak. But her refusal of food was, in fact, a kind of utterance.

Frank suggests that being one of the tallest girls at the school, and the oldest, made Emily's body size important: at seventeen, she had been placed in a low grade and surrounded with young girls half her age—and half her size.

Once Branwell's opium addiction took over his life, according to Frank, he haunted his father and sisters and held them "hostage at home." His behavior was so unpredictable—lewd, violent, and suicidal—that some nights Charlotte, Emily, and Anne wondered whether they would live till dawn: fires were numerous, and after their father went blind, only Emily could handle the raging man. For the years of Branwell's decline and madness, until he finally died of tuberculosis in 1848, Emily was his nurse and caretaker. No wonder she contracted his highly contagious illness, surviving him by only a few months.

As Frank makes clear, however, Emily's death came as much because of her starvation as her consumption: "The light-headed dreaminess of hunger gave way to the distorted and delusional thinking of starvation. Once a certain point of emaciation has been reached, the brain too becomes starved by internal imbalances induced by fasting. As the body becomes frailer, the psychological sensation of power and transcendence over the purely physical must be protected. Hence Emily's rejection not only of food but of medical attention as well." In 1990, the long-standing enigma of Emily Brontë's behavior, and perhaps her magnificent gift, was solved through a biographer's probing the possibility of a serious medical condition.

In these two brief histories of biographies of George Eliot and Emily Brontë, the more recent books have been written by women biographers, using approaches based on current information about female development. That paradigm, however, does not always hold true. Women biographers, like women readers, are often themselves caught responding to women's lives in stereotyped ways, their imaginations flooded with ideas about which women deserve biographies. Even in the cases of Eliot and Emily Brontë, women who are valued primarily for their art, an interest in their personal and sexual behavior almost overshadows their work. That may be the reason so many biographers—both male and female—are most comfortable with women as biographical subjects when they have chosen acceptable social roles—when they have married successful men. To write about a woman who is a wife gives the biographer additional parameters: the subject is not only female but probably heterosexual, dependent in some way on her husband, and accustomed to living in the real world as half a couple. For a woman to accept such social conformity may mean a less idiosyncratic, or a less mysterious, persona.

5

The Biographer's Problem: Women as Wives

> I believe that what woman resents is not so
> much giving herself in pieces as
> giving herself purposelessly.
> Anne Morrow Lindbergh

Of all the stereotypes of women that today's culture still accepts, that of wife (and mother) has—if anything—gained in value. The privileging of the heterosexual and the even more recent conservative privileging of the woman who lives to make a home for husband and family suggest that Susan Faludi's *Backlash* (1990) was accurate: society's much-publicized emphasis on the need for a return to stable, traditional morality was a means of encouraging women to leave the work force. In the 1990s, there is a growing sentiment that the truly good and useful woman is the homemaker. For women biographers, the climate of book acceptance and publication has changed accordingly. Of the many women who purchase biographies, nearly 40 percent are homemakers.

Within the category of "biography of wife," however, there is room to maneuver, and several recent books about wives have made clear how much choice the biographer has in describing a woman's role in marriage. Recent biographies of Nora Joyce, Hadley Hemingway, Abigail Adams, and Eleanor Roosevelt show a range of approaches to the difficult problem of keeping a wife's character separate from that of her spouse.

The Search for Nora Joyce

Brenda Maddox's 1988 *Nora*, the narrative of Nora Barnacle, wife of modernist writer James Joyce, is a model of the wife's story that becomes a dual biography of wife and husband. Like Milford's *Zelda, Nora* provided an unfamiliar perspective on a number of events in Joyce's life. More importantly, and again like *Zelda*, the book brought to life the woman who had long been derogated to the role of Joyce's sex partner—in this case, a coarse, even illiterate playmate. Maddox didn't entirely relinquish that appeal, however: whereas in England, *Nora* was subtitled *A Biography of Nora Joyce*, in the States the subtitle became *The Real Life of Molly Bloom*. This capitalization on the erotic appeal of the Molly Bloom section of Joyce's *Ulysses* was reinforced by the fact that throughout her book Maddox identified Nora with Joyce's women characters. Just as F. Scott Fitzgerald had modeled his fictional women on his wife, Zelda, sometimes directly borrowing from her letters and diaries, so Joyce portrayed Nora—at least one part of Nora—repeatedly in his writing. The subtitle was effective: sales were high, and the book in its U.S. publication won a *Los Angeles Times* Book Prize.

To appreciate Maddox's book requires knowing the kind of portrayal Nora had received in standard biographies of Joyce—especially Richard Ellmann's 1959 book and the 1982 revision. Appearing for the first time a quarter of the way into the Ellmann biography, after an extensive and sympathetic rendition of Joyce's unpleasant personality traits, Nora was introduced in the character that was to remain constant, according to this biographer, through the next thirty-seven years: "a tall young woman, auburn-haired, walking with a proud stride." Employed in "a slightly exalted rooming house," Nora was given no credit by Ellmann for her ability to make her own living at what was the best hotel in Dublin (and where she was chosen from her peers to do the most responsible work available). With more education than most women of the time had, Nora was ambitious, a shrewd judge of people, and a witty conversationalist (though not, as Ellmann emphasized, an "intellectual"). Ellmann, however, saw Nora as someone to condescend to. He spoke of her simplicity and her alcoholic father; he opened the paragraph in which he attempted to describe the woman who might somehow have been worthy of Joyce with this sentence, "To any other writer of the time, Nora Barnacle would have seemed ordinary." The reader understands that, at least to Ellmann, Nora would have seemed very ordinary.

For all his proven ability to write Joyce's life, this biographer missed the complexity of his subject's most enduring relationship. Ellmann had decided that Joyce's primary tie was to his brother Stanislaus; by emphasizing this tie, he could effectively discount Joyce's liaison with Nora. From Joyce's disappointment that Nora had not kept their date in June 1904, to his request that her bed be placed close to his as he lay dying in hospital, his passion for her was a driving force in his life. But in Ellmann's account, such passion remained puzzling.

In describing the couple's meeting after Joyce's initial disappointment, Ellmann is guilty of using Joyce's fictional date of Bloomsday, June 16, to claim that Joyce and Nora finally walked out on that day. Maddox questions the date, however, and also corrects Ellmann's assumption that the two had intercourse at that time (Ellmann used as proof Joyce's later comment to Nora, "You made me a man"). Given Nora's sense of propriety, Maddox believes that act occurred only after the couple left Ireland together, months later. In their view, elopement replaced conventional marriage (they were not married until 1931, and then under the pressure that their two children were, by law, bastards). Nora's being a common-law wife contributed to her defamation by critics and biographers: not only was she supposedly unlettered, sexual, and a bad cook (the order of importance among these reprehensible qualities varied with biographer), Nora was not even Joyce's legal wife. That she might have been years ahead of her society, wanting a union based only on love, was never suggested.

In *Nora*, Maddox told a different story. The Barnacles were no lower in class than the Joyces. Both families were dysfunctional; Joyce's father, too, was an alcoholic. Nor was Nora uneducated. Considered pretty, she also had several well-born suitors, and part of Joyce's urgency in taking her away from Dublin was to separate her from the most recent of them, a man whose family was far superior to the Joyces. Yet, even though Joyce's jealousy was a prime motive in their elopement, Ellmann chose not to mention that Nora had other beaux until midway through the book, a hundred fifty pages past his introduction of her.

When Maddox tells Nora's story, the Joyce narrative becomes human. Unable to find work, Joyce lives in misery; three weeks after their first child, Giorgio, is born, Nora takes in laundry to earn money for their living. Anger, poverty, trickery, sex good and bad, cruelty—the life of Jim and Nora Joyce is colored with emotion. In Ellmann's telling, however, Joyce exists as a sterile but brilliant trickster, criticizing friends and especially his brother for their failures to provide money for his living expenses. Nora barely exists, except as she is mentioned occasionally in letters to Joyce from friends. In Maddox's biography, Nora plays one of the leading roles. For example, it is Nora's unhappiness with Italy—and with Joyce during that time—that leads to his early bouts of heavy drinking; in Ellmann's account, Joyce simply drinks, with no provocation. In Maddox, Nora's sleeping head-to-feet away from Joyce is explained as a kind of inexpensive birth control, whereas in Ellmann the practice is only aberrant.

The differences in the perspectives of the Maddox and the Ellmann biographies are extensive, but even more important for the reader's sense of both Nora and James Joyce is the male biographer's historical privileging of the male subject in Anglo culture. While Maddox pointed out that Joyce probably learned some of his objectionable behavior toward women from his father, it is Ellmann whose vivid—but strangely nonjudgmental—sentence rings true: admitting John Joyce's alcoholism, Ellmann wrote that he often returned home to "tonguelash his sons and perhaps whip any small daughter who happened to be within reach. 'An insolent pack of little bitches since your poor mother died,' he would say, and rebuke them for fancied ingratitude." That Ellmann was here quoting from Joyce's *Ulysses* further muddies the attribution. If the reader is being told that Joyce's biography exists whole and factual in his fiction, then the dangerous implications of father-daughter incest to be found there will also have to be reckoned with.

Ellmann's biography of Joyce emphasized two relationships—his tormenting dependence on his brother and his obsessively erotic protection of his second child, Lucia. Once it became clear in her early adolescence that Lucia was psychologically unstable, Joyce grew obdurate about caring for her. He fought institution-alization for her. While Ellmann saw his defense of his daughter as admirable, Maddox questioned his refusal to accept the obvious. As Hélène Cixous wrote in her study of Joyce about his fascination with the theme of incest, "surely the complex relationship between Joyce and his daughter Lucia must have provided inspiration for the ardent, guilty father who refused, against the general opinion, to admit his daughter's madness, insofar as he could not but feel himself responsible." Joyce's concern, Cixous pointed out, was in-congruous. In life, he seldom noticed his children and left their rearing to Nora. Once Lucia's condition became apparent, Joyce tried to escape admitting her illness through his absorption in writ-ing *Finnegans Wake*. Although he found Ireland, sexuality, the muse, and the life force in both Nora and Lucia, he yet denied his dependence on either.

Despite such assessments by feminist readers and critics as Ci-xous, when Ellmann in 1982 published the much revised version of his 1959 biography of Joyce, he simply reprinted verbatim the sec-tions about Nora. Ellmann remained confident that Nora Barnacle was the classic nonentity—a wife truly inferior to Joyce, who was, in his words, "one of the most rarefied minds of the century." For Brenda Maddox, however, Nora was "important because she be-longed to Joyce and because she never did. She was the stronger of the two, an independent spirit, who had far more influence on him than he upon her."

The Several Hadley Hemingway Stories

Maddox's summation of Nora in her wifely role to James Joyce might be transferred to describe another often-underestimated wife, Ernest Hemingway's first partner, Hadley Richardson of St. Louis. In the many biographies of Hemingway, all written by men, Hadley was the large, older woman he had married at twenty-one as if, in a classic Freudian act, he was replacing the mother with whom he had quarreled. Although their Paris friends considered Hadley beautiful, the fact that she gained a substantial amount of weight while pregnant with their child, John (Bumby), somehow justified Hemingway's leaving her for the fashionable, small, and rich Pauline Pfeiffer. Hemingway himself never suggested this; in fact, much of *A Moveable Feast*, his memoir of the Paris years, laments his divorce from Hadley.

The two biographies of her, written nearly twenty years apart, present a tough woman who was willing to move on rather than cope with her young husband's immaturity, temper, and infidelity. In Alice Hunt Sokoloff's 1973 biography, *Hadley, The First Mrs. Hemingway*, the reader cannot forget that Hadley Richardson is interesting because of that initial marriage. According to Sokoloff, after Hadley decided she would give Hemingway a divorce so that he could marry Pauline, that next spring (1927) she met journalist Paul Mowrer, and they were married, after his divorce, in 1933. In Gioia Diliberto's 1992 *Hadley*, because more correspondence of both Hadley and Ernest had come to light, Hadley's relationship with Mowrer, which dated to 1923 when they played tennis together, may have influenced her decision to give Hemingway the divorce. Diliberto describes Mowrer's arranging a meeting with Ernest during the fall of 1926 so that he could discern what Hadley's status as a separated woman actually was. While the more recent book still emphasizes Hadley's marriages, it also clarifies a number of details that have remained vague—even in countless biographies of Hemingway. For instance, Diliberto says bluntly that during the 1920s both Hemingway and Ezra Pound lived primarily on income from their wives' trust funds.

The Diliberto book adds some necessary context to much of Sokoloff's information. The two biographers describe Grace Hemingway's call on Hadley soon after her marriage to Ernest to instruct her about love and how to make her son happy. Sokoloff calls the visit a "tasteless intrusion." But it is Diliberto's mentioning that throughout the visit Grace held Hadley's hands between her own—"as in a trap"—that brings the scene to life. Both books make clear that though literary history has given Hadley Richardson Hemingway only a fraction of the attention that her young husband has received, their many letters show that much of his literary education came from his widely-read and intelligent first wife.

The Presidential Wife Saga

A more startling case of a wife being discounted as negligible to the career of her husband is the biography of Eleanor Roosevelt. Yet the story of this young Roosevelt orphan who married her Hyde Park cousin, Franklin Delano, questions patriarchal power from the start: Eleanor didn't even need to change her name. While their marriage, particularly in its early years, appeared to be all too traditional, Eleanor grew from the role of naive—and eventually betrayed—wife into that of an independent and loving woman, able to find happiness separate from her life with her husband.

The biographer of any political figure faces the task of redescribing history in order to tell the personal story. Wives of literary figures, too, are caught in history to some extent—at least the history of book publication. Nora Joyce's life was often described as pre-*Ulysses* and post-*Ulysses*, even though the more important chronology for her during the 1920s traced the state of her daughter's health. But the historicizing of literary event is nothing compared with the way historical event dominates the narratives of wives of political figures. The process is obvious in the narrative of that often-profiled presidential wife, Abigail Adams, as it is in accounts of Eleanor Roosevelt.

Whether or not these women were interested in history as it surrounded their families, the shape of their existence in biography is pegged on elections, legislative action, and wars. There is little attention to what was happening in their personal lives. No matter how outstanding the political wife is in her own charitable or career field or within her family, the biographer tends to take one of three approaches. One possibility is to subordinate all personal narrative to visible external history. During the decade when Abigail Adams lived and cared for her five children in the States while John lived abroad as minister to France, Holland, and Britain, she was lonely and depressed. She often wrote imploring him to return, sometimes threatening him that she would leave. In his absence, she delivered a stillborn child, struggled to remain calm during actual battles, and kept their farm solvent despite high inflation and Adams's failure to send her money. Yet in nearly all biographies of either John Adams or the Adamses as a couple, these are the years of the Revolutionary War. The books chart important battles and decisive acts; the Adamses' intimate history is seldom mentioned.

Another common approach is to emphasize the wife's political acumen, even if she has little. To raise her to a level of quasi equality with her political husband means making her an expert in his field. (As recently as 1987, one biographer of Abigail Adams refers to her marriage as "a partnership" of skilled political figures.) While Abigail was a very capable woman—and a better farmer than John—she was married at nineteen and quickly had seven children. At this stage of her life, she was no politician—there was no reason for her to be. This admission does not diminish her abilities; it rather points again to the fact that women's biographies need to have a different set of emphases, just as women heroes may have different qualities from male heroes.

Yet a third way of rendering a visible wife harmless, diluting any threat a woman with power might have, is to emphasize her moral goodness. When Elizabeth Ellet, one of America's first biographers, wrote about Adams, it was with praise for "her republican simplicity of manners." Ellet further claimed about Abigail that "her close observation, clear judgment and discrimination, enabled her to exercise an influence widely acknowledged." The biographer's tactic here was not to make Adams a politician but rather to leave vague her spheres of influence.

In an early stage of her reputation as First Lady, Eleanor Roosevelt was considered heroic because of her consistent work for the poor and the marginalized. The social reforms that Franklin Delano Roosevelt initiated were largely the vision of his wife and his advisers. But because her ennobling image was tied to her physical appearance later in her life, when her tall angularity and strong facial planes made her seem less than feminine (displayed in photos chosen to emphasize her properness rather than her considerable charm), her generous spirit seemed linked with what the media portrayed as her ugliness. Twelve years of being the First Lady had also brought her enough enemies that caricature and detraction were familiar.

The truth of her life, however, was almost the opposite of this caricature. As the oldest of the alcoholic Elliott Roosevelt's children, she was subject to his most aberrant behavior. Her mother, Anna Hall Roosevelt, a naive beautiful socialite when she married, was herself so defeated and demoralized by his erratic, abusive behavior that she died during routine surgery in 1892. Eleanor, then eight, lived reclusively with her grandmother Hall until her father's death five years later, when she was sent, happily, to Marie Souvestre's school in England. From 1899 to 1902, she became confident, learning to dress fashionably and to present her mind and her height to advantage. When she returned to the States and made her debut, she was considered something of a beauty.

Unfortunately, returning to her grandmother's home meant reliving the trauma of an alcoholic household: her young uncle behaved much as her father had years before, and now there was physical threat to a woman of her age. At nineteen she became secretly engaged to Franklin Roosevelt, her fifth cousin, despite the reservations of Franklin's commanding mother. When Eleanor's uncle Teddy gave her away at the 1905 wedding, some observers felt that Franklin gained more than she.

During Eleanor's child-bearing years (six children, one of whom died before his first birthday), her lack of self-esteem caused depression and unease. She was always unsure of herself, partly because she could not satisfy her mother-in-law. According to Blanche Wiesen Cook's 1992 *Eleanor Roosevelt, 1884–1933*, she resented being made to become only a wife to a husband who was so desperately ambitious that everything he did—including, perhaps, marrying her—could be attributed to political aims. Rather than share their abilities, as they had during courtship and the early years of their marriage, FDR after 1913 relegated Eleanor to the roles of mother and housekeeper and began the most important affair of his life—with Lucy Mercer, Eleanor's social secretary and friend. When in 1917 Eleanor discovered some of Lucy's love letters to Franklin and offered him a divorce, Eleanor, then thirty-three, lost all will to live. Even though her five children were under eleven, she could not attend to them; she barely had strength enough to drive to Henry Adams's monument to his wife, Clover, the Saint-Gaudens statue she called Grief, in the Rock Creek Cemetery in Washington, where she spent most of her days. A victim of eating disorders during this period, Eleanor had teeth and gums so weakened from starvation and vomiting that her upper teeth protruded further and further.

During the next years of agony and emotional separation from her husband, Eleanor lost what little self-esteem she had left. But the battle over Franklin's giving up Lucy—which he did, for the most part, evidently because of his mother's firm stand on the matter—gave her some power, and she was eventually able to turn away from him to pursuits she found interesting. She threw herself into work for women's issues; she became friends with two lesbian couples, Esther Lape and Elizabeth Reed and Nancy Cook and Marion Dickerman, and with them built a hideaway house called Val-Kill; and she also began the affair, till recently shrouded in mystery, with Earl Miller, her husband's bodyguard and twelve years her junior. Even though Franklin had forged a new romantic liaison with another blue-eyed secretary, Missy LeHand, his erotic life was now less threatening to her.

By the time of FDR's contracting polio in 1921 and then needing to live in the South (rehabilitation at Warm Springs, Georgia, was necessary for the rest of his life), Eleanor, still truly supportive and continuing to play the role of loyal wife and mother, had developed her own personal life.

According to most biographers of Franklin and of the Roosevelts as a couple, however, Eleanor was a somewhat boring woman who lived joylessly after her discovery of the affair with Lucy Mercer. Some historians concluded that her constant visits to the Saint-Gaudens monument and her obvious withdrawal marked the end of her growth as a person. They saw her turning to charitable works as a kind of vengeance for having been scorned as a woman. Even family friend Joseph P. Lash who wrote the story of her discovering the affair in his 1971 *Eleanor and Franklin* gave it less than a page and focused on Franklin's recognition that divorce would end his career rather than on Eleanor's illness and depression—which go unmentioned.

As recently as 1985, in his *FDR: The New York Years, 1928–1933*, Kenneth S. Davis summarized the situation with little mention of Eleanor's anguish: "He seriously considered divorcing Eleanor so that he might marry Lucy. This would have meant the end of his political career, as Eleanor, wounded almost to death, pointed out to him in offering him his freedom." Davis's emphasis throughout stresses the crucial role Louis Howe played in FDR's career; yet, while that friendship is important, it hardly supplanted Roosevelt's relationship with his wife and family. Davis portrays Eleanor as the manipulative wife, taunting her husband with the sure loss of a successful political future if he divorces her. No other historians' accounts have repeated this tone; most have respected Eleanor's pained correspondence and the obvious devastation her discovery brought her. Years later, in her own three-volume autobiography, Eleanor never mentioned the Lucy Mercer affair—or the name Lucy Mercer.

Silence was her tactic regarding Earl Miller as well. Her memoirs and letters, then, followed the public lead, presenting her as long-suffering wife, staunch champion of her husband's ambition, without regard for his flirtations or more serious extramarital involvements (she does mention Missy LeHand and her role as Roosevelt's hostess when he entertained at Warm Springs, where Eleanor seldom visited). She herself adopted the conventions of the political biographer—that the wife of a politician has no identity other than that of wife, subject largely to external event. She did this partly to maintain her own elevated position (after her husband's death and her numerous charitable contributions in connection with the Second World War, Eleanor Roosevelt was viewed as such a saint, she would surely not have contributed to any notion of scandal in her memoirs). She may also have used this strict, external approach to shield herself from having to acknowledge the incredible pain FDR's infidelity brought her. And in some still-devoted way, she continued to protect his image as president and international leader.

The photographs accompanying the text of Eleanor Roosevelt's memoir are also public and political: they are of Mrs. Roosevelt in public ceremonies, going on good-will flights, with her colleagues and friends (but never with Franklin). In contrast, the many more personally intimate photographs that Cook chose for her recent biography show Eleanor as exuberant, loving and lovely, and usually accompanied by friends. These photos appear in no other biographies of either Eleanor or Franklin.

The fact that from the time of the Lucy Mercer affair Eleanor and Franklin led essentially separate lives was kept a secret from the American public. So separate had their existences become that Eleanor faced panic in 1932 when she realized that her husband could well be elected president. To a friend she wrote an outspoken letter about her possibly refusing to move to the White House. She would not give up her satisfying private life, Eleanor said; she would instead elope with Earl Miller. At Louis Howe's insistence, the friend destroyed the letter. While Kenneth Davis termed the missive "hysterical," Eleanor was undoubtedly trying to explain the hypocrisy she felt at pretending to be FDR's long-suffering helpmeet. After fifteen years of silence, she was finally expressing herself. Yet in her autobiography, though she admitted that "the turmoil in my heart and mind was rather great that night," she attributes her panic to the change in her private existence: "As I saw it, this meant the end of any personal life of my own. I knew what traditionally should lie before me; I had watched Mrs. Theodore Roosevelt and had seen what it meant to be the wife of a president, and I cannot say that I was pleased at the prospect." Eleanor's usual pose of serenity came to her rescue, however, and she added that not wanting Franklin to be president "was pure selfishness on my part, and I never mentioned my feelings on the subject to him." These comments suggest that even when the First Lady broke her silence on some topics, her watchful writing about them might be less than truthful.

Later in her life, Eleanor became the lover of Lorena Hickok, a prominent *New York Times* reporter, and after the passion of their liaison ended, they remained devoted friends for the rest of their lives. Eleanor guarded their secret well: the American public at midcentury, or today for that matter, would not have welcomed any glimpse of a bisexual First Lady.

For the researcher of Eleanor Roosevelt's life, there is almost as much information to be gathered from what is missing as from what is visible. There is no correspondence between Earl Miller and Eleanor, although it is known that he wrote her long letters every day from 1928 to her death in 1962: thirty-four years of daily letters. Eleanor's personal photographs and films show a steady stream of outings, plays, swims, and other intimate times with Earl alone and with his friends. This photographic record is indisputable, as is the fact that in it Eleanor looks like a new, a loved, woman. No longer the strained and fearful wife of the New York governor, in these photos Mrs. Roosevelt was the woman she had promised to become after her years of British education—charming, poised, knowledgeable, and confident in her sexuality.

BOTH ELEANOR ROOSEVELT and Abigail Adams were themselves writers, so their representations of themselves (whether in autobiography, memoir, letters, or diaries) serve both to counter and in some ways to inform the biographers' views. Just as biographers draw from the husband's written persona, so they can draw from the wife's. In most biography, *research* means the reading of correspondence and other archival materials. If the wife goes unrepresented there, the biography of necessity becomes one-sided. Because of Abigail Adams's letters and Eleanor Roosevelt's extensive writing, including her three-volume autobiography, the biographer interested in the lives of these political wives has a storehouse of information about not only the times and family events but about the characters and voices of the women in question.

Any such written record, however, must be read with at least some suspicion: wives of presidents are still, in a very great sense, public property. Their writings all too frequently are shaped to support the necessary public image.

6
A Woman's Self: Wives and Writers

> Women will starve in silence until new
> stories are created which confer on them
> the power of naming themselves.
> Sandra M. Gilbert and Susan Gubar

While Eleanor Roosevelt wrote a cautious tale of her personal life, leaving out more crucial information than she included, other women writers have been more willing to speak about the full range of their experiences in their own voices. African pilot and horse trainer Beryl Markham, for instance, though a married woman much of her life, portrayed herself in her memoir *West with the Night* (which may have literally been written by her third husband Raoul Schumacher) as adventurous, independent, and as free as the wind that carried her plane. But for Anne Morrow Lindbergh, the woman married to the most famous flier of the century, speaking in her own voice was difficult, possible only in the diaries that she finally published thirty years after they had been written. Even though she made money from her other writing about both flying and ecology, she seldom broke out of the aura of wifehood with which she carefully surrounded herself. Her own creation of herself in her writing and the two 1993 biographies that tell her story show the kinds of ellipses that occur when a woman's story is submerged in that of her husband.

The Lindbergh Legends

The problem with being Anne Morrow Lindbergh, the writer, was that she remained, always, Charles A. Lindbergh's wife. Few people in the twentieth century have been able to carve out lasting personal fame, but young aviator Charles Lindbergh did so. When he made the first nonstop solo flight from New York to Paris in 1927, those thirty-three hours etched his lanky boyish image on the world's imagination, and he and *The Spirit of St. Louis* became icons of romantic change. Nothing had captured the human fancy in the 1920s like air travel, and pilots were in a class by themselves when it came to adventure.

Part of Lindbergh's charm was his adventure of flying across the Atlantic so modestly, a paper bag of sandwiches seemingly his only preparation. Another part was physical. His lean body and smiling face made him appear even younger than the twenty-six he was. As the boy next door, Lindy was everyone's little brother, the one who didn't seem as though he'd ever amount to much. (Child of separated parents, he had been reared by his teacher mother, and one of the photographs that endeared him to the public was of him with his attractive mother leaving Lindbergh's plane after a flight. Mom was also a buddy.)

Quickly taking to fame and what would be his public relations role for aviation, Lindbergh next captured the world's imagination by marrying the lovely Smith graduate Anne Morrow. Although her father, a wealthy Morgan partner, was ambassador to Mexico, and her mother acting president of Smith College, the media disguised the family's prestige and made Anne into the girl next door: the Lindberghs became the perfect American couple. Anne, the maverick English major who wrote poetry and loved Virginia Woolf's novels, was delighted to accept Lindy. No matter that he had first dated her older sister; no matter that his first criterion for choosing a bride was her ability to learn to fly (on their first date, Lindbergh took Anne up in a plane and gave her the controls). No matter that, in her own words from her 1927 diary, "His coat doesn't fit him . . . the wrist watch shows way up his wrist." Despite her omnipresent consciousness of class and background,

Anne was captivated by the flier's youthful acceptance of his immense fame—and the fame itself.

Becoming Mrs. Charles A. Lindbergh in effect erased Anne Morrow. Lindbergh's life in the air become their life, for he was not joking that Anne was to be his crew—she made long flights with him even during pregnancies. She lovingly accepted the subordination of being a helpmeet to this airborne dynamo. Fittingly, the most familiar photos of the couple, taking off for other record-breaking flights (for Anne did become a good navigator and co-pilot), show her garbed in a flight suit, teddy bear fashion, looking like a miniature replica of her tall husband.

The Lindberghs would have undoubtedly settled into a manageable level of fame, had it not been for the kidnapping and murder of their first child, Charles A. Lindbergh, Jr. In a comparatively safe 1930s world, this carefully planned attack—taking the sleeping twenty-month-old from his bedroom in the lavish New Jersey home—dominated the news for months. The agonizing period while Lindbergh met the kidnappers' ransom demands ended ten weeks later with the discovery of the child's decomposing body several miles from their home.

The three years of publicity—during and after the kidnapping and then the trial and execution of the supposed criminal, Bruno Hauptmann—forced the Lindberghs further into the privacy they had tried to construct from the start of their marriage. One of the most important effects of the tragedy was the metamorphosis in Anne, who changed from being a somewhat cynical young wife to a woman capable of both understanding and passion. She subsequently dedicated her life to protecting her family, and she also chose to do that by validating her existence—and her family's—through her writing. The tragedy of the loss of her child was her crucible as writer.

Biographies of Lindbergh throughout the years have mentioned the kidnapping and murder of his son, but sometimes briefly and always in the perspective of his life as aviator. Joyce Milton's 1993 biography *Loss of Eden: A Biography of Charles and Anne Morrow Lindbergh* makes the event central to the marriage as she treats the tragedy from the perspective of the couple's life, shattered from such grief. She devotes one-third of the book to the kidnapping and the Hauptmann trial and execution, mining back files of newspapers all over the country. She also describes the way Lindbergh worked through his grief by spending his days in physical efforts to find the kidnappers, turning their home into an unofficial police station with twenty telephone lines, and then by playing an integral role in the suspect's prosecution. Anne, however, had no such outlets. Instead, she bore a second son and then faced the indescribable worry of trying to protect him.

Ironically, the completeness of Milton's crime narrative adds little to the reader's understanding of the tense relationship between Lindbergh and his wife. Regrettably, she seldom used Anne's published diaries from these years, diaries that record the fear, pain, and loneliness of the bereft young wife. Of the several volumes of diaries, Milton quotes only a terse comment that Charles Lindbergh made a year after his son's death, "I went through it last spring—I can't go through it again," as if to suggest that this was the only, or a typical, comment. By isolating the sentence, rather than quoting it in the context Anne gives it in her diary, Milton imposes a tone on the couple's dialogue that may be inaccurate, a tone that disappears if one reads Anne's February 5, 1933, diary entry published in *Locked Rooms and Open Doors*. There, the exchange seems to be part of an ongoing discussion that dominated their lives. Both tried to face their grief, but there were great—and perhaps predictable—differences in the way they dealt with the loss of their child and with each other. Anne, writing in response to her husband's inability to empathize fully with her continuing pain, concluded, "There is a difference between men and woman. I never went through it really then. I never accepted it. I never experienced it and I will *never* be through with it. I feel sometimes frantic, battling against time—this strange time that I thought marched along in orderly fashion to the tick of the clock. And now it does not move, it stays frozen inside of me."

Her diary entries during that winter reflect the depth of her disorienting grief. They make repeated references to sleeplessness: "Bad night. C home at 2." "Bad night. . . . The Terror—it goes and is unbelievable in morning light." "Terrible night," followed by the question, "'Do you think about it so much, Anne?'" and her stream-of-consciousness answer, "All the time—it never stops—I never meet it. It happens every night—every night of my life. *It did not happen* and *It happened.* For I go over the possibilities of its not happening—so close, so narrow they are. So hard do I think about it that I almost make it unhappen."

Anne Lindbergh's evocative, almost artless, accounts of her distraught grieving show all sides of her persona. In a January 1933 entry, affronted by lower-class subway passengers, she admits to blaming her child's kidnapping on such people: "Down in the subway express, trying not to cry, terrified of a smashup. All those people—listless, tired, already dead. The pale fish-faced boy poking his mother, who reads the *Mirror*. Horrible horrible-looking people. I wanted to say, 'And which one of you killed my boy?'" Even her focus on the boy bothering his mother is disdainful. The son-mother pair could be her son and herself, yet she, as mother, would not be caught reading the *Mirror*. Disappointing as her snobbery is, the recall of the scene leads her to muse again on what the death of her child means: "When someone dies in your family you don't accept it as *Death*. It isn't death at all but something else—terrible and shaking and personal, something no one else ever suffered."

In writing about the kidnapping, Anne Morrow gave voice to that most poignant of narratives, the mother's lament for the death of a child. Her most effective writing occurs in the diaries from those years, *Hour of Gold, Hour of Lead: Diaries and Letters, 1929–1932* and *Locked Rooms and Open Doors: Diaries and Letters, 1933–1935*. Her later *Gift from the Sea* (1955) speaks indirectly to the difficult years when she and her husband were considered pro-Nazi: Lindbergh was not allowed to serve in any military capacity, and the family chose to move for a time to England to avoid U.S. journalists.

It is fortunate that Lindbergh wrote at least some of her own story. The 1993 biographies—Joyce Milton's of the couple and Dorothy Herrmann's *Anne Morrow Lindbergh: A Gift for Life*—draw heavily on her accounts, but perhaps not heavily enough: in both books, Anne is of interest largely because she is Lindbergh's wife. The Milton book begins as if it were a biography of only Lindbergh; with no mention of Anne at all, it devotes seventy pages to his ancestry, family, childhood, and career to 1926. Then his narrative joins that of the Morrow family summering in Europe, with Anne a twenty-year-old college junior. Milton's book takes on an expansive historical cast as she describes the interrelationships of government agencies concerned with aviation, but she gives little new information about the Morrows or Anne herself.

Herrmann's biography of Anne forces the reader to think of her as Lindbergh's wife because it opens with a preface describing her wedding day. Chapter 1, entitled "The Sleeping Princess," continues the fairy-tale analogy, but instead of focusing on Anne, it traces the history of her father, Dwight Morrow, "one of the most famous men of his time." Although Herrmann claims that Anne was closer to her mother and her two sisters than to the men of the family, little of the first chapter is about those women. More of it describes Anne's father and the psychological instability of her brother. Herrmann's second chapter, "A Modern Galahad," spends only a few pages on Anne's college years. As its title suggests, this chapter is about Lindbergh. The result of the book's structure is that early in a biography of a woman the reader has been introduced more thoroughly to her father, brother, and husband-to-be than to her—or to the women who were said to have been crucial to her life. Still in 1993, Anne Lindbergh is portrayed as daugher, sister, and wife. Because of the death of her child, she then becomes the unsuccessful mother, criticism that haunted her because she continued to make long flights with her husband, leaving behind her second child. The five children she bore and raised to maturity are scarcely mentioned.

The most effective portrait of Lindbergh—her sentiments and her voice—remains her diaries. While her writing in them may be guarded about some aspects of her life, they at least suggest that the woman married to Charles Lindbergh was capable of having her own ideas about most events in the couple's world. As she matured, and particularly after the deaths of both her child and her father, Anne often made wiser choices than did her spouse. The later tragedy of the Lindberghs' life was that her husband so seldom listened to her.

Women's Stories of the Exotic

Anne Lindbergh became a published writer in response to the public's interest in flight. In the 1920s and 1930s, with great reader demand for stories about aviation, fliers were encouraged to write about their experiences—and books by Amelia Earhart, Jean Batten, Nevil Shute, John Grierson, Antoine de Saint-Exupéry, and William Faulkner (his novel *Pylon)* resulted.

It was also the age of autobiography, with countless books written by anyone who either was famous or had known famous people—witness Mabel Dodge Luhan's four-volume autobiography, which mentioned D. H. Lawrence, James Joyce, Gertrude Stein, Pablo Picasso, and many other friends in Paris, Florence, New York, and Taos, New Mexico.

The small but important 1942 book by Beryl Markham/Raoul Schumacher fits into both categories. *West with the Night* is both the memoir of Markham's years flying, including her 1936 record-setting flight from England to Nova Scotia, and a tribute to the men who flew or hunted big game in the early 1930s in Kenya, Rhodesia, Tanganyika, and the Sudan—Baron Bror von Blixen, Denys Finch Hatton, and Tom Campbell Black.

At twenty-nine, Beryl Clutterbuck Markham learned to fly, and, at thirty-nine, she wrote about the period from 1931 to 1936 when she flew small planes, carrying mail and scouting elephants for hunters in East Africa. Leaving behind her horse-training business, as well as her son and his father, Mansfield Markham, she considered her plane her home: "Harmony comes gradually to a pilot and his plane. The wing does not want so much to fly true as to tug at the hands that guide it; the ship would rather hunt the wind than lay her nose to the horizon far ahead. She has a derelict quality in her character." Markham liked that derelict quality. She made a number of foolhardy but often successful flights, including her solo to Nova Scotia, which set a record for the east-to-west crossing of the Atlantic.

West with the Night is a highly selective account. For every adventure Markham records, dozens are omitted. Because the book begins with her childhood—spent with the native Murani children in the East Africa that became her home when she was four—and includes her career as horse trainer on her father's farm, more than half the book relates her life before she learned to fly. But it is the almost spiritual adventure of flight that captures her best self—and the best writing. There is ample reason for Ernest Hemingway's high praise of it.

In Errol Trzebinski's 1993 biography, *The Lives of Beryl Markham*—the chief emphasis of which is that Markham used everyone she knew, including Schumacher—the notion of how one writes becomes the issue. Schumacher, a ghost writer by trade, may have been the author of Markham's life; surely some of the passages the book is remembered for—the writing that earned Hemingway's praise—were his, based on his careful reading of both Hemingway's work and a number of flight memoirs. But Trzebinski also mentions the sheaf of pages of Markham's stories in her handwriting. Perhaps Schumacher's authorship was a rewrite process. Perhaps the fragmentation of the chronology stemmed from the process of Markham's writing about what she thought were the crucial events in her life and Schumacher's revising and elaborating on those key descriptions. There is also evidence that the publisher insisted on a quantity of rewriting and reshaping before publication—a process that further refined the raw materials of the book.

The possible influence of a male author may be one reason the Markham persona in *West with the Night* appears as an almost mythic figure: the erotic white woman. Not only was her skin white, but her white costume reinforced the difference of her role: Markham was female, light, purity, and beauty in a field dominated by the darkly powerful masculine. Through her flying, she had usurped male power. The week of her Atlantic crossing, two male fliers, Richard Merrill and Harry Richman, planned a similar flight in a much larger plane with a 1000-horsepower engine (Markham's engine in *The Messenger* was only 200 horsepower). Delayed by the dangerous weather, which Markham flew in, the men left days later. They, too, crashed.

The mythic quality of *West with the Night* was also enhanced by the restraint with which Markham's personal life was presented. The book omits several of her well-published affairs, for example, and the men who are included are not identified as lovers. They were also people readers might recognize. The Baron Bror von Blixen was an internationally known hunter, who had already published autobiographies. Both Denys Finch Hatton and the man who taught Markham to fly, Tom Campbell Black, had been killed in plane accidents during the mid-1930s; both deaths made international headlines. Finch Hatton crashed his Gypsy Moth shortly after takeoff on a flight he had invited Markham to make with him. Several years after this, just days after Markham's successful crossing of the Atlantic, Tom Black's small plane was run into by a light bomber on an airstrip, the latter's propeller slashing through Black's left shoulder and lung.

While *West with the Night* gives the men high praise for the lives they carved out of the possibility of Africa, vignettes about them stand separate and seem to impact little on Markham's life. Not surprisingly, in the first biography of Markham, Mary Lovell's *Straight on Till Morning*, these men figured prominently. Lovell claimed that Tom Black had been Beryl's great love and that she may have been pregnant with Finch Hatton's child when he died. Except for this emphasis and for its providing more context for the episodic scenes in Markham's memoir, the Lovell biography does not essentially change—or improve—the Markham narrative.

Errol Trzebinski's *Lives of Beryl Markham* benefits from years of continued reader interest, and continued research, as she presents a more complex woman, one whose tendency to create her own publicity enhanced rather than undermined her persona. That persona, however, in Trzebinski's view, was so self-absorbed as to be close to inhuman. The biographer's proof of her view is, regrettably, tied to Markham's treatment of Schumacher, and the macabre scene of Markham's driving her third husband to a meeting place so that a friend can shelter him, leaving him close to death, is a vivid one. As the biographer accepted the narrative of the friend who took Schumacher to an emergency room and secured the services of a fine physician who specialized in Malta fever, the proof of whatever illness had set upon the writer is long lost to hospital records. His blood was drained three times, and the malady was supposedly held in check so that he could be released after a week in the hospital, followed by a long recuperation in a nursing home. To attribute this illness entirely to Markham's abuse of her husband, when Schumacher was a consistently heavy drinker, seems somewhat naive—especially when Markham and Schumacher lived together subsequently.

The Trzebinski biography, like *West with the Night* itself, draws on the fact that flying was as exotic and erotic as it was adventurous. There is no question that part of the appeal of Markham's memoir was its location in Africa and the validation of her image as the beautiful Englishwoman crossing gender lines to lead a man's life training horses and then flying mail planes. Her life of adventure and freedom as a divorced woman is carefully played off against those qualities of middle-class America that gave the boyish Lindbergh his attraction. While in 1927 he reached his destination, Paris, Markham gave the sense of being equally heroic even though she did not make hers, instead crashing into a swamp, her fuel cut off by ice in the line. Markham was easy for readers to admire partly because she was so attractive—"Garbo-esque." She wore a white silk suit and a carefully fitted white helmet, her chic appearance contrasting vividly with that of Anne Lindbergh in her bulky flight suit. In the longest tradition of biography, that of portraying lives of exceptional people, Markham became the woman-as-man, a tough and brave pilot seemingly impervious to physical danger.

By the time of Lovell's biography in 1987, the names Markham, Blixen, and Finch Hatton had already been given new currency through the writings of Blixen's former wife, Karen, now known as the writer Isak Dinesen. In her 1937 memoir, *Out of Africa*, Dinesen captured the continent's exotic appeal—as she had done in her tales since returning to Denmark after the African coffee plantation had failed. For Dinesen, who had flown often with Finch Hatton in the year before his death, flying with him was her "most transporting pleasure. . . . You are taken into the full freedom of the three dimensions, after long ages of exile and dreams the homesick heart throws itself into the arms of space." Most of her memoir, however, is not about flying; it rather concerns the coffee growing, hunting, and storytelling that made up her life on the farm and with Finch Hatton. In a mournful eulogy, Dinesen memorializes her lover's last years: "Denys had a trait of character which to me was very precious, he liked to hear a story told." "Denys and I, whenever we were together, had great luck with lions." "Denys taught me Latin, and to read the Bible, and the Greek poets." At the same time, she carefully makes herself a part of everything Finch Hatton did.

Beautiful as the austere writing is, however, Dinesen's account of her last months with her lover is entirely suspect from the perspective of biographical accuracy. When she wrote about Finch

Hatton's last flight to Voi, she admitted that she asked to go along. But she replaced the story of his refusal (because he had invited Beryl Markham) with the explanation that he worried about her health and thought that the necessary camping out would be difficult for her. In contrast to Dinesen's story, her biographer Judith Thurman wrote that the two argued and Denys asked for the return of his ring, after which Karen tried to commit suicide at the home of friends.

In most accounts of the couple's involvement, their life as a couple overshadows what Dinesen was to claim was her primary attraction—her love for Africa and its people. For all the superficial similarity in place, personalities, and adventuresomeness, Karen Blixen and Beryl Markham wrote very different stories of their East African lives. While *West with the Night* is a reasonably accurate, discreet account of Markham's experiences, Dinesen's *Out of Africa* uses the guise of memoir to validate events that are often fictionalized.

Dinesen's steadily growing public called for the biographies of both Finch Hatton (Trzebinski's 1977 *Silence Will Speak*) and herself (Judith Thurman's 1982 *Isak Dinesen, The Life of a Storyteller*). The Thurman biography was the last in a series of books—in several languages—which included *Titania: The Biography of Isak Dinesen* by Parmenia Migel (1967), *Romance for Valdhorn* by Ole Wivel (1972), and *My Sister, Isak Dinesen* by Thomas Dinesen (1975). All were followed by the film *Out of Africa*, in which Robert Redford played Denys to Meryl Streep's Karen.

For the Baroness von Blixen, her fiction allowed her to assume the role of wife by pretending to be Finch Hatton's widow, even as she knew he had, just days before his death, permanently left her. His death returned him to her, and she fictionalized even the account of his funeral, with friends paying her the respect due a bereaved wife. She could then take refuge in the role of widow and return to Denmark—ill, frantic with pain some of the time, but able to write the tales that linked her imagination with that of the man she loved. Reading Isak Dinesen is both ennobling and saddening, for her fictions show how powerful cultural pressure was and is: for all her independence of spirit, Dinesen believed firmly that women should be married. She accepted the premise that only women who are loved by worthy men are themselves worthy. In her case, it was not a biographer who forced her life into the wifehood paradigm. Isak Dinesen the author created the role, and Karen von Blixen played it to perfection, leaving the 1990s reader with a kind of conundrum to face, unravel, and perhaps challenge.

7

The Power of Naming

Both biography and autobiography lay claim to facticity,
yet both are by nature artful enterprises which select,
shape, and produce a very unnatural product.

Liz Stanley, *The auto/biographical I*

Anne Lindbergh dodged the issue of writing her autobiography
by publishing her diaries, grouped in years that reflected meaningful divisions in her life. By presenting to the reader (in the
1970s) her writings from 1928 to 1933, for example, she avoided
having to comment on her life then: what the reader wants to
know, of course, is whether she regretted marrying Lindbergh.
For all her writing, she never answered that question.

Some of the autobiographers I have discussed have also avoided
writing the truth. Certainly, Isak Dinesen's memoir of her African
years was a self-justifying one, hardly a complete and truthful rendition of that part of her life, and Beryl Markham's *West with the
Night* was a partial, highly selective account of her life to middle age.

Markham's autobiography, however, provides a metaphor for
the fluidity of the possible narrative, the essential tale the writer
attempts to tell. In the opening chapter, "Message from Nungwe,"
Markham asks, "How is it possible to bring order out of memory?
I should like to begin at the beginning, patiently, like a weaver at
his loom. I should like to say, 'This is the place to start; there can
be no other.'" She continues,

> But there are a hundred places to start, for there are a hun-
> dred names—Mwanza, Serengetti, Nungwe, Molo, Nakuru.
> There are easily a hundred names, and I can begin best by
> choosing one of them—not because it is first nor of any im-
> portance in a wildly adventurous sense, but because here it

69

happens to be, turned uppermost in my logbook. After all, I am no weaver. Weavers create. This is remembrance—revisitation; and names are keys that open corridors no longer fresh in the mind, but nonetheless familiar in the heart.

Markham is willing to question the writer's pose of knowing which structure to choose. It is a posturing like that of being able to tell fiction from fact or autobiography from fiction. All writing is some incomprehensible mix of impulse and reason, strands of memory crossing immediate details and provoking the writer to telling—or to naming. Recounting the experience, or perhaps only the emotions connected with it, is the writer's naming, making concrete words out of vague, suffused feeling.

Lillian Hellman's Memoirs

In this context of recognizing that overarching mystery that writing is, one of the most fascinating pieces of women's autobiography in the past twenty years is playwright Lillian Hellman's fourth memoir, *Maybe: A Story.* Almost unnoticed after her well-received *Unfinished Woman, Pentimento,* and *Scoundrel Time,* this fourth book is an utter mystery. It breaks all rules of either autobiography or biography, even though it is ostensibly about Sarah Cameron, a woman with whom Hellman crossed paths, and roles, occasionally. At first Cameron takes Hellman's lover away from her, though she does not do so maliciously or even intentionally. The lover leaves Hellman for Cameron; Hellman then finds out who she is and wonders about her. It is the resonance of Hellman's wondering, visualizing, and fantasizing about Cameron's life that binds the segments of the book together as story, Hellman's subtitle for the book.

But it is the problematic identity or lack of it that makes the work as autobiography intriguing. Who is Cameron? By implication, then, the author's technique suggests, who is Hellman? What meaning does this woman have in Hellman's life—or does Hellman have in hers? Hellman admits that she is not sure. Important enough to be the focus, and perhaps the subject, of an entire book,

Cameron lives through the kaleidoscopic presentation of her moving quietly through this crowd, that cocktail party, this airport. And Hellman, never quite sure she is seeing her, may be finding in the adventurous woman a mirror image, a double, but the reader is never told. We start to believe that it is not in our power to understand, just as it is not in Hellman's power to understand, what the meaning of these intertwined lives might be. But rather than name the work or the relationship in any way, Hellman titles her book *Maybe*.

Since she had called her second and most emotionally powerful memoir *Pentimento*, evoking the image of one painting worked over another, the finish enriched by the layering of substance and color even if the artist was unsure about intention, readers might have looked for some clue, some introduction to method, that would make reading *Maybe* easier. Bewilderment is not a happy state for most readers. But perhaps *Maybe* is also a directive title, in its own way, because by using it Hellman calls into question all kinds of literary and genre divisions. What does it mean for a reader to be told that something is, indeed, autobiography? Or biography? Or fiction? Or story? If all genres have broken out of their definitional confines, why rely on them for any meaning? Joyce Carol Oates describes the changes among once-impermeable genre boundaries: "Like rock strata, genres shift through time. Form and content always seem inevitable, yet the one is easily detached from the other, when purpose and intention alter." In the past several decades, such change—particularly in writing by women—has accelerated.

In the same vein, are women's lives either separable or distinguishable? In the case of their initial crossing, both Hellman and Cameron were identified as the same man's lover. He was an unusual man, then, an exceptional man in the way that a hero is; he gains his exceptionality from his role in these two women's erotic histories. Hellman's last memoir asks whether one woman's life role is distinguishable from that of another.

Her other autobiographies, published between 1969 and 1980, attempt to narrate through disguise. Through severely fragmented structures, Hellman intentionally confused the reader. For all her seeming disdain for propriety—writing about an early abortion, her alcoholism, and her many years as the sometime companion of detective novelist Dashiell Hammett—Hellman's narrative presents the proper Southern woman in all her defiant guilt. In effect, her four-part memoir insists that woman's lives must be seen in bits and pieces rather than whole if they are to avoid the terrible censure society administers so readily.

The structure of *Pentimento*, for example, both hides and reveals Hellman's sexual history. It is not in the narrative about herself that the sexual text reveals itself but rather in the wonderfully poignant story of Bethe, the scandalous young aunt who relinquished good name and family for her passionate love of a gangster; of adventurous women like Julia who were passionately committed to political undertakings; of wise—and passionate—black women like Helen (and here Hellman's identity as both Southerner and misplaced Southerner, the legacy of her Jewish father, becomes key to understanding her ambivalence toward women of color). These ostensibly separate narratives never formally coalesce in *Pentimento*, but they are brought sharply back to the reader's mind in the concluding sections of the memoir, when Hammett is dead and Hellman's lost passion threatens to blank out what remains of her life. Even for the contemporary, successful woman, discourse about living life as a sexual woman remains forbidden.

Rather than mentioning the many remarkable external events of her life as America's most successful woman playwright, Hellman wrote memoirs that were so interior they were almost fantasy. One would have had to know from other sources the brilliance of her career as playwright and public literary person: her memoirs disclose little of that life. In this respect, she may have been using some of the same postmodern autobiographical license that Norman Mailer made famous in his 1959 autobiography, *Advertisements for Myself*.

Stein, Woolf, and Parody

Women's autobiography also has its own cache of defiant humor. Part of the feminized rewriting of literary history, and of literature itself, consists of questioning the name of this style or that mode. To rewrite, as Gertrude Stein said wryly that she had rewritten Robinson Crusoe, called attention to the differences between Crusoe and *The Autobiography of Alice B. Toklas*. Stein is able to achieve this fascinating comparison quickly, by juxtaposing the two works with confidence and leaving the details of comparison to her readers. The understatement that characterizes Stein's comment adds to the impression that her work is a joke, a parody, a giggle in the midst of serious literary history.

Stein was aiming for such an effect, of course. By the time of her writing of Toklas's autobiography, which was really Stein's biography—except that, written by Stein as it was, it would then have been Stein's autobiography, spoken in a voice that resembled Toklas's voice so that the book reverted into being Stein's biography as told by Alice Toklas—she had learned that traditional, conventional genre description was useless. By the time of this writing, in the fall of 1932, Stein had been a serious writer for nearly thirty years. She had published little but had had enough acclaim from other writers that she could overlook the absurd image of her as a cubist writer that was current in the States. She often, in fact, took whatever opportunity she could to inflate the public image of her and her work in order to publish and make money. Living in France in the 1930s was not nearly so cheap as it had been a decade earlier, and neither Toklas nor Stein had any means of increasing their modest stipends except by selling Gertrude's writings.

In the autumn of 1932, then, enjoying the unusually warm weather in Belley, Gertrude wrote away on the manuscript of Alice's autobiography. So close to Alice's voice was the language, so close a replica of the old stories as she had so often told them (for Alice was the storyteller in company; Gertrude forgot important details), that many readers who knew the women were sure Alice had written the work. In some ways, she did.

In the manuscript version of *The Autobiography* at Yale University, housed with the thousands of other sheets and notebooks of Stein's writing, is a different beginning for the work. This start sounds a great deal like Gertrude, with its heavy repetition, its tendency to begin in the middle, its awkward phrasing and rhythm. But later in the notebooks appear several handwritten sheets in

Toklas's small writing, and those sheets are the beginning of *The Autobiography* as it was published. I think that Stein, trying to write Alice's story, initially could not shake herself loose from her own voice, her own pattern of naming, to hear Toklas's language. With the best will in the world, Gertrude could not approach what being Alice B. Toklas sounded like. She could hear her voice, but she could not find a way to write that voice. So Alice gave her the start that enabled Stein to continue and to mimic the voice that had told her stories for more than twenty-five years. It was a symbiotic effort, with Toklas typing each day's writing and overseeing Stein's accuracy (this is one of the few manuscripts that Toklas did correct, although usually in very minor ways) and Gertrude writing again later in the day, ploughing her way through what she thought was significant about Alice's life—which was largely Alice's life with her—until the end.

The joy in Stein's assumption of the name of *autobiography* and its twin *biography* and her sense that neither had any unbreakable conventions made this work, like so much of her writing, postmodernist. But *The Autobiography* is particularly important because it was a female-voiced text, the story of two American women leading outrageously unconventional lives in France, that yet placed itself in the grand, male, conventional British literary tradition by its connection with Crusoe.

At the same time that Stein was publishing *The Autobiography of Alice B. Toklas* in 1933, Virginia Woolf was publishing her parodic biography of Elizabeth Barrett Browning's dog, *Flush*. Drawing from the letters of Elizabeth and Robert Browning and other historical sources, Woolf succeeded in writing an impassioned story of the aristocratic spaniel. Discounting so-called appropriate subject matter, Woolf filled the short book with typical biographical phrases: "historians tell us," "the task of the biographer," and a marvelously comic section of notes that ridicule the biographer's tendency both to hedge statements and to add pages of nonessential information. She also included Nero, Jane Carlyle's suicidal dog, as a means of subtly attacking both Thomas Carlyle and Elizabeth Barrett's father (and perhaps her own) for their heavy-handed patriarchal control.

Before this comparatively innocuous work—though Elizabeth

Browning might not have thought it innocuous—Woolf had seriously questioned the conventions of biography and autobiography in her wildly untraditional *Orlando* (and in 1906, when she wrote the equally parodic *Journal of Mistress Joan Martyn*). When *Orlando* appeared in 1928, it included Woolf's thanks to Defoe and other British stalwarts in its preface, so Stein's mention may have indicated her knowledge of this earlier spoof. The existence of *Orlando* seemed to contradict Woolf's very positive essay on biography in 1927, when she claimed that good biography was art rather than a work of skill. She praised the new biography that read like a novel, because people were interested in character rather than event. A few years later, however, in "The Art of Biography," her view had changed, and she criticized most biographers for their reliance on simple facts. In contrast, Woolf wrote, the biographer should be giving the reader "much more than another fact to add to our collection. He can give us the creative fact; the fertile fact; the fact that suggests and engenders."

Woolf's lifelong saturation in conventional biography—her father was the editor for most of his career of the *Dictionary of National Biography*, a twenty-volume project published between 1882 and 1901—meant that she wrote *Orlando* with full knowledge of the rules for writing biography. Within her fictional biography, she broke every conceivable convention, concluding *Orlando* with this sentence: "The true length of a person's life, whatever the Dictionary of National Biography may say, is always a matter of dispute." If a person's death date can be negotiated, any reliance on fact—even creative fact—is doomed from the start.

Both Woolf and Stein saved themselves from the heavy-handed self-justification that was the norm for successful literary women's autobiographies. Edith Wharton and Ellen Glasgow, both best-selling novelists, were so conscious of their social and intellectual positions that they wrote their memoirs as if they had led asexual, completely intellectualized, lives. To today's readers both Wharton's *A Backward Glance*, published in 1934, and Glasgow's *The Woman Within*, published in 1954—posthumously, at her direction—seem evasive and heavily self-censored. Wharton omits nearly all her romantic life, including the painful liaison with journalist Morton Fullerton; Glasgow includes an oblique account of her first serious affair but pretends that successive romances did not occur. Both women elide difficult relationships with their families and friends over their professional authorship (for women of their social position, work for pay was unsuitable), their unchaperoned travels, and their comparatively bohemian life-styles. In their stately sentences, which create the tone of a gracious old aunt deigning to tell a story or two, both take on a role of a dignified personage who is in many ways sexless. Although Glasgow gave her memoir the heretical title that promised an interior, gendered history, readers have been consistently disappointed in its revelations.

In many ways, women who write autobiography—usually women who have had successful careers—face the same problems as do women biographers of women. There are few models, and the necessary choices are difficult. Wharton and Glasgow were not the only women who disguised their life stories: as we have seen, Eleanor Roosevelt and Isak Dinesen followed the path of nondisclosure, or of self-protective disclosure. So, too, did Mary Antin, Mabel Dodge Luhan, Mary Austin, Anzia Yezierska, and Isadora Duncan. What often happens when literary women write autobiography is that they create another fictive persona. The process of writing autobiography is in some ways the same as writing fiction: creating a character to set on a narrative path, selecting events that will make the plot both plausible and dramatic (sometimes difficult in women's largely domestic lives), and telling the story so that the protagonist (who has the awkward history of also being the writer) gains both readers' admiration and their compassion. Most novels are not bound by so many confines.

So the difficulty of a woman's writing her autobiography is one of skillfully maintaining narrative interest, set against a complex of social injunctions about appropriate—and proper—women's lives. Considering that both Wharton and Glasgow avoided disclosing the central romance of their lives, Stein's outright presentation of the love between herself and Toklas in *The Autobiography of Alice B. Toklas* was years ahead of the practice in women's autobiography. Heterosexual liaisons were more acceptable than homosexual, but the problem of relationships existing outside marriage meant that discretion was imperative. Silence about sexuality was a tradition in women's autobiography: the daring radical Emma

Goldman, in her 1931 two-volume *My Life*, did not reveal her ten-year-relationship with Ben Reitman, and Margaret Sanger's 1938 *An Autobiography* omitted her two marriages, a divorce, and her intimate friendship with sexologist Havelock Ellis. When in 1927 Isadora Duncan made a number of sexual disclosures in *My Life*, the autobiography received bad reviews. (Reviewers said they were disgusted by her informal "breathless" style, but no doubt her sexual text also discomfitted them.)

Critical Reaction

Biographers of women subjects do not have the luxury of silence that Ellen Glasgow, Edith Wharton, and countless other women writing autobiography chose; nor can they be so selective about what to include and how to structure their narratives as Lillian Hellman was in her four memoirs. Biographers are held by reader expectation to plausible, and readable, narratives. While they may be able to focus those narratives on internal as well as external events, they are still bound by the chronology of the subject's life and the need for enough contextualized history that readers are able to set the events of the narrative within a recognizable world.

When the biographer fails to meet the most traditional of biography's rules—to provide a structure of external event as a setting for the subject's life story—critics are disgruntled. Even in books about women who write, who may well lead lives much more interior than those tied to outer events, the biographer has to keep some focus on real-world chronology. Ann Hurlbert's *The Interior Castle*, her biography of American novelist Jean Stafford, presents Stafford's interiority and the unusual emotional events that shaped much of her life. Accordingly, some critics had difficulty with the book considered as biography. In his *New York Times Book Review* essay (June 21, 1992), William Pritchard, obviously attempting to put biography back into a more traditional mode, wrote,

> These days, there is a general assumption, mainly unexamined, that a biography, by probing its subject's childhood, sexual and domestic conflicts, obsessions and compulsions,

leads to our better understanding of that subject. In fact, the more fully we become acquainted with people—in real life or in biography—the more ultimately mysterious and unfathomable they may become. With Jean Stafford, the probing, as Ms. Hurlbert firmly but tactfully practices it, is directed at her unhappy relations with her father, a small-time California walnut grower who wanted to be a writer and who squandered his inheritance in the stock market, then, in straitened circumstances, moved his family to Colorado.

Pritchard's disdainful tone suggests that he, the biographer of Robert Frost and Randall Jarrell, is more uncomfortable with the *kind* of personal in this biography of Stafford than with its presence per se. His review hurries from point to point, saying reasonably complimentary things—but without relish. One might guess that what Pritchard finds unpalatable, and perhaps unprofessional, is the physical brutality of Robert Lowell's relationship with Stafford—as when Lowell drove their car into a wall after she refused to marry him, seriously injuring—and disfiguring—her. Pritchard's anger, however, seems directed less at Hurlbert's psychoanalytic method than at Stafford's life, especially her continuing attraction to her unsuccessful father. There is a definite sense in the review that Pritchard disapproves of much about Stafford, as well as much about the interior, the truly personal, in this biography.

Not to object to the book saves face. One biographer to another, Pritchard can give Hurlbert a reasonably good review and still plant the notion that the current trend in biography displeases him. He also sets the writing of women's biography back a few years because disallowing this kind of personal information about Jean Stafford is, in effect, erasing the story of a woman trained from infancy to obey male authority. Most of the biography of this accomplished, and still underrated, writer is embroidery on the theme of her search for a self that could live without male approval. How to remove certain kinds of "probings" from that narrative is hard to imagine.

When Joyce Carol Oates complains that the current flood of biography panders to readers' interest in the sordid or seamy details of subjects' lives, she is voicing a similar kind of unease with the power of biographers—some of whom may be unscrupulous, or at best uninterested in complex motivations for people's acts. The scandal of those acts may be the reason these biographers are writing the books, attracting wide readerships, and making money. Most serious biographies, however, do not make much money—so the profit motive cannot be blamed. What has happened in much of late-twentieth-century biography is that more information about sexual and psychoanalytic matters has become available; and to most readers, that information is of interest. Oates's sense that prurience has taken over serious biography is exaggeration; her coining the term "*pathography*" to replace *biography* does a disservice to recent trends that allow the inclusion of new kinds of psychological and physical information. Particularly for biography of women, whose private lives have often been marked with such events as abuse, rape, and psychological manipulation, allowing discussion of painful subjects has been useful—even crucial. Oates's complaints about the biographer's focus on "dysfunction and disaster" discount the fact that many women's stories include such elements.

For readers who are satisfied with the current parameters of literary classification, who really do not want change within genre, a more fruitful approach in reviewing biographies of women might be to recognize that people have much less practice in writing biography about women subjects and to be willing to let adventurous biographers explore. Arnold Rampersad said recently that writing about women's interior lives remains difficult:

> So many biographies and histories have been written ascribing very little to women's interior lives except in very conventional ways—in particular, ascribing very little to women's intellectual lives. And now all that has changed. The mind of a woman is now certainly on the same level as the mind of a man as a field of investigation for the scholar, the biographer. New terms are being invented and developed—a whole new way of approaching the subject.

While Rampersad characteristically puts the best face possible on changing modes, reviewers and readers still chafe at visible difference. Where biographies of women are concerned, quibbling and critical attack will come over the degree of the biographer's displaying "the psychology of the human being." Some psychologies are more approachable, more understandable, more comfortable, than others. As we have seen, those distinctions often fall along gender lines.

Phyllis Rose rejects general terms about biography for those of deep-force psychology, saying that biographers should uncover "really, really deep structures, really, really deep assumptions." The biographer must go past fact and create from the merely factual text of a person's life the reasons he or she made key decisions. "What I'm interested in, I would say, is ideology, structuring the way that people's personal frameworks for understanding make their lives turn out the way they have." Rose's work with subjects ranging from Virginia Woolf to Josephine Baker suggests that she has decided that whatever will convey the personal force of each subject is fair.

Unfortunately, no scholar is trained to intuit, to uncover, these kinds of deep structures. A biography course, a class in historical research, even psychology courses will leave the writer with only terminology, nothing close to accurate insight. So if this modern, and perhaps feminist, biography cannot be learned by wending one's way through the established biographies of the century or by studying related disciplines in the usual academic way, how then does one assume to be qualified in the skill? (The whole designation of biography as art, long controversial, continues to be elusive.)

What is at stake here is, in fact, the process of being able to define both art and its categorization. As countless feminist critics and historians have suggested in past decades, the power to name is the real seat of control. While critics recognize, as Lutzeler says in "Fictionality in Historiography and the Novel," that "narration can be viewed as one of the primary tools of knowledge, and it determines the structure and aesthetic form in the presentation of a real or a fictional event," the numerous arguments over narrative as it appears in fiction, biography, autobiography, nonfiction, and poetry are more divisive than harmonic.

The argument has been carried into the field of history, with work by Hayden White and others questioning whether the fact that a narrative was historically true meant that it was accurate history. As White insisted in *Metahistory*, "no sequence of events—

by itself—is a story; it is the task of the historiographer to transfer the events, the facts, to the narrative framework of a story." So long as the author/historian is allowed the power to create his or her own structure, his or her own tapestry of information, the merely factual can be challenged. Critic Dorrit Cohn questions the whole notion of biography as a stable genre by describing a variety of mutations from the form: historical biography, fictionalized historical biography, historicized fictional biography, and fictional biography. Cohn's point is simply that the reader has difficulty distinguishing among these supposedly different modes.

Important theoreticians have taken on the responsibility of naming anew, but as with most expansions of genre, the actual practice is far in advance of critical terminology. Even as Lillian Hellman was writing four separate volumes of memoir that created both new structures and new rationale for the art of autobiography, and Gertrude Stein was shaping a parody that challenged both the idea of authorship and the idea of subject, and Virginia Woolf was spoofing the entire premise that important biography could be written only about important people, the conventions of mainstream biography remained in place. Forty, fifty, sixty years after these remarkable books appeared, criticism has finally begun to deal seriously with them.

It is no accident that these are books written by women or that they have long been considered idiosyncratic aberrations rather than books that break existing traditions as a means of preparing for future experimentation. How carefully the canon has excluded the most interesting work of the twentieth century, by defining out of each genre some of its most fascinating writing. In literary history as in art, women need to become namers. They need to stop repeating the conventions that history, and the largely male academy, inscribes and look carefully at what has been written and published throughout the century. In some respects, earlier critics were more charitable, more accepting of difference than have been critics of the past twenty years. At times we must look back into published criticism and literary history to see more flexible patterns of appreciation than we are currently privy to.*

*If the nineteenth century had been as hidebound as ours in its literary traditions, readers would never have known Herman Melville's *Moby-Dick*,

We seem to be caught, in the last decade of what has been the most artistically experimental century in history, in a grudging battle of attrition to stifle the variety that was earlier encouraged. Intent on limiting the canon so that it becomes manageable (for the first time in fifty years), established critics often criticize even long-approved new directions. One of the most insidious methods of curbing experimentation is the recent tendency to legislate morals, if only by withholding funds for the production of art or literature that might be offensive to some viewers or readers. At odds with the more usual humanistic mode of avoiding censorship, cultural watchdogs today make the general public all too conscious of so-called subversive and improper themes or representations.

History proves that cultural focus on issues of propriety and suitability usually turns back on women's art and women's themes in writing. Most obviously, in women's writing and art, readers object to unseemly body parts and such physical processes as menstruation. They also face the conundrum of names or, more accurately, the need to rename. Feminist writers through the past fifty years have called for renaming, yet cultural patterns have changed only slightly. Women still abandon their surnames for those of their husbands. Women writers still use pseudonyms and often write under both a pseudonym and their own name. The outrage because Sylvia Plath wrote under her own name in North Tawton, the small Devon town where the Hugheses lived, gave rise to speculation that she and Ted were not married. When mail came addressed to Plath, the postman let other residents know about the irregularity. There is surely a connection between women's feeling free to take their own name—or any name they want—and their feeling empowered to take their own stand about whatever matters—politically, literarily, or personally.

What most theoretical issues come down to, finally, is whose story, for whatever reasons, deserves telling? And the corollary to

---

Ralph Waldo Emerson's essays, Henry David Thoreau's *Walden*, Edgar Allan Poe's *Eureka*, Walt Whitman's *Leaves of Grass* in all its expanding versions, or Emily Dickinson's carefully bound poem fascicles. The idiosyncratic texts of nineteenth-century American literature rightfully became its classics, but the boundaries of form and convention have nearly strangled twentieth-century works that should have been honored, as well as accepted, long ago.

that central question is, who deserves to tell it, using what kind of language or syntax or structure? In the past several decades, culture has seen the social power of naming, particularly in concert with so-called women's issues. In 1904, Ellen Glasgow wrote about an abused wife searching for help by running to a neighbor's house on a stormy night. A casual vignette in *The Deliverance*, a book about women's friendships, the episode was never commented on. Literary critics believed such tales were the stuff of melodrama or soap opera, not serious fiction. Even though Henry James hints at Isabel Archer's psychological abuse—from the betrayal of both her husband and Madame Merle, whose friendship she once valued—he does not give the reader any other stage of that abuse, such as physical threats and beatings. Disguised as a class issue, husbands' abuse of wives was one of those improprieties that the literate (middle- and upper-class readers) would not face.

Naming has given the world a vocabulary for such unmentionable subjects. The simple act of giving a name to such abuse has done as much to provide help as have concentrated social movements. Glasgow's fearful abused woman, today, could have run to a shelter, a place of secrecy and aid run by the local council against domestic assault. Or if she were past the stage of fear, she could have called the local police and, if she were lucky, expected some kind of intervention. In 1993, several states passed anti-stalking regulations so that angry people cannot haunt other human beings. Similar victories—in both language and law—have been won as sexual harrassment and various kinds of pornographic exploitation have been named. Once a name exists, society can respond by enacting legislation.

Women had learned these lessons about language at their grandmothers' knees (witness the power of the names "virgin" and "good" as opposed to "whore" and "bad" as agencies of social control) and Mary Daly's *Webster's First New Intergalactic Wickedary of the English Language* plays on the ultimate negative characterization of powerful women as "wicked" or "witchlike" as it creates language that changes traditional dictionary definitions. Daly's work shows how crucial male control of language through history has been. Unfortunately, much of the world remains oblivious to Daly's efforts, along with those of hundreds of other women linguists, writers, historians, and anthropologists, by relegating any clamor for change to the devalued category of women's issues. Such ghettoization has long been a successful model of social control. In the case of language and its coinage, women cannot be content to accept that ghettoization; they must be willing to create new words to embody the themes and emotions of their narrative.

8
Listening to Women's Stories

Soon now they would enter the Delta. The sensation was
familiar to him. It had been renewed like this each last
week in November for more than fifty years—the last
hill, at the foot of which the rich unbroken alluvial
flatness began as the sea began at the base of its cliffs,
dissolving away beneath the unhurried November rain
as the sea itself would dissolve away.
William Faulkner, "Delta Autumn"

Faulkner's hunting story is written; therefore, it is called literature.
Part of the haunting attraction of Faulkner's work, however, is its
rhythmical pace: it often sounds like speech. Yet for all the recent
attention such writers as Leslie Marmon Silko, Lee Smith, Toni
Morrison, Paula Gunn Allen, Gloria Anzaldúa, Eudora Welty, and
others have given to basing their fiction on the art of storying, the
English-speaking literary world prefers non-oral art. The written
word, and only the written word, constitutes literature. Ironically,
Faulkner's eminence as a writer stems partly from his ability to use
spoken stories within his novels, but when women use the same
technique, it is often devalued.

Readers have few early models that teach them to appreciate
the nuance of women's stories. A deft ability to characterize, to
build plot, to repeat motifs, and to strike to the heart of narrative
with exactly the right detail has brought women little prominence
in the world of letters. Until very recently, unless a text is written,
unless a narrative is published in some form that the literary world
recognizes—a novel rather than a memoir, a short story rather

than a diary entry—women's prowess as storytellers would be ignored.

The activity of women in groups sharing narratives is usually described pejoratively. Sometimes called gossip, women's talking together has often been derogated—the power to name, once more, categorizing women's activities as valueless. *To gossip*, according to *The Oxford English Dictionary*, is to be a godparent and, in a second definition, to bear information. In contemporary terms, however, to gossip is to be guilty of telling tales about others, tales that have been characterized as bothersome, meddling, and harmful. When men talk together, even though they discuss golf scores, the conversation is business. When women talk together, they are criticized and patronized, as are their narratives.

Contemporary women writers have taken the image of the gossiping woman and subverted its negative connotations. One prominent publisher of ethnic women's writing, Barbara Smith, has chosen the name Kitchen Table Press, evoking an implicit defense of women's storying. One of Rayna Green's most anthologized stories, "High Cotton," also defends the orality of women's culture. It begins,

> Is everything a story? Ramona asked her.
> It is if a story's what you're looking for—otherwise, it's just people telling lies and there's no end to it. Grandma waited to see how she took that and she started in again, smoothing out the red-checked oilcloth on the kitchen table as she talked.

In the carefully woven text that follows, Green uses pace to separate direct quotes from author's description—so that the effect of the whole is of Grandma's voiced stories, with the child, Ramona, listening. At the kitchen table, three generations of women share wisdom and humor in their poignant tales.

Culturally and literarily, the content of women's talk, as compared with men's talk, has been consistently diminished. Groups with power retain authoritative speech. Correspondingly, the narratives women told—as contrasted with men's—have also been denigrated. When a reader begins the Faulkner story quoted as epigraph to this chapter, years of literary training come into play. The reader's learned response is that this must be a piece of writing about some crucial confrontation between man and nature, between an established culture about to disappear and the reverence modern man has for it. The short sentences that open the passage meld swiftly with the incremental rhythms of the longer sentence, reassuring in its sonority. Subconsciously, the reader thinks, surely the effect of good writing is supposed to be like this—learned, solemn.

On the other hand, the opening of the Green story sends no such comforting signals. We have heard this syntax all our listening lives; how could this diction, set in a simple narrative, approach the Faulkner text above in greatness? Because Green's is a different kind of writing, aimed at re-creating life as we hear it.

If gaining power means gaining control of language, as Clifford Geertz, Deborah Tannen, Cheris Kramarae, and other linguists and anthropologists insist, a woman writer may have to detour back into the mainstream provinces of literature in order to gain that first positive recognition (of being a serious writer, of being one of the boys) before writing what she would normally undertake. It is a career pattern that Edith Wharton, Ellen Glasgow, and Willa Cather all used, though they were less conscious of the need to play the male literary game than my comment suggests. When Glasgow and Wharton were writing their first fiction, in the 1890s, the novels they used as models were European, Russian, and British, all very masculine in language and theme. The normal literary sentence was what could be called masculine. A sentence from Charles Dickens's *Pickwick Papers*—"He had always been looked up to as a high authority on all matters of amusement and dexterity, whether offensive, defensive, or inoffensive; and if, on this very first occasion of being put to the test, he shrunk back from trial, beneath his leader's eye, his name and standing were lost for ever"—was hardly swift moving or speech based. One aim of serious nineteenth-century writing was to impress the reader with the writer's vocabulary, ease of syntactic movement, and sonority. If one managed to tell a good story along the (long) way, so much the better; but as Dickens discovered with *Pickwick*, the story was secondary to the lushness of the prose.

Ellen Glasgow was delighted when her first novel, *The Descendant*, published anonymously in 1897, was credited to the controversial Harold Frederic. At the same time, Edith Wharton succeeded in publishing her masculine, plot-dominated short stories in good magazines. Women's writing, then, early in this century, was still very much like writing by men in its language and plots, with themes drawn from a pool of suitable subjects that were not distinguished by gender. All serious literary stories were, in effect, men's stories.

Willa Cather did even better. After her first novel, the realistic *Alexander's Bridge*, sold badly, she wrote about two heterosexual love stories in *O Pioneers!* In this novel, and in *My Ántonia* and *A Lost Lady*, however, she never cast the woman protagonist as her narrator: the story was told by a man and could well have been read as if the male voice was that of the protagonist. In her later fiction, too, Wharton often used a male narrator. These two American women novelists thus gave their work enough traits of acceptable fiction by men that they could be seen as serious writers, even while they were portraying women's lives and, often, criticizing patriarchal culture.

In England, Virginia Woolf's fragmented *Jacob's Room* used both her "women's sentence" and a structure dependent less on chronology than on "moments of being," key scenes in Jacob's emotional life. Rather than create a narrative that bore little relation to any linear plot, as she was to do in *Mrs. Dalloway* and *To the Lighthouse*, Woolf followed Jacob through the ruin of his postwar existence, expressed in countless flashbacks. While the style might have been feminine, Woolf's narrative was about a man—because, as she understood the minds of her reading public, who else could one write war novels about?

There were other kinds of wars, of course, and women writers were all too familiar with embattled lives—but they tried to avoid risking the return to the literary limbo of "sentimental" or "domestic" writing. They moved their women protagonists into more adventurous settings (Isak Dinesen, Doris Lessing, and Nadine Gordimer mined an exotic continent) or gave them more critical roles to play in familiar cultures: the widow who took charge of her children's lives, the Appalachian woman who brought her family to the Detroit auto plants, the Southern black woman demanding dental attention for her son, the Southern white woman leaving home to live at the post office. Writers like Harriette Arnow, Maya Angelou, and Eudora Welty wrote about apparently real events, many with a sharp comic edge. Such others as Dorothy Parker, Jane Bowles, and Djuna Barnes wrote comedy to puncture the high seriousness of traditional fiction.

As important as changes in plot, character, and tone was the all-important shift from the author's use of omniscient point-of-view to first-person perspective—and voice. A hundred years ago, in Charlotte Perkins Gilman's "The Yellow Wallpaper," readers heard the voice of a woman protagonist for itself. Without intermediary, without explanation, Gilman's unnamed woman storyteller wrote her "letter to the world," and readers today are finally learning to listen:

> It is very seldom that mere ordinary people like John and myself secure ancestral halls for the summer. . . . John is practical in the extreme. He has no patience with faith, an intense horror of superstition, and he scoffs openly at any talk of things not to be felt and seen and put down in figures. John is a physician, and perhaps—(I would not say it to a living soul, of course, but this is dead paper and a great relief to my mind)—perhaps that is one reason I do not get well faster. You see he does not believe I am sick! . . . If a physician of high standing, and one's own husband, assures friends and relatives that there is really nothing the matter with one but temporary nervous depression—a slight hysterical tendency—what is one to do?

With amazing concision, Gilman sets the stage, explains the narrative dilemma (the learned man does not listen to his wife, and therefore she has stopped talking, taking refuge instead in her writing) and introduces the reader to the modest, sensible, and miserable woman who is to go mad during the course of the story. Readers of the tale during the 1890s identified it as an Edgar Allan Poe gothic, without realizing that the voice was female, as was the problem, postpartum depression. But Gilman's accomplishment was to tell the story in a way that broke through centuries of narrative conventions: just as women's stories deserve to be told, so do they deserve to be told in voices that are germane. As so many women writers have said, and are saying, women need the power to tell their own stories, using whatever techniques the literary world will accept.

The force of the woman character's voice that Charlotte Perkins Gilman claimed for her unnamed narrator in "The Yellow Wallpaper" recurs again and again in first-person writing by women, the use of recognizable voice seeming particularly apt for autobiography or memoir. Yet it was not until several decades ago that such use of voice penetrated even this form. Margaret Mead's 1972 *Blackberry Winter: My Earlier Years* creates much of its interest through the terse, overly serious expression of her teacherly speech. Readers were interested in Mead's book, which was a book club selection, because they were interested in her life as early anthropologist, sexologist, and lively, practical woman. To illustrate her point that "today's children have to find new ways of anchoring the changing moments of their lives," she re-creates her vision of her childhood home, captured in the tangible objects of her mother's room: "There were treasures on Mother's dressing table, too—a Wedgwood pin dish, a little porcelain Mary and her lamb, the pale green, flowered top of a rose bowl that had broken, and Mother's silver-backed comb and brush and mirror. All these things held meaning for me. Each was—and still is—capable of evoking a rush of memories."

In 1970, Maya Angelou's *I Know Why the Caged Bird Sings* used a number of oral speech techniques to pull readers into the first volume of her autobiography. Although she did not have the same kind of name recognition that Mead had, Angelou was a writer: readers believed, and liked, the convincing voice of the young black protagonist, whose love of metaphor seasoned her bleak narrative of growing up in the segregated South:

> The Angel of the candy counter had found me out at last, and was exacting excruciating penance for all the stolen Milky Ways, Mounds, Mr. Goodbars and Hersheys with Almonds. I had two cavities that were rotten to the gums. The pain was beyond the bailiwick of crushed aspirins or oil of cloves. Only one thing could help me, so I prayed earnestly that I'd be allowed to sit under the house and have the building collapse on my left jaw. . . . I lived a few days and nights in blinding pain, not so much toying with as seriously considering the idea of

jumping in the well, and Momma decided I had to be taken to a dentist.

Complemented by decades of work in interviewing both in oral history and anthropological ethnography, writers have turned increasingly to the use of real speech as the basis *for* narratives and *as* narratives. Among recent books that illustrate this trend toward creating valid biography from spoken and recorded language are Vera Laska's *Women in the Resistance and the Holocaust: The Voices of Eye Witnesses* (1983), Barbara Omolade's *It's a Family Affair: The Real Lives of Black Single Mothers* and Elizabeth Fishel's *The Men in Our Lives: Fathers, Lovers, Husbands, Mentors* (1985), Vicki L. Ruiz's *Cannery Women, Cannery Lives; Mexican Women, Unionization, and the California Food Processing Industry, 1930–1950* (1987), Susan Tucker's *Telling Memories among Southern Women: Domesticated Workers and Their Employers in the Segregated South* and Sydney Stahl Weinberg's *The World of Our Mothers: The Lives of Jewish Immigrant Women* (1988), Mikio Kanda's *Widows of Hiroshima: The Life Stories of Nineteen Peasant Wives* (1989), and Alison Owings's *Frauen: German Women Recall the Third Reich* and Mary Romero's *Dignity for Domestic Workers: Maid in the U.S.A.* (1993). As their titles suggest, these grouped individual stories create a new, composite voice and give the telling of these experiences a different kind of validity. The technique works regardless of subject, class, or national language, but it is particularly important in creating voices for people who are not themselves professional writers.

Without such innovation, stories remain unwritten, unheard even when told. Isak Dinesen's story, "The Blank Page," has given readers a chilling metaphor for voicelessness. Told by the "old coffee-brown, black-veiled woman who made her living by telling stories" (and who had learned the art from her mother and her mother's mother), the narrative describes a display of bed linen, marked with the bloody fluids of virgin brides on their wedding nights. Dinesen's emphasis is on the one unmarked sheet, "the blank page," framed in its whiteness as a striking contrast to the other linens. Its purity gives rise to the viewers' most imaginative stories, but it also makes the lessons of the ruined linens even more frightening: in this culture, the only voices woman have are those of their sexual expression. The blood of their defilement is their only ink. Without such inscription, Dinesen's story makes clear, the observing world made up the missing narrative for itself. The tragedy of the story remains unvoiced: the woman of the blank page never expressed the authentic version of her experience, the legend that today we might claim as *herstory*.

In some of the most effective women's writing of the past decades, the themes of traditional literature are spoken in women's voices—possibly for the first time in the history of letters. Susan Griffin's 1978 prose poem *Woman and Nature* takes on the large theme of human beings relating to the natural universe, as if responding to Faulkner's male-centered paradigm. The fourth segment of Minnie Bruce Pratt's title poem from her prize-winning collection, *Crime Against Nature*, illustrates that theme ironically. This is her opening stanza:

> No one says *crime against nature* when a man
> shotguns one or two or three or four or five
> or more of his children, and usually his wife,
> and maybe her visiting sister. But of the woman
> who jumps twelve floors to her death, no I.D.
> but a key around her neck, and in the apartment
> her cold son in a back room, dead on a blanket . . .

Shock, paradox, disbelief are all Pratt's allies in her relentless description. In stanza two, the monologue conjectures explanations for the tragedy, admitting that those conjectures might well be fantasy:

> Some are quick to say she was a fraud hiding
> in a woman's body. Some pretend to be judicious
> and give her as an example of why unmarried sluts
> are not fit to raise children. But the truth is
> we don't know what happened. Maybe she could not
> imagine another ending because she was dirt poor,
> alone, had tried everything. Or she was a queer
> who hated herself by her family's name: *crooked*.

Pratt then asks, Who has the right to name? Is the lesbian woman "crooked," in her family's terms, or is she, simply, lesbian?

Implicit, too, is the question of who has the right to tell a woman's story. Her last stanza states defiantly that the woman's story is her own and that, without her voice, no reader can reconstruct her life or her death.

> Maybe she killed the child because she looked
> into the future and saw her past. Or maybe
> some man killed the boy and pushed her, splayed,
> out the window, no one to grab, nothing to hide
> but the key between her breasts, so we would find
> the child and punish the killer. The iron key
> warm, then cooling against her skin, her memory,
> the locked room. She left a clue. We don't know
> her secret. She's not here to tell the story.

Questioning the woman's place in society and nature, either alienated from culture or victimized by it, Pratt uses voiced language to speak her objective narrative. In the Hemingway-like phrases that close the poem, she lets the assumed facts of the protagonist's life and death carry the weight of the story. Her writing—although it speaks of anger, desolation, and loss—is surely as powerful, as evocative, as Faulkner's prose. And even in the telling of the bleak narrative, the act of recounting the story creates a community of readers who care about the unnamed protagonist of Pratt's "Crime Against Nature."

9

Writing about Mothers

> It is hard to write about my own mother. Whatever I do
> write, it is my story I am telling, my version of the past.
> Adrienne Rich, *Of Woman Born*

Pratt's poem about a dead mother and child twists the image of the Pietà, Mary mourning the death of her son Jesus, into a stinging scene of contemporary waste. But most women's writing about mothers or grandmothers or sisters or daughters reverses the postmodern mode of disillusion. In thinking back through our mothers, to use Virginia Woolf's phrase, women writers are usually compelled to acknowledge any ambivalence they might harbor but at the same time put the maternal subject in the best possible light. For most women, at least one of the dominant voices in their lives—perhaps the voice that literally gave them language—was their mother's.

If the act of writing is a way of giving name and identity to a person, then to bestow that gift on one's mother seems appropriate. Yet because writing about loved ones has been called sentimental, the fact that a writer writes about her mother or other family members can undermine the reception of the best writing.

Women who write about mothers are moving directly into the cross hairs of a number of theoretical issues, many of them feminist. As Marianne Hirsch has recently described in *The Mother/Daughter Plot*, theorizing motherhood has been an important critical project of the past twenty years. It began in the mid-1970s when a group of three influential books marked the beginning of the extreme self-consciousness that crowds into any writing about a woman's mother. In 1976, Adrienne Rich's *Of Woman Born: Motherhood as Experience and Institution* established a woman's right to question the reverence usually given motherhood. As both a daughter and the mother of three sons, Rich spoke with full aware- ness of the many painful decisions each role entailed. In 1977, Nancy Friday's *My Mother/My Self: The Daughter's Search for Identity*, a popularized narrative of some of the psychoanalytic problems in mother-daughter relationships, disseminated current critical think- ing to thousands. It was followed in 1978 by Nancy Chodorow's definitive *Reproduction of Mothering: Psychoanalysis and the Sociology of Gender*. Women readers now had language to describe some of the age-old conflicts, and the hundreds of essays and books that followed were evidence of the effectiveness of this writing.

There is always a gap between the academy and the critical establishment's countenancing of theoretical issues. In later-1970s circles of commercial publishing and reviewing, women's writing about mothers was still called sentimental. But men who wrote about parents were receiving serious attention. One book that caught reviewers' eyes, and obliquely improved the quality of reader response to memoirs about parents, was Geoffrey Wolff's 1979 *The Duke of Deception: Memories of My Father*. Praised by novelists Tim O'Brien and John Irving, the book was called "part biography and part autobiography" (by O'Brien) and "a first-rate autobiography," as well as "a wholly instructive and provocative biography of the father and swindler" (by Irving). The latter's highest praise was that the memoir read like a novel. But the real issue, of whose story was paramount—Geoffrey Wolff's difficult boyhood or his charming scoundrel-father's even more difficult adulthood—was never tackled.

Both reviewers praised what they considered Wolff's attempt to get at the truth, but they were admittedly charmed by his mix- ture of attitudes. "Harsh but affectionate," said Irving; "straight and tough," echoed O'Brien. Cast in the format of a novel, then, Wolff's memoir was never held to meeting standards of traditional biography or autobiography.

When Tobias Wolff repeated his half-brother's feat a decade later with *This Boy's Life* in 1989, the turn to fiction was even more noticeable. Few reviewers bothered to distinguish between memoir and novel, or between biography and autobiography, but the book was termed "engrossing," "candid." Joel Conarroe in the *New York*

Times Book Review wrote that Wolff was "by his own admission, a fabricator who learned at his father's knee that it is pointless to stick to facts when fantasy is so much more rewarding."

By the time of Philip Roth's 1991 *Patrimony*, a book about his father Herman's later life and dying (and his own substantial role in that process), the literary world had decided that men writing about fathers was a new genre, a hybrid that could stand alone. Peter Prescott called *Patrimony* Roth's best book in a decade and described it as "a book about fathers . . . and how to treat them." Prescott's praise was undiluted. And although some questioned Roth's turn away from his fictional comic genius, most reviewers liked *Patrimony, A True Story.* They accepted Roth's self-conscious moralizing and his plotting for reader sympathy, even as they accepted his play on the contradiction between *true* and *story.* The line between the supposedly factually-based biography and the imaginary novel had been subsumed in this re-creation of the male world.

Yet in 1987, midway between the Geoffrey Wolff memoir and the Roth, Vivian Gornick wrote an even less traditional narrative of her mother and herself in *Fierce Attachments, A Memoir.* A heavily sexualized text, Gornick's story of her life to maturity in a continuum of biographies of neighbor women and other women relatives, in addition to her mother, received comparatively little comment. Whereas the Wolff books received front-page placement in the *New York Times Book Review*, Mona Simpson's review of *Fierce Attachments* appeared inside the supplement. And rather than seeing its indeterminate genre as an advantage, Simpson described the book as sociology: "What the narrator seems to want to write about is the discovery of the life of the mind, the cyclical barrenness and frustration of living alone and working . . . the fate of women in her generation."

Simpson's description had little to do with the book as I read it, though she did also say that *Fierce Attachments* was "the story of an abiding, difficult love over time." She did not see it as primarily a mother-daughter conflict, although Wendy Gimbel, reviewing it for *The Nation*, thought the portrait of the mother was "brilliant." For her, however, sympathy for the two characters in conflict was absent. She described the mother and daughter as creations from

Samuel Beckett, something out of *Endgame*, "fixed forever in a hopeless but symbiotic existence."

The difference in the tone of these reviews is instructive. When a woman writer experiments in the biography/autobiography genre, her work is compared to that of an absurdist (male) playwright and novelist. The warmth that Gornick manages to create for the mother figure evaporates in the language of the reviewers, and what remains is a grotesque Siamese-twin female coupling. Compared with the enthusiastic acceptance of the men's memoirs, these reviews appear even more negative.

Gornick would probably be the first to point out that she was asking, if anything, more difficult questions. Her characters were not aberrant or fantastic, nor were they on the edge of death; they were people the reader would recognize and, perhaps, dislike. The truth the male writers and male reviewers liked to claim was present in the Wolff and Roth memoirs seemed less than realistic when contrasted with the narrative Gornick created.

In recent memoirs and biographies by Gloria Steinem, Letty Cottin Pogrebin, Margaret Mead and her daughter, Mary Catherine Bateson, Sissela Bok, and Kim Chernin, the range of realism and clarity about, and charity toward, the mother varies widely. Each writer has used distancing strategies so that autobiographical elements are often repressed. Unlike the memoirs by Roth and the Wolffs, which purposely fuse the biographical and the autobiographical, these memoirs by women writers try to keep the narrative focused, where possible, on the figure of the mother. As the epigraph to this chapter suggests, the difficulties of writing biography increase exponentially when the subject is someone who shares the biographer's private life.

Absent Mothers

One of the most direct, and in some ways traditional, memoirs of a mother is Gloria Steinem's 1983 "Ruth's Song (Because She Could Not Sing It)." Written more than twenty years after the life events told in the memoir, the moving biography describes the broken woman it was Steinem's duty to care for when she was barely ten. Ruth Nuneviller Steinem had been a successful journalist. Then she married an impractical man whose various dreams—acting in show business, running an isolated Michigan resort—demanded that she give up the career she loved. Plagued by real financial worries and groundless worries about the well-being of her young daughters, the "energetic, fun-loving, book-loving woman" suffered a series of nervous breakdowns. Sedated by her doctor and divorced by her husband, Ruth cowered in paranoid fear in the Toledo, Ohio, apartment she shared with Gloria—except for the nights when the coatless woman worriedly met her daughter at the bus stop. As Steinem summarizes, "That's why our lives, my mother's from forty-six to fifty-three, and my own from ten to seventeen, were spent alone together."

Steinem avoids some of the pathos inherent in the story by setting her recollections of her mother's life in the wider context of the mystery of family relations: just as no one knew what happened to change her uncle from a competent engineer to the town handyman, so no one noticed what happened to the vivacious, capable Ruth. Dedicating her writing to her mother, Steinem uses the combination of poignant immediate detail and the distance of time past to create a mosaic of evocative memory. The reader comes away with images both of the younger Ruth and the drugged, bedfast woman dependent on her daughter's care.

Steinem makes the sad portrait bearable by focusing on her grandmother's avoidance of Ruth's medical problems (an enigma, since her grandmother was a suffragette, supposedly interested in the rights of women), as well as her own. She remembered her tactic of distancing herself from her mother and their life: "My ultimate protection was this: I was just passing through, a guest in the house; perhaps this wasn't my mother at all."

Even as she recognizes the absurdity of her dodge, however, she concludes, "Pity takes distance and a certainty of surviving." From an Eastern college and a later career in journalism, Steinem watched the healing and changing of her mother, now institutionalized in Baltimore. The pathetic story of a lost woman, ignored because her "functioning was not that necessary to the world," has a comparatively positive ending. Before her death, Ruth became less dependent, and her agoraphobia was controlled. Her illness, never diagnosed, diminished with the security of being well cared for. But Steinem does not avoid naming the tragedy of her mother's being so used—and so unwilling to stand up for her needs— all those long years. As she concludes, "I miss her, but perhaps no more in death than I did in life."

Letty Pogrebin's chapters about her mother and grandmother in *Deborah, Golda, and Me: Being Female and Jewish in America* (1991) are a similar mix of factual recollection—studded with concrete details—and personal assessment. Pogrebin's memoir is an attempt to link herself to the heroines of her Jewish culture—the Biblical Deborah, Golda Meir, and key women in her family. The extension of *family* to include the women named in the title is a useful move to create links between contemporary women and matriarchal tradition. Because Pogrebin's mother died when she was only fifteen, her reminiscence is reflective. It is also autobiographical. While she misses her mother, she also sees that "her death forced me to live a different life." Content to be the loving Jewish homemaker, Ceil Cottin would have wanted the same kind of life for her daughter. Instead, Pogrebin went away to college and then worked in journalism before marrying.

Pogrebin's memoir avoids outright praise of her dead mother by structuring Ceil's narrative as her own story. The book begins with her being told by a taunting cousin that her mother and father have each been married before and that each has a child from that previous life. While Pogrebin is their child, her beloved older sister is only a half sister. Shattered by this revelation and ashamed that her parents have lied to her, she has no sympathy for Ceil. Only later does she realize that her immigrant mother so desperately wanted a "normal" American life for her children that she would have put up with almost any marriage to give them a two-parent home. When her second marriage also failed, she was terribly ashamed. Later, dying of cancer, she apologized to Pogrebin for having twice chosen the wrong man. Even then, she defined achievement in a woman's life in terms of marriage.

In moving between her childhood and her mother's life, and her own maturity, Pogrebin allows room in her text for authorial comments: "I can bemoan the years she [Ceil] wasted on undeserving men, the needless humiliation she felt on behalf of her impoverished, unassimilated family." She also, however, calls Ceil "a miracle worker" because "She invented herself. Then she invented the family life she thought she and her daughters deserved." And while Pogrebin did not want the same kind of American dream, she was able, in constructing her own, to use "survival skills and tools of invention" reminiscent of her mother's.

Part of the legacy from Ceil's narrative was Pogrebin's conviction that her father was a false, pretentious man. Rather than express that, however, she describes him with understated irony:

> I don't like to write about my father.
>
> During more than twenty years as a writer, I've poured out thousands of words about my mother, but my father, who lived until 1982, has earned only a sentence here or there. I've written extensively about my husband, my children, my colleagues, my friends, but I don't like to write about my father.
>
> I'm afraid to read what I have to say. . . .

Although she lists her father's commendable traits, they do not seem creditable, shadowed as they are by this stark beginning. Whereas Steinem wrote less about her father, Pogrebin counterpoints Ceil's story with the child's view of the handsome man.

Famous Mothers

Twenty years earlier, Margaret Mead's alternation of chapters about mother, father, and grandmother created a similar multifaceted effect. *Blackberry Winter: My Earlier Years* (1972) illustrated her belief that people are determined by families and family practices. Just as she shaped her autobiography to begin with her infancy and childhood, the book closed with chapters about the birth of her daughter, Cathy, her development, and the later birth and development of Mead's granddaughter. For all her time spent studying foreign cultures and her own various living arrangements, Mead held the firm conviction that any woman's sense of herself is intricately woven into, and from, the life of her immediate family.

Describing the self—the purpose of all autobiographical writing—almost mandates describing both parents. Lillian Hellman's father appears often in her memoirs; Gertrude Stein's remains an indelible presence. Anzia Yezierska's portraits of her Russian-Jewish scholar father fuel much of her writing. Germaine Greer's *Daddy, We Hardly Knew You* (1989) draws the portrait of both her complex parent and, in a later chapter titled "The Heroine of This Story," her grandmother Emma Wise. Ursula Owen's edited collection, *Fathers, Reflections by Daughters* (1983) includes moving and sometimes perplexing memoirs by Sheila Rowbotham, Adrienne Rich, and Doris Lessing, among others.

Similar in tone to the memoirs of both Steinem and Pogrebin, Mead's autobiography is much more kindly when she writes about her daughter than is that daughter's account of her parents. Mary Catherine Bateson's *With a Daughter's Eye: A Memoir of Margaret Mead and Gregory Bateson* (1984) speaks critically about her infancy and youth as a scientific specimen—the continuous photographing (whatever she did, beginning with her birth, was grist for her parents' research) and the continual observation. While Mead mentions that their child was an ideal subject for anthropological work, she does not specify instances. Bateson herself, however, remembers the tricks she did to show her physical development and later being kept from throwing away childhood paintings because she "had no right to do so." Those paintings, her mother reminded her, were part of her archive. She had probably had "the best-documented childhood in the United States."

Herself an anthropologist, Bateson frequently states her family's position as though she agreed with it: "In my family, we never simply live, we are always reflecting on our lives." The tone of her memoir suggests, however, that she may not accept that premise, or many others. "Margaret always had a multiplicity of rationales for her arrangements," begins one passage that lists disturbing child care arrangements ironically, each a new stage of efficiency from her mother's point of view, each leaving her daughter with a new nurse and robbing her of either parent's company. In contrast, Mead fondly describes their lives in various extended households: "Thinking back to my grandmother and my mother and the kind of mother I had tried to be and remembering all the different kinds of mothering people who had cared for my daughter in her childhood—her English nanny, her lovely young aunt Mary, and her devoted godmother, Aunt Marie." Bateson, however, bitterly quotes her parents saying proudly that when she was six weeks old, they "let the nurse go and took care of her ourselves for a whole weekend." She meditates on her parents' seemingly genuine belief that forty-eight hours of care was adequate for them to understand their child as an infant.

Bateson's most pervasive censure is for her parents' separation and eventual divorce (in an age when few families experienced that breakage). Although she was to be photographed in her infancy to show that children develop trust and self-confidence from the very start, her environment of trust was ruptured when she was two years old—by her father's leaving the family. Three years later, when Margaret went to California, where Bateson and her father were spending the summer, to tell her that they were divorcing, the child's reaction was the natural one—guilt, sorrow, feelings of complicity and shame, and the hope that Mead and Bateson would someday remarry.

Part of the drama of *With a Daughter's Eye* accrues from Bateson's practice of quoting from her mother's autobiography and then questioning the assumptions that Mead clearly thought she and her child shared. The fallacy in Mead's thinking was in not recognizing that although she was an adult, her beloved daughter could be only a child. Bateson comments, too, about the difficulty of writing her memoir, saying "This book cannot be the child's interpretation, for that child is now an adult, and what I write about that period is a reconstruction." What the reader finds compelling here is an ambivalence spelled out more clearly than it is in Steinem's biography of her mother or Pogrebin's of hers.

Some of the harshness, too, may stem from Margaret Mead's fame: throughout her life, Bateson heard her mother deified. Yet she also had to deal with a very natural anger—at being left with other people; at being the unusual child, the one with divorced parents; at being, perhaps, some kind of experiment. Her anger—because it seemed unreasonable to her mother—was seldom acknowledged. Steinem and Pogrebin were writing about women whose lives needed to be salvaged from the abyss of memory. Margaret Mead, as the *Blackberry Winter* jacket notes, was already a legend.

What her only child could contribute to what the world knew

about this most famous anthropologist was the slight and often fragmentary track of her mother's most private life. When Bateson writes, near the end of her rich but sorrowful book, "We talk in this country often about property rights, but we talk more rarely about the shares people have in each other's lives, and about people's rights to participation and pleasure, especially at the moments of passage: the right to throw a handful of earth on a coffin, the right to stand up to catch a tossed bouquet." The lingering tone of *In a Daughter's Eye* is one of regret—that this single and special daughter felt so bereft of her parents' attention that her book commemorating their roles as parents in fact became the vehicle for her insistence that she had been an essential part of those famous lives.*

Sissela Bok's 1991 *Alva Myrdal: A Daughter's Memoir*, her biography of her Nobel Peace Prize–winning mother, shares an equally complex pattern of praising with one anecdote and criticizing with another. Famous and beloved as her mother was, Myrdal was also weary and sometimes unable to hear what her daughter's needs were. Bok's biography, however, begins at the start of her mother's life rather than her own and tells a fascinating story of the independent fifteen-year-old Swede who broke all social rules in her search for education and love. At seventeen, Alva met the young Gunnar Myrdal, who was to become an internationally known economist. While her own evolution to a position of personal prominence was torturous, by the time sixty difficult years of marriage had passed, the Myrdals were the only couple who had ever won Nobel Prizes in different fields.

Bok's charting of the life stories of her two brilliant, ambitious parents gains immeasurably from her access to their letters and to her mother's journals. Using their words allows her to remain a fairly objective biographer, although she makes good use of a

---

*Rosalind Rosenberg in a 1991 essay accepted Mead's assessment, saying that "motherhood changed Mead's life" and noting that "she set about creating an extended family to help her raise Cathy." But Jane Howard's definitive biography, *Margaret Mead, A Life*, recognizes the discrepancies between Mead's theory of child rearing and the practical implementation of that theory in Cathy's life. (See chapter 12 for discussion of the Howard book.)

modern interrogation—as when she describes Alva's reticence to tell people she is pregnant. This is Bok:

> About this time in her life, I now wish that I could ask Alva more, request further explanations. To be sure, women were much more discreet at that time when it came to pregnancy. But why did she conceal her condition from the family in particular? [Alva hid in bed when Gunnar's sisters visited, so that they would not see her obvious pregnancy.] It is possible that the earlier miscarriage led her to wish to guard against all who would otherwise come running with good advice and warnings, perhaps begin to knit or sew for the baby in whose arrival she did not yet quite dare to believe.

Salvaging the personal from the abstract, Bok then incorporates her own memories: "I remember how she wrote to me when I was expecting my own first child, also after a miscarriage suffered through in anguish, that it was not worth 'awakening joy in advance in too many hearts.'"

While Bok draws extensively on her mother's letters and journals, she also writes with the authority of the professional biographer—as when she describes the first-born Myrdal and Alva's reaction to caring for him:

> Alva, meanwhile, was at home with Jan, increasingly nervous and exhausted. She took poorly to his frequent wakefulness at night and to his crying, especially since this irritated Gunnar . . . [who] wanted to be at the center of her world and found everyone else's demands on her time invasive. Looking back, she remembered feeling so locked in that she wanted to scratch the walls. While she continued to read for a higher degree in psychology and began to plan a dissertation, her time was no longer her own.

Although Alva never earned a doctorate, she wrote professionally, at first collaborating with Gunnar, as on their controversial book *Crisis in the Population Question*. Bok's skill as involved biographer shows in her combination of the heated reception of this work—which advocated stringent birth control and limitation of the size of families—with the announcement of her own birth in December 1934. Maligned because they continued to have children despite the state of the world, the Myrdals met the bitter reaction to their calls for welfare and social reforms (among them free health care and communal nurseries) by calling Sissela "Krisan" (Little Crisis).

During these years, Alva and Gunnar's careers ran parallel; as they later diverged, with Alva finding the will to break out of the wifely role Gunnar expected her to play, family life all but evaporated. While Gunnar was lionized, Alva made a home for the family, paying bills, arguing with adolescent children, and worrying about her husband's overwork—all the while maintaining her own professional status. She was sometimes curt with the children, trying to save some of her energy for her own research and writing. Bok neither minimizes nor exaggerates the family tensions in her diplomatic biography, but she does manage to keep reader attention on Alva and therefore ensure that her story is clearly told.

Scandalous Mothers

While Bok's biography follows a traditional chronology, ending with each parent's death, Kim Chernin's *In My Mother's House* (1983) takes its entire structure from her mother's language. Chernin's biography of her Communist mother, Rose, begins with a family scene—grandmother Rose welcoming Kim and her daughter, Larissa, who has just been accepted at Harvard—but the narrative of the book quickly becomes Rose's, as her granddaughter wants to hear her stories about her life. "The First Story My Mother Tells: Childhood in Russia (1903–1914)" is followed with another family interchange, but then that present-day scene is followed with "The Second Story My Mother Tells: America, the Early Years (1914–1920)." Asked by her aging parent to write her life story, Kim Chernin realized early that the most effective telling of Rose's life narrative would be her own. As the poet-daughter, Chernin played recorder—at least until the third section of the book, when she began telling her own life story.

While both Mary Catherine Bateson and Sissela Bok recalled

their mothers telling them stories, neither biography has the force of spoken language that Chernin's has. The texture of *In My Mother's House* alternates between the narrator's description of the three generations enjoying each other's presence, and Rose Chernin's narration of her life events. The latter provides the rhythmic pace for the biography. She tells about her life as an immigrant factory girl at twelve, living in the shtetl culture where spoken Yiddish, Russian, and English blurred lines of nationality. When she went to school, very much an outsider, she would not relinquish her principles; she insisted on speaking truth even when she corrected her school principal in touchingly awkward language:

> "I am here to tell you the papers did not tell the truth about Kate Richards O'Hare."
>
> That was a moment. In it what comes after is already there. Character shows itself. At the time you have no idea of this. Thinking back you realize. Was it for nothing Paul Kusnitz came up to you? Was it for nothing you responded to the *Call*? Was it an accident you stood up there in the school assembly? An immigrant girl, standing up to the principal?

For all her later radicalism, Rose makes clear to her daughter and granddaughter that radicalism is determined by belief in something and not by resentment about class or impoverishment. Her own commitment to change began in the early years of the Depression: "I'll tell you. It's a good story, because in those days we began to organize. We formed Unemployed Councils. They were spontaneous people's organizations and I want you to know about them because I helped to organize them from the first days. . . . This was the way we changed the terrible thing that was happening to . . . all of us, into productive action. We got into control of our lives. We were no longer victims."

Chernin's narrative choice, to replicate her mother's speech, makes her biography work. After the eight sections of Rose's narratives, the reader is almost disappointed when Chernin takes over telling the story. But McCarthyism from a child's point of view—especially the trauma of her mother's imprisonment when she was eleven—is riveting.

The Chernins also remember enough Russian that they use

that language for their most poignant interchanges, particularly as Rose grows older (the interviews for the book span seven years of the women's meetings) and she relies more and more frequently on phrases from her childhood. The tonal shifts from spirited and objective labor history to the sadness of her approaching death are often conveyed through a bilingual text. In the closing scene, Rose quotes the poet Lermontov, in Russian, and the following interchange is about the beauty of life, its essential loneliness sharpened with its haunting promise. Yet Chernin's last paragraph is rendered in English, and it concludes the intertwined stories of mother and daughter, Russian and American, activist and writer, without ambivalence: "It is late. My mother is tired. She reaches over to hold my hand. Suddenly, she speaks familiar words in a voice I have never heard before. It is pure feeling. It says, 'I love you more than life, my daughter. I love you more than life.'"

With the exception of Chernin's biography, which reads as much like a collection of family stories as biography, the narratives I have discussed have been plagued with the problems of over-involved narrators. Some writers show their hurt or ambivalence; some try to be objective rather than eulogistic; some rearrange chronology to avoid the predictable. Even as women biographers try to write more emotionally involved, and involving, narratives—Blanche Wiesen Cook insists that "personal involvement is central"—they are more restrained than the men who write memoirs about their fathers. In the matriarchal tradition, the role of storyteller has its own kind of impersonality.

On more than one occasion, however, telling a woman's story has been a way to correct the person's image, and when Eve Curie wrote *Madame Curie, A Biography* in 1937, she used her work to wipe clean the scandal of her mother's existence, which was sexual rather than political. Eve's narrative was of the Marie Sklodovska Curie whose career included two Nobel Prizes—one, in physics, shared with her husband, Pierre, and the other, in chemistry, awarded to her later, before she died of the uncontrollable anemia that her work with radium provoked.

Using the extensive family correspondence, Eve's book was a classic daughter's telling of her saintly mother's life. She pictured her mother as a superwoman and described her parents' unorthodox wedding in the most favorable light possible, avoiding what being freethinkers might have meant to the European culture in which they lived. The heart of her biography, however, privileges the mother alone. It focuses on the hardships Marie Curie experienced after the early death of Pierre, when she was refused membership in the French Academy of Sciences. In order to keep her mother's life exemplary and martyred, Eve quietly omitted the crystallizing event for this persecution, which was probably Marie's romantic involvement with her younger, married colleague Paul Langevin.

In Rosalynd Pflaum's 1989 *Grand Obsession: Madame Curie and Her World*, the complex story of the family's scientific involvement is told as a means of putting Marie's romance with a married man in perspective. (Her account of the public outcry about Marie and Langevin is poignant, realistic, and full, and she succeeds in showing that intellectual women can also be sexual beings.) Her biography is focused on the lives not only of the Curies but of their older daughter, Irene, who also won the Nobel Prize, and her husband, Frederic Joliot; and stresses that science was the passion that bonded the family. Her accounts of the daily risks taken in their laboratories—even as they are surrounded by coworkers and friends who are dying from leukemia, bone disorders, and mysterious maladies—depict the blindness of this age of science. As late as 1925, Marie Curie suggested that fresh air was the best remedy for contamination. That both she and Irene would die of illnesses caused by their work was one of the most moving sections of Pflaum's work.

Another was the account of the political persecution both Irene and Frederic underwent for years after World War II (in 1950, because of her sympathy with communism, Irene was forbidden entry to New York and detained in an Ellis Island camp overnight). Pflaum doesn't make the point that both Marie and Irene, as women scientists, were suspect because of their national origin, their fame, and their almost superhuman endurance in the laboratory. But she does give voice to their narratives, however scandalous, and thereby corrects the inaccuracies of earlier versions of their biographies.

CAROLE IONE TAKES on the problem of writing about accomplished women in her own family in her *Pride of Family: Four Generations of*

American Women of Color (1991). She traces her lineage through three generations of strong black women: her journalist and mystery writer mother; her great-aunt, who was one of the first black women doctors in Washington, D.C.; her great-grandmother, who was a Boston abolitionist; and various others. Realizing how helpful family stories are, Ione scatters them throughout the historical narrative. More like a Virginia Woolf fiction than biography, however, the mélange of her experience is achronological, moving thematically and emotionally from episode to episode, across time.

The isolation she experiences, for example, is like that of her mother and her actress grandmother: "As the only daughter of an only daughter of an only daughter, I have all my life felt the pure lineage of my mother's childhood sorrow as my own." Living abroad much of her adult life, Ione finally returned to the States and, like her strong female ancestors, insisted on carving out a home for her children and her remaining women relatives. In her wide-ranging series of family biographies, she re-creates those homes and, through them, the pride of family that sustained her.

A much less personal approach to telling the mother's story through the daughter's life was that of Monica Sone, whose 1953 *Nisei Daughter* was ostensibly an autobiography of her Japanese-American childhood in the internment camps of World War II but was also a story about her parents' resilience during that harsh time. The title also signaled the real narrative of the story, that the nisei, second-generation Japanese-Americans, were allowed to leave the camps long before their parents were: "By 1943, scarcely a year after Evacuation Day, the War Relocation Authority was opening channels through which the Nisei could return to the main stream of life. It granted permanent leave to anyone cleared by the FBI who had proof of a job and a place to live. Students were also released. . . . The West Coast was still off-limits, but we had access to the rest of the continent where we could start all over again." The last segment of Sone's story, then, is her life in the Middle West, without her beloved parents.

As these books show, writing a successful biography of one's mother can take multiple shapes and speak with various voices. Making the attempt is worth doing, though none of these books has won prizes. It was in 1917 that the Pulitzer Prize for biography went to Laura E. Richards and Maude Howe Elliott, daughters of

Julia Ward Howe, the author of "The Battle Hymn of the Republic" and much more, including a biography of Margaret Fuller. Their biography of their mother was titled simply *Julia Ward Howe, 1819–1910,* and countless references within its more than four hundred pages were to "our mother." No need to dodge the issue early in the century: people wrote about those they loved. Drawing extensively from their mother's letters and her own two-volume *Reminiscences,* the biography gives the reader the sound of a moderate, loving, and thoroughly committed writer-mother. Novelistic in its use of scene and dialogue, the book is readable, accurate, and suitably reverential. In the strange way literary fashion has of circling, the subjectively based biography—voiced both through Howe's written memories and those of her daughters' recollections—seems refreshingly current.

Women of accomplishment are often represented as comparatively unattractive females. Marie Curie, who won two Nobel Prizes during her important career, was notorious in France for an affair with a married colleague. Yet she is usually pictured in her primitive laboratory, wearing a humorless and appropriately selfless expression. (The Bettmann Archive)

The same kind of stereotyping occurs with anthropologist Margaret Mead, often portrayed with exotic art objects and in poses that are less than feminine. Here, with the samples of Manus art she collected during her seven-month stay in the Admiralty Islands in 1954, she smiles broadly—but not alluringly. The fact that she had three husbands and other lovers of both sexes is never emphasized, and scarcely acknowledged—even today. (UPI/The Bettmann Archive)

Women writers have often been portrayed as eccentric, different from the women of their times, as if to ridicule their accomplishments. These images contrast with the more familiar photos of both Gertrude Stein and Edith Wharton: Stein, stolidly heavy and all-too-often unsmiling, and Wharton as the stony-faced genteel "Mrs. Wharton," which people called her twenty years after her divorce from Wharton.

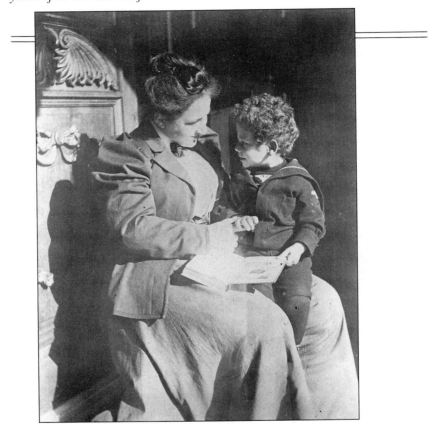

At the turn of the century, Gertrude Stein, a magna cum laude graduate in philosophy from Radcliffe College, visits her California brother's family and smiles down into the face of her only nephew, Allan Stein. A medical student specializing in women's medicine at the Johns Hopkins Medical School, Stein treasured her visits to Michael and Sally's home. Because she was thoroughly frustrated with current thinking about the treatment of women's illnesses ("womb disease" and "neurasthenia" were the usual categories of description), she did not finish her degree, but she did postgraduate research in the development of the brain and published her findings at several points in her education. A few years later, Mike, Sally, and Allan moved to Paris (as had Gertrude and her brother Leo) and became the famous collectors of Henri Matisse's work. (Courtesy of the Beinecke Rare Book and Manuscript Collection, Yale University Library, New Haven, Conn.)

Edith Wharton at the time of her first best-seller, the 1905 novel *The House of Mirth*. A member of the New York Jones family, she was always elegantly dressed and knew how to enhance her tall frame. Several years after this photo was taken, she began an affair with the younger journalist Morton Fullerton, a liaison that brought her much joy and—for the first time—sexual fulfillment. One can imagine her saying something similar to Gloria Steinem's quip when told that she did not "look forty" on her birthday. Steinem's comment was "This is what forty looks like." Wharton here was close to forty-five. (Courtesy of the Beinecke Rare Book and Manuscript Collection, Yale University Library, New Haven, Conn.)

Women of color have the same kinds of image restrictions. This less-familiar photograph of novelist and poet Alice Walker, taken soon after she won the Pulitzer Prize for her 1982 novel *The Color Purple*, emphasizes her purposely ethnic hair style and dress. Like her close friend Steinem, Walker is implicitly saying, "This is what an African-American woman writer looks like." (UPI/The Bettmann Archive)

First ladies have an almost intolerable role before the camera: they probably should not be shown as sexy, or happy, or tragic. Eleanor Roosevelt was all of these things, but the usual image of this astoundingly stable and productive wife of Franklin Delano Roosevelt presents an unattractive, even dour, woman. In contrast, here are the Roosevelts honeymooning in Strathpeffer, Scotland, in 1905—Eleanor not only joyful and smiling, but holding a cigarette. (Courtesy of the Franklin Delano Roosevelt Library, Hyde Park, N.Y.)

This 1933 portrait, taken years after the heartbreak of her husband's affair with Lucy Mercer (and Eleanor's resulting anorexia), shows her steady beauty as a mature, independent woman. Her official role was wife of the governor of New York, about to become First Lady of the country, but by this time she was leading a private life entirely separate from Franklin's. (Underwood and Underwood, courtesy of the Franklin Delano Roosevelt Library, Hyde Park, N.Y.)

One of the enduring satisfactions of Eleanor Roosevelt's private life even as she served the country as its First Lady was her long-term relationship with Earl Miller. Previously Franklin's bodyguard during his first term as governor of New York, Miller was a companion who maintained a daily contact with Eleanor throughout their lives, friends say writing her a letter every day for more than thirty years. Her hand resting on his knee suggests the intimacy they shared. (Courtesy of the Franklin Delano Roosevelt Library, Hyde Park, N.Y.)

At times, a woman's appearance has been made to serve as justification for a number of her husband's acts. Perhaps unintentionally, this late-twenties photograph of Hadley with Ernest Hemingway and their son, John (Bumby), often appears in biographies of Hemingway that explain his leaving Hadley for his petite second wife, Pauline Pfeiffer. The usual rationale is that a heavy Hadley, who was also eight years older than the young writer, began to look something like Hemingway's mother, Grace Hall Hemingway, with whom Ernest had a troubled relationship. To the couple's Paris friends, however, Hadley was the vivacious and kind beauty of the lower photograph, a woman whose physical size was thoroughly fashionable. (Courtesy of the John F. Kennedy Library, Boston, Mass.)

Although Anne Morrow Lindbergh was, in fact, often the copilot for her husband's record-setting flights, the flight suit and helmet she wore made her seem a dwarflike miniature of the tall Charles Lindbergh. (Most photographs of the famous Lindy, sometimes called "the last American hero," are of him alone or with groups of other men. His image is an indelible part of this country's history.) Although the couple had five children, after the kidnapping and death of their first son, family photographs were rare. Unfortunately, this typical photograph of Anne makes her an exact, small, replica of her husband. (UPI/The Bettmann Archive)

Beryl Markham's Garbo-esque flight jacket and slacks, which she wore during the early 1930s (the same period as the Lindberghs' photograph), show the possibilities of women finding ways to appeal to the public imagination. Markham's flight from Europe to the States was not successful, but she became an American celebrity because of her beauty and her panache. (UPI/The Bettmann Archive)

It is every woman's dream to appear in photographs as a sentient, sensual, and intelligent human being. In Man Ray's photograph of the mature Woolf, the author of *To the Lighthouse, Mrs. Dalloway, Orlando,* and other of the most important texts of modernism (and postmodernism), we can see the fragile yet sturdy brilliance that gave her the will—and the energy—to change the shape and content of twentieth-century writing. (Copyright © 1994, ARS, New York/ADAGPP/Man Ray Trust, Paris)

10
Taking Control of Story: Women's Voices

My voice formed from my life belongs to no one else.
Susan Howe, *My Emily Dickinson*

One of the reasons daughters' biographies of mothers may be problematic is that a subjective, or loving, or personal, tone strikes some readers of biography as unprofessional. It is oversimplifying to say that any story told in a woman's voice has certain characteristics, but there have been countless times when a woman's narrative becomes a different story told in the voice of a male biographer. Few traits of biography are more firmly entrenched than the conventions of voice, tone, and perspective: the biographer purportedly maintains objectivity. Drawing from a largely factual base, he or she tells the subject's story through wise selection of event and scene. What should drive the narrative, some critics say, is the choice of episode—the story of what happened—not the biographer's attitude toward the subject or the biographer's way of recounting the life.

But as we have seen in the case of George Eliot, for example, such male biographers as Sir Leslie Stephen selected events from her womanly life so that she could be portrayed as though she had been a man. With recent critical attention dominated by French theorists' discussions of the power of the male gaze, and women placed in the position of observed subjects under that gaze, readers of biography have come to recognize that the perspective of most biographies of women is male. The male biographer studies the woman's life and then—with what some readers would call appropriate detachment—presents his assessment of that life.

Unfortunately, at times the biographer's objective tone keeps the reader outside the narrative, so that reading the biography is not an interactive process. A traditional male biographer writing a woman's life may be guilty of several mistakes. Among the most common are (1) an undue emphasis on external history, to the jeopardy of paying adequate attention to internal event; (2) the omission of events crucial to the woman subject's development— either because the biographer thought them unimportant or because they went unnoticed; (3) the belief that there is one story, an "appropriate" story; and (4) the tendency to chart a woman's life in terms of her friendships and liaisons with men rather than equally through her associations with other women. While it is clear that not all men fail as biographers of women, praise such as Susan Belasco Smith's for Charles Capper's *Margaret Fuller: An American Romantic Life, The Private Years* is rare. In a June 1993 review, Smith wrote, "Capper is the first biographer to pay close attention to the details of Fuller's childhood and adolescence, in particular her relationship with her mother." In this emphasis on Fuller's matrifocal life, then, Capper avoided writing traditional biography.

Smith's comment reflects the fact that women readers distinguish among narrative voices when they approach biography. The point of view of the narrator may be one of the most significant elements in shaping a more responsive approach to telling women's lives. Observing women's lives may require a different kind of sensitivity, an eye for different kinds of details.

The Kate Chopin Biographies

Many of today's women biographers inherit the narrative of their women subjects' lives from earlier biographies, books that were probably written by men. Emily Toth wrote her 1990 biography of Kate Chopin to tell a different story of the Louisiana writer. To unearth the facts that had been obscured by earlier biographies took years of research.

The first Chopin biography, Daniel Rankin's *Kate Chopin and*

Her Creole Stories (1932), had created a pious, widowed Kate, devoted to rearing her children and writing only to make a living for them. Himself a Catholic priest, Rankin pictured Chopin as a self-sacrificing martyr, not, in Toth's words, "an eccentric, an inveterate smoker and bridge player," a sensual woman who was also an ambitious writer. When Per Seyersted's biography appeared in 1969, he echoed Rankin's often-fanciful tales about Chopin, although, more interested in Chopin's texts than in her life, Seyersted did some good in correcting Rankin's emphasis on Chopin as only a "local color" writer. But biographical information about her remained seriously inaccurate.

Toth's biography, ten years in the making, was a much-needed corrective to all this misinformation, particularly since readers familiar with *The Awakening* always questioned how Chopin understood illicit passion so well. Toth found, through personal interviews with descendants of friends of the people in Cloutierville whom Rankin had interviewed fifty years earlier, that Kate Chopin had indeed taken a lover. In *The Awakening*, Alcée Arobin was a clear picture of the suave, already married Albert (pronounced *Al-BEAR*) Sampite, and Chopin used him, and his wife, in other of her fictions as well. This information informs Toth's careful, helpful reading of the novel, as when the biographer points out: "When she named Edna's lovers, Kate Chopin gave them each a part of Albert Sampite's name: Al-cée (Al. S——é) and Ro-BERT. Alcée is the man who appeals to Edna's body; Robert is, she thinks, the mate of her soul. Albert Sampite, of course, proved to be neither, and *The Awakening* can be read as a cautionary tale about the promises of men."

Parallel with this kind of discovery was the fact that Chopin had been a highly motivated student with an exemplary record; male biographers, however, had been uninterested in her academic aptitude. She also had grown up in a matriarchal household, filled with strong, independent, and loving women, and she had probably learned her skill of storytelling from her great-grandmother, Madame Victoire Verdon Charleville. (It was also a crowded household, with more than a dozen people living together at times, so she did not have the lonely childhood Rankin described.) Chopin also formed close friendships with women throughout her life, particularly during her teenage years. Yet even though Rankin had corresponded with Chopin's best friend, Kitty, from whom she was separated during the five years of the Civil War—between the ages of thirteen and eighteen—he did little with her crucial relationships with women. Even though Chopin's life clearly foreshadowed the themes she would express in her writing, Rankin and Seyersted overlooked the biographical details that would have made such themes understandable.

In Toth's words, her attempt to rewrite Chopin's history was frustrated because of the impact of these earlier biographies; once readers thought they knew the story, change was difficult. Toth makes clear that Rankin was "not a villain—but he shared the unacknowledged biases of countless biographers of women." Toth comments that Rankin's forcing Chopin's life into the "love-motherhood-loneliness paradigm" kept readers from further investigating her work and life. His 1932 book, in its oversimplification, "closed lines of inquiry."

Toth's *Kate Chopin, A Life of the Author of "The Awakening"* was meant to open those lines. Toth could not, and did not, claim to have found information about every aspect of Chopin's life. She could not prove that Chopin had had more than one affair, but she was willing to speculate that the young widow's sexual appetites continued after her liaison with Sampite ended. But even as she gave readers directions for further investigation, critics attacked Toth because she did not have answers to all her inquiries. Despite the excellence of the book, reviewers made clear that speculation—even well-grounded speculation—was not the province of the biographer.

The Edith Wharton Biographies

While Toth's biography corrected readers' base of factual information about Kate Chopin and supplied a more empathetic interpretation of her life as self-supporting writer, other kinds of revisioning may be more complicated. The prize-winning *Edith Wharton, A Biography* by R.W.B. Lewis remains a good book, even twenty years after its publication. But in its somewhat limited focus on Wharton's sexual and personal dilemmas—first through her mother's unsympathetic eyes, then through her husband's uncomprehending vision, and later through the critical view of her lover Morton Fullerton—Lewis gives the reader a circumscribed picture of this most imaginative and perceptive woman. It is as if these sources of acute pain for Wharton are interesting to Lewis only as markers of her all-too-typical femininity. What Lewis purported to find interesting about Wharton was how intellectual—that is, masculine—she was.

The best sections of Lewis's biography are based on Wharton's own writings. They speak with the authenticity of the author's journal and save the rest of Lewis's well-described social history from becoming sterile. Together, Wharton's words and Lewis's ability to evoke the times create a good scenario—but one that leaves questions in the minds of readers who already know Wharton's fiction. The woman Lewis drew in this biography sometimes had little to do with the woman who wrote the hundreds of short stories and novels during the first thirty-five years of this century, the woman who moved easily between being a novelist of manners and a modernist. What is memorable in Lewis's biography—Edith's begging her mother before her marriage for information about intercourse, only to be referred to the nude statues she had seen; her pleading with Morton Fullerton to write to her; her confessions to friends about the misery her divorce occasioned—comes from either Wharton's unpublished memoirs or her letters.

Shari Benstock's recent biography of Wharton differs from Lewis's partly in matters of tone. For example, when Lewis discusses Wharton's early dealings with her publisher, Scribner's, he describes her expectations as unreasonable, verging on "paranoia." By drawing from more diverse sources, Benstock is able to show that Wharton complained justifiably (Scribner's was not doing enough advertising) and that she usually wrote her letters of complaint at the direction of her friend and mentor, the lawyer Walter Berry. Far from being unreasonable, Wharton only wanted her work to have a fair chance to sell.

Lewis's descriptions of what he refers to as Wharton's breakdowns are similarly exaggerated: "It was a stretched-out nightmare of exhaustion, depression, and nausea . . . ten days of it." This depression followed her fortieth birthday, but, although Lewis mentions the date, he does not establish any causal relationship. In Benstock's account, Wharton's malaise seems less whimsical. Exhausted from finishing *The Valley of Decision*, her two-volume novel, struggling while ill with the flu to entertain house guests, and also facing the inauspicious birthday, Wharton wrote angrily to her equally debilitated friend Sally Norton, "Don't I know that feeling you describe, when one longs to go to a hospital & *have something cut out*, & come out minus an organ, but alive & active & like other people, instead of dragging on with this bloodless existence." Benstock also provides enough information for readers to comprehend the ties between illness and women's roles during the early years of this century.

Benstock is not afraid to point the reader toward the explicable causes of Wharton's neurasthenia: feelings of guilt about her writing, disillusion with marriage (and guilt over her own lack of sexual pleasure), her mother's terminal illness (more guilt), and her own unresolved identity issues. For Lewis as biographer, Wharton's psyche remained a mystery. For Benstock in that same role, her various mood changes seemed almost normal for a woman so divided, especially for a woman writer whose "long and often-interrupted literary apprenticeship" made her so happy and her husband and family so unhappy.

One of the most useful services the new Benstock biography of Wharton provides is to make even her early fiction clearly *her* fiction. Readers of Wharton have often denied that there are extensive autobiographical elements in her work. (Benstock quotes reviewers who are puzzled because the wealthy, fashionable Mrs. Wharton writes so well about pain and unhappiness, as if only material wealth was significant.) In her discussion of the early stories "The Lamp of Psyche" and "The Journey," for example, Benstock shows how conflicted Wharton the author felt as friends advised her: some said that as a now-famous author, she should surround herself with the literati in London or Paris; others urged her to become more involved in elite New York society. Yet as her fiction showed, in Wharton's seemingly satisfying life, nothing was as it appeared. The Benstock biography creates the poignance of that chimera for the reader, as it gives us Edith Wharton as writer.

A Husband's (or Brother's) Control

The history of biography provides a number of situations in which a successful woman's story is told by her husband, particularly if he outlives her. Even when he has access to unpublished letters and diaries, his selection will reflect the parameters of his view, and all too often the husband's voice creates its own version of the wife's narrative. As we have seen with the three-volume biography of George Eliot by John Cross, her young husband of half a year, the husband's presentation then influences all subsequent biographies. It benefits from the authenticity of intimacy.

John Middleton Murry's careful handling of his ten-year marriage to Katherine Mansfield took the form, after her death in 1923, of editing her journal and letters. For the next thirty years, he wrote about her, and in 1959 his influential essay appeared in a small book titled *Katherine Mansfield and Other Literary Portraits*. Here Murry explained that he had edited and published Mansfield's journals, scrapbooks, and letters (several versions of them) because he believed that she was like Keats—her "life and work were one and inseparable." The pure flame of her creation was what he admired, he said, and it remained for later biographers to describe how painful his treatment of Mansfield had been during their marriage, especially while she was dying. In his 1978 biography, Jeffrey Meyers suggests that Murry may have been the carrier of the pulmonary tuberculosis that killed Mansfield (and his second wife as well).

Claire Tomalin's view in her *Katherine Mansfield, A Secret Life* (1988) is that Murry was more concerned about his own comfort and security than he was about his wife's art. Though Mansfield preferred living in Paris, Murry insisted they return to London (where they lived for some years on her allowance from her father). Tomalin also believes that Murry did not recognize the severity of her tuberculosis, even though she lost weight and coughed blood. They were living separately, in fact, during the winter of her death, and Murry arrived to see her only the day of her last severe hemorrhage.

About Murry's zealous publishing of Mansfield's work, both

D. H. Lawrence and T. S. Eliot said his effort was self-publicity; Lawrence noted that Murry "made capital out of her death." Another friend, Sylvia Lynd, spoke of Murry's "boiling Katherine's bones to make soup."

Depicting Mansfield as a writer possessed, somehow apart from the human condition, gave Murry a way both to avoid guilt for his failure to help her live longer (she died at thirty-three) and to comfort himself as he kept her work in print and proselytized for recognition of her fiction. In his comments about her and her life, however, he virtually erased her earlier marriages and affairs, saying that he and she had met and married, not that they had lived together for six years before Mansfield's divorce, after which they did marry. He also disguised her willful rejections of him and his social climbing (it was at her request that she lived alone toward the end of her life).

For all Murry's attention to Mansfield's unpublished writings, it is biographer Claire Tomalin who describes the fragments of Mansfield's lost autobiographical novel, *Maata*. Murry's including this work in some of his collections of her writing would have been useful. But because she had written it after reading D. H. Lawrence's *Sons and Lovers* and intended it to be emotionally accurate, he may have been uncomfortable with the woman persona it presented.

Olive Schreiner, too, whose 1883 novel *The Story of an African Farm* (published under the pseudonym Ralph Iron) led to her recognition as an early feminist, was the subject of an idolizing biography written by a husband. She may have married Samuel Cron Cronwright-Schreiner (after refusing to marry any of her lovers, including Havelock Ellis) in order to have a child. Thirty-eight when she met the virile farmer, she gave birth the next year to a nine-pound daughter who lived less than a day. Schreiner held the dead child in her arms for ten hours; much later, at her own death, her body was buried with the baby's casket. Rather than emphasize the poignant story of Schreiner's desperate longing to be a mother, Samuel's biography told the story of his wife as "the Greatest of Women . . . someone holy."

Among the many changes he made in the actual story of Schreiner's life, Cronwright discounted her politics and her interests (among them, the book on sexuality she planned to write, either with Ellis or alone). Stressing his wife's artistic temperament, which he described as impractical and impassioned, he deified what Schreiner had accomplished. But because he was not interested in social reform, his biography omitted Schreiner's commitment to ending racial inequity in South Africa, righting the abuse of sexual power in relationships, and leading her own life. Working from her personal papers and correspondence, he used what documents fit his thesis and threw away the rest.

Living apart from her during World War I, Cronwright-Schreiner did not recognize Olive when she came to greet him at the door of her London flat in 1920: nearly eight years older than he, she had aged terribly during the conflict. As it became clear that she was ill and her great wish was to return to Cape Town, he used his own poor health to avoid making the trip with her—in fact, he did not even take her to the dock. With Havelock Ellis, Cronwright-Schreiner accompanied her only as far as the train station. Several months later, Schreiner died, alone, in a Cape Town hotel room.

Sanitizing the life of the troublesome woman writer was a duty William Michael Rossetti also undertook: his biographical memoir of his brilliant poet sister, Christina, appeared in his 1904 edition of her poems (*Poetical Works*). In 1906 he published *Some Reminiscences*; two years later he edited *The Family Letters of Christina Rossetti*. While William did not have to hide illicit sexual experience in his sister's life, he did try to create religious myth from her existence.

In his characterization, Christina was the martyred sister who gave up two engagements—one at twenty to James Collinson, another in her mid-thirties to Charles Cayley—so that she could remain a part of the Rossetti family and nurse her aging mother. The passions of her relinquishment voiced in her poetry—especially the three hundred poems that remained unpublished because they were too personal—seem to have escaped her brother's notice. Recent biographers suggest that it was likely that she broke with Collinson over his Catholicism and with Cayley because she did not love him with the same intensity as she had loved Collinson.

In their self-creation, achieved through their paintings, writings, and the family newspaper *Hodge Podge*, the four Rossettis shaped both their lives and the public response to those lives. Early on, Dante Gabriel's painting of Christina in *The Girlhood of Mary Virgin* established the sweet purity of his younger sister. She fed that image by publishing poems of inward repression, filled with locked rooms and walled-in gardens, just as she dressed to fulfill the Madonna-like role. Later she destroyed her papers and letters. Like Emily Dickinson, the American poet whose life resembled hers, Christina was sometimes thought to have had a grand sexual passion in her life. W. B. Scott has been a candidate for the secret passion, but Kathleen Jones, Rossetti's most recent biographer, thinks that Christina's fulfilling friendship was with Scott's wife, Laetitia, and that friendships with women were her comfort in her mature years.

In 1977 biographer Stanley Weintraub told the story of *The Four Rossettis*, finding in them the perfect narrative for a family biography. Thirty years before that attempt, F. O. Matthiessen had told such an intertwined tale of the American James family—Henry James, Sr., his two sons, William and Henry, and his daughter, Alice. Fifteen years before Matthiessen, Clinton Hartley Grattan's *The Three Jameses, a Family of Minds: Henry James, Sr., William James, Henry James* made the point more clearly: any intellectual history of letters lived only in the male line of descent. In every case, the biographers' view followed patriarchal power: the people of interest in these composite portraits were the fathers and their male heirs. Within their families, both Christina Rossetti and Alice James were fey and diffident, puzzling misfits in a visibly achieving group.

Just as Samuel Cron Cronwright-Schreiner had suggested that his wife, Olive, may have been an hysteric, so the maladies of Christina and Alice were treated as if they were inexplicable. Part of the inferiority of women/sisters/mothers was this tendency to poor health. Yet often there was little mystery about women's illnesses. During Alice's 1882 relapse, for example, when she hemorrhaged from the vagina, her brother William (who was trained in medicine) suggested a uterine examination, but such extreme measures were performed only by specialists—Alice was not examined. And while the Rossetti household coped with Dante Gabriel's laudanum addiction and resulting madness, it found Christina's languishing fevers of only mild interest. Women who were ill were advised to make the best of their lives despite their poor health; men were given what medical attention there was.

In 1980, both in response to women readers' interest and as part of the move to broaden the traditional base of biography, Jean Strouse wrote a biography of Alice James. Here, the sheltered life of the James sister became the stuff of drama. Readers responded by making the name Alice James more familiar than that of her older brother, William. Strouse later said that while her initial attraction was to the life that seemed to have gone unlived, after five years of writing the book she understood that Alice, a fierce competitor, was struggling all along to make her mark on her family and friends. Strouse then said, "who Alice James was in fact was much more interesting than who she might have been."

The problems of writing about a woman subject were complicated because much of Alice's writing had been considered unimportant. There is no trace of her writing until she was eighteen, at which time some of her letters began to be saved. She did not keep a diary until she was forty-two, and then she lived only a few years longer. (She did, however, consider the diary "her dialogue with the future.") She would not attempt any kind of memoir, because she saw herself as society saw her—without value. A supportive and brilliant sister, Alice was known as "poor Miss James." Another such sister, Dorothy Wordsworth, living the last two decades of her life under the curse of Alzheimer's disease, was referred to as "poor Miss Wordsworth." The role of the proper unmarried lady, no matter how well read and witty, was to encumber her father's house.

As Strouse tells Alice's story, she was surrounded with loyal women friends—including her lifetime companion, Katharine Loring—and their support probably led to her living as long as she did. Yet the narrative of women's lives late in the nineteenth century remains a marriage plot, and while Alice watched her good friends become engaged, marry, and establish households, she had to doubt their love for her. She was, once again, different. She could never be an essential cog in her brilliant family because her intelligence worked differently from her father's and her older brother's, and now she was shut out of the world of women because she was unmarried. As Strouse phrased Alice's dilemma:

And what would happen to her after Quincy Street was no longer home? Her parents were getting old. Some day her father would not be there to require her companionship. He had written to Henry in Europe that he hoped she would always "enjoy her husband's appreciation to the same extent her mother does mine." Would she find a husband and establish a family of her own? It was time, as her marrying friends and William's exhortations repeatedly reminded her.

Strouse does not whitewash Alice's use of her physical debilities. Her first serious breakdown occurred late in the 1870s, after most of her friends had married, on the occasion of her brother William's engagement to his own Alice. Too ill to attend the wedding, Alice traveled with Katharine and forced her family to discuss suicide with her. While she grew to accept it as a choice, she was troubled when first Clover Hooper Adams and then Ellen Hooper Gurney, her sister, chose to die—Clover by drinking photographic fluid, Ellen by walking into a freight train. The latter's death Alice called "hideous . . . ghastly."

After her own mother died in 1881, Alice's health improved enough that she could care for her bereft father. Then, after his willed death from virtual starvation—a macabre comment on Alice's care of him—her health deteriorated once again. In fact, it fluctuated, seeming to depend on the nearness of Katharine Loring. When Loring was called on to care for her own family, Alice broke down, necessitating Loring's return. There were stays at sanatoria, quiet years in England, and an eventual, painful death from breast cancer.

Leaving her diary to Katharine, Alice seemed to have been content with her quiet life and death. One of her late entries mentioned the choice of suicide:

> I am being ground slowly on the grim grindstone of physical pain, and on two nights I had almost asked for K's lethal dose, but one steps hesitantly along such unaccustomed ways and endures from second to second; and I feel sure that it can't be possible but what the bewildered battle hammer that keeps me going will very shortly see the decency of ending his distracted

career; however this may be, physical pain however great ends in itself and falls away like dry husks from the mind.

Never the subject of any biography of her own before Strouse's, Alice James found her way into literary history through the 1964 publication of her diary (the book had been privately printed several times before). That she had become a writer of repute on her own terms—and in her own style of writing—would have pleased her. That the first publication of the diary, limited to four copies for family members, was the idea of Katharine Loring would also have pleased her. The acuity and acerbity of her woman's voice was the only memorial Alice James desired.

For biographers of women's lives, the problems of telling the story of a woman subject who was essentially, and sometimes literally, voiceless may be insurmountable. According to theorist Liz Stanley, such problems exist beause the conventions of biography (and all writing about the person and the self) have been so slow to change. What is needed, and may be appearing during the 1990s, are serious questions about the process of writing biography: "The past [told] from whose viewpoint? Who says this? or What would be the effect of working from a contrary viewpoint?" Underlying these questions is the basic one, Who decides which lives are interesting and therefore worthy subjects for biographies? Even if Alice James did not understand how meaningful her life story was, a perceptive woman biographer did.

11

Families of Women

I long to speak out the inspiration that comes
to me from the lives of strong women. They
make of their lives a Great Adventure.

Ruth Benedict

So long as biographers accept a Western, historical definition
of family, they must write about siblings and parents related by
blood. Some women's biographies today, however, are creating
new family configurations. When writers view women as members of differently defined families, they change the category of
"family biography." Just as some biographers of the Henry James
family wrote about only the father and two of the four sons, as if
Mrs. James, Alice, and the two younger boys were not parts of the
family, so some of today's biographers locate significant relationships for women subjects in different kinds of groupings. The
larger notion of a community formed by women who share interests and work, or simply like each other, has influenced the choice
of many recent women biographers.

Biographies of Women in Groups

Millicent Dillon pairs painter and dancer in her 1990 *After Egypt:
Isadora Duncan and Mary Cassatt* (although not intimate friends, the
women shared some of the same liberating experiences). In *Women
in Romanticism* (1989), Meena Alexander groups Mary Wollstonecraft and her daughter, Mary Shelley, with Dorothy Wordsworth,
showing the power each writer gained through her work. In the
same year, Susan J. Leonardi's biography of women at Oxford has

124

the effect of pointing out similarities that separate biographies would not have achieved, and Jean Fagan Yellin's *Women and Sisters, The Antislavery Feminists in American Culture* describes lines of both friendship and influence between black women and white, lower class and upper. Margaret Forster's 1985 *Significant Sisters: The Grassroots of Active Feminism, 1839–1939* combines biographies of such leaders as Emma Goldman, Florence Nightingale, Elizabeth Blackwell, Margaret Sanger, Caroline Norton, Josephine Butler, and others.

The now-classic group study of women's lives in the context of both cultural and personal forces is Shari Benstock's 1986 *Women of the Left Bank, Paris, 1910–1940.* Working from separate discussions of Margaret Anderson, Djuna Barnes, Natalie Barney, Sylvia Beach, Colette, Bryher and H.D., Stein and Toklas, Janet Flanner, Anaïs Nin, Jean Rhys, Wharton, and others, Benstock sets the women's lives in Paris in conjunction with each other. Her work provides new information about, and new perspectives on, both the women writers and modernist culture per se. Similarly, on a smaller scale, Mary Ann Caws explores bisexual patterning as part of the intensely creative lives of her subjects in *Women of Bloomsbury: Virginia, Vanessa, and Carrington* (1990). Writing about Virginia Woolf, her sister Vanessa Bell, and their friend the painter Dora Carrington as a trio of unusual women serves Caws's announced purpose: "This interwoven story of three women, with its fragments partially braided and sometimes frayed, wants to be a tale about understanding, which necessarily (if implicitly) includes the self writing as well as those written about."

Making explicit how distorted claims of objectivity often are for biographers, Caws speaks directly about her own involvement in this project: "I have stated in several places in this book my own point of view about these lives: these choices and these situations, however unusual, seem to me in some sense intimately involved with the creativity of these women." She admires particularly the fact "that they all should have taken their greatest and most profound joy in such a particular mixture of work and solitude, of creation and love and companionship within the idea of work itself, of work and their own radical alterations of mood in regard to it and to life."

Caws's portraits of the women *as artists,* with her resulting emphasis on their work rather than on their sexuality, are both memorable and corrective. Her description of Virginia Woolf's suicide, for example, shows the balance her approach provides:

> Just before her sixtieth birthday, with the rumors of German invasion at any moment and under the stress of the repeated air raids, [she] felt she was going irretrievably mad, hearing birds' voices until she could no longer stand the thought of it or of being unable to write again, for her madness. Considering what it would do, yet again, to Leonard's life, she walked into the nearby river with a large stone in her pocket, making her decision irreversible. On the bank she left her walking stick, and in the house she left notes for Leonard and Vanessa, explaining her action and its reasons, expressing her gratitude to Leonard for that great joy he had given her: "I don't think two people could have been happier than we have been."

What Caws's group biography does for scholarship on Woolf is immense: it regularizes a number of situations that some readers have taken as evidence of Woolf's mental instability—or at least of her idiosyncratic taste. Treated out of the isolation that often surrounds her, Woolf becomes conventional (for her circle). Caws's book also corrects the limiting biographical practice of tracing a woman subject's life through the lives of her male friends, people who were usually better known, whose papers and correspondence were more likely to have been saved.

Biographer Dee Garrison describes the difficulty of relying on possibly biased sources in her essay about writing the biography of Mary Heaton Vorse, journalist, *Masses* editor, and labor activist. Surrounded by novelists, playwrights, and Marxists whose names are better known today, Vorse led a radical life: married several times, she boarded her children out so she could lead the life she wanted; an organizer of the Provincetown Players (the early productions were staged on her property); a foreign correspondent, she was still publishing major essays in *Harper's* at nearly eighty. Yet as Garrison acknowledges:

> Much of what I knew about Vorse was written by men. It was more difficult to see Vorse through the eyes of women, for few

of them left papers or published memoirs. Yet the views of women, their judgment of meaning and importance, are usually so different from that of men, as each of us knows from our own experience. The scarcity of recorded female vision distorts almost all historical findings. A few letters and interviews with women friends and neighbors helped me to widen the span of evidence. . . . Still, I will never know how much the sparsity of extensive female input may have misshaped my story of Vorse's life.

Theorist Liz Stanley points to the absence of what she calls the "friendship biography," describing "a need to conceptualize women's patterns of friendship in biography, as well as to record these. . . . Once friendship is admitted to be an important aspect of biographical investigation, unresolved issues remain concerning how this investigation should be carried out as well as the significance that should be accorded to its textual product."

Biographies of Friends and Foremothers

The wealth of women writing biographies of other women suggests that women have recognized the importance of caring about their subjects, even if there is no critical theory that acknowledges that bond. Often, the woman biographer who chooses to write about a woman subject has formed a passionate attachment to her and often that attachment is the reason for the book—as in the cases of Margaret Mead writing on Ruth Benedict, Margaret Drabble on Virginia Woolf, Agnes DeMille on Martha Graham, Violet Hunt on Elizabeth Siddal, Alice Walker on Zora Neale Hurston, and Melva Joyce Boyd on Frances E. W. Harper.

In 1959, when Mead prepared her edition of Ruth Benedict's poems, papers, and essays, it became clear that she needed to write biographical commentary to accompany her friend's work. Mead saw her biography of Benedict, which she wrote informally so that it would give the effect of oral history, as commemoration both of their twenty-five years of friendship and of Benedict's great contributions to the study of anthropology. What Benedict had considered essential during the 1920s, 1930s, and 1940s was innovative and brilliant, but without Mead's biographies about each stage in her friend's life, the reader might not understand her professional acumen.

As a married woman of some means, Benedict chose the poverty of being an unpaid assistant to her mentor Franz Boas; after her divorce, she again chose to take low-paying positions in order to stay near Boas and Edward Sapir. Like Mead, Benedict never achieved the academic rank she deserved, although her influential books—*Patterns of Culture* and *The Chrysanthemum and The Sword*—made her world-famous.

Mead's book is intended to be a personal statement as well as an objective one. She describes Benedict's career in terms of three other anthropologists—Boas, Sapir, "and myself, her first student, fifteen years younger but anthropologically almost a contemporary." Mead also describes Benedict as a poet who published under the pseudonym of Anne Singleton in the circle of their friends Léonie Adams, Louise Bogan, and Genevieve Taggard, and she includes part of the first writing Benedict did, a series of essays on Mary Wollstonecraft, Olive Schreiner, and Margaret Fuller. Benedict's moving biographical essay on Wollstonecraft remains evocative, and much of what she says about her applies to her own pioneering work. By the time the reader comes to Benedict's essay on Wollstonecraft, which appears last in the collection, Mead's biographical sections have shown her friend, too, as a daringly unconventional woman.

True to Stanley's premise that women who share work—or the appreciation of each other's work—often bond intimately, Agnes DeMille's 1991 biography of Martha Graham speaks to the fact that they were both dancers. DeMille was Graham's student (much as Mead had been Benedict's) and had lived to see her mentor age and change but still create her brilliant art as she envisioned it. In *Martha, The Life and Work of Martha Graham*, DeMille tells the story of the "genius" choreographer and dancer, who reshaped dance and stage aesthetic as passionately as she led her private life.

To begin, DeMille tells of being a twenty-three-year-old dance student when she met Graham, then thirty-five. She recognized instantly that Graham—both in movement and in words—was sheer energy: "Martha cast her remarks up like flowers into the air and they fell every which way as all listeners grabbed to snatch at their loveliness. More frequently they were like a flight of darts or arrows. One was not convinced; one was impaled and stood like a Saint Sebastian. . . . Blood flowed and that was enough. Danger proved life." DeMille's authoritative voice gives the fascinating details of Graham's involvement in Denishawn, Ruth St. Denis and Ted Shawn's school; Ted's touring company; her two years in the *Greenwich Village Follies*; her teaching at Eastman, where she began forging her own concepts into dance (twenty-nine new pieces in 1926; sixteen the next year, among them *Revolt*, to music by Arthur Honegger). The thirties were euphoric, intense, and productive; by their end, Graham was a name to be reckoned with, in the midst of a career that lasted another fifty years.

During World War II, Graham's company tours grew harder— ambitious programs, scarce food, poor accommodations. In DeMille's prose, "the tours, the arriving late, the going to the theater, the unpacking, the ironing of the costumes with the help of one or two hired local women, the concert, the midnight snack, the unpacking of the single personal suitcase, the exhausted sleep, the early-morning departure, the repetition. Martha used to do a great deal of the ironing herself . . . and the girls used to help. While she ironed, Martha talked in a very relaxed and informative way, mainly about love and life." Only an insider, and a woman, would emphasize these details (that the dancers were onstage for two numbers, and then ironed costumes for the next two); the book convinces through its incontrovertible base of knowledge, and its insistence on the subtle power of interaction both physical and mental. Such a wealth of information continued through Graham's death, though she had last danced in 1968, at age seventy-two: her choreography went on through the 1980s even though, in DeMille's words, "she was old, badly crippled, and depleted, with one of the most extraordinary minds of this century, the valor of a warrior, and the untiring instinct of an animal. . . . Martha released living ideas. They thrive. They are free. They have their own direction and trajectory, and they cannot be caught and held."

Alice Walker's essays on Zora Neale Hurston called for women writers to admit their need for women as models. As she wrote in "Zora Neale Hurston: A Cautionary Tale and a Partisan View," "I became aware of my need for Zora Neale Hurston's work some time before I knew her work existed." Admitting the need is the first step to finding help. What Walker admired about Hurston's writing, once she had found both her folklore and her fiction, which were then out of print, was her view of "racial health; a sense of black people as complete, complex, *undiminished* human beings." Reading Hurston gave Walker the sense that as an African-American woman writer, she had at least one entire culture to write about, a culture that was not inherently crippled or angry or depraved, but varied and interesting.

Her personal need to discover what she could about Hurston led her to search for Zora's unmarked pauper's grave, a process described in her essay "Looking for Zora." Only after Walker had paid what she thought were fitting tributes to this earlier writer, which included putting a stone on her grave as well as editing a collection of Hurston's work, could she continue with her own life.

These essays on Hurston were integral to Walker's message in the title essay of her 1983 collection *In Search of Our Mothers' Gardens*: that women must learn from women who love them how to be themselves, how to find the wellsprings of their own creativity, how to sustain themselves. In giving readers this generational imperative—that they look to families both actual and extended—Walker also acknowledged that finding a woman's lineage might be difficult. Names change, as do public records, and nothing is matrifocal. But rather than lament the difficulty, Walker issued the directive that women learn to redefine creativity. Women have been making beautiful quilts, needlework, and knitting for centuries; women have been cooking exquisite food, arranging furniture, and planting breath-taking gardens through the history of domesticity. What the aspiring artist, or the aspiring human being, can learn from these models of women's art and work is inexhaustible and priceless.

The Marginalized Subject and Readers

Walker's injunction that women look into the lives of women who preceded them was one rationale for poet Melva Joyce Boyd's 1994 biography of Frances E. W. Harper, also a poet. Boyd's study of Harper emphasizes the immense creativity of the African-American writer she felt was an ancestor figure for her. While *Discarded Legacy: Politics and Poetics in the Life of Frances E. W. Harper, 1825–1911* is on the one hand a traditional, well-researched biography, Boyd interjects subjective comments throughout. Of her title, for example, she notes, "A legacy is not static. It is not suspended in the time frame of the birth and the death of the person. Rather, it is like a poem. It imparts to each person who encounters it an affirmation, a confrontation, or an indulgence. The conceptual framework of the book is developed around the voice of Harper speaking directly to the reader, and my voice speaks over her shoulder in another verbal dimension."

Boyd intentionally fixes herself, and her voice, in the portrait of Frances Harper, an orator like Maria W. Stewart and the Grimkés as well as a writer of poetry, prose, and political essays. Boyd's process of writing the biography, then, tries to approximate the multivocality that characterized Harper's life and connects both Harper and Boyd with the dialogism in women's lives and its re-creation through women's history.

Boyd also emphasizes the creative side of Frances Harper, as she places her in the long American literary tradition of engagement with political themes. As she explains, her focus in the biography "merges from the intersection of her [Harper's] poetry with her political and cultural stature as an abolitionist and as a feminist. It demonstrates the integral presence of a black woman on the axis of democratic challenges of the nineteenth century and the unique perspective she cultivated through her work." And because Harper's insight was developed during an era rife with violent enforcement of racism, sexism, and classism, her story provides a viable ideological framework for contemporary radical thought.

Boyd also considers Harper as writer, showing how her novel *Iola Leroy, or Shadows Uplifted* grew from her earlier short fiction, her long poems, *Moses, A Story of the Nile* and "Sketches of Southern Life," and her serialized novels, "Minnie's Sacrifice," "Reaping and Sowing," and "Trial and Triumph." But Boyd's book avoids being simply a critical biography, with emphasis on Harper's writing, because of the blend of personal interrogation (the author's own comments) within the historicized text. More a literary study than is Erlene Stetson's *Glorying in Tribulation: A Biography of Sojourner Truth* (1994), which treats Truth as a powerful determinant of history, or Kay Mills's *This Little Light of Mine* (1993), which focuses on Fannie Lou Hamer's role in the Civil Rights movement, Boyd's book avoids some of the pitfalls of writing about the marginalized subject.

The problems of writing serious biography about women of color, lower-classed women, lesbians, and/or so-called scandalous women sometimes seem insurmountable. It is clear that in today's publishing world there is a comparatively scant market for books about fairly famous white, middle- or upper-class women subjects. In this context, it seems foolhardy for a biographer to write about a woman subject who has little name recognition, especially when that subject does not represent a substantial book-buying readership. A small audience is the reason most biographies of ethnic or otherwise marginalized subjects are published by university presses rather than commercial ones.

The issue, however, is more complicated than such an emphasis on economics suggests. As Arlyn Diamond recently pointed out in her review of the Mills biography of Hamer, "Not to write about Fannie Lou Hamer is to reproduce the racist scholarship we have been guilty of in the past. To write about her is to run the risk of appropriation, of using her to consolidate our own ideas and positions while we leave her behind. Hamer herself for some was too black, too poor, too uneducated, too female to walk through the doors she had paid so much to open." Echoing more than a decade of complaint that only certain minority writers will ever be accepted by elite literary readers, Diamond bluntly states another of the problems. Readership for biography wants the kind of comfort that comes with identification. If the subject comes from too remote a place, either geographically or financially, or from too different a culture, the oddity must be prestigious rather than threatening. As a result of knowing how difficult the problems are, any biographer who works in these newer fields must be visibly self-conscious. And while the literary world waits for the publication of Nell Painter's book on Sojourner Truth and Margaret Wilkerson's biography of Lorraine Hansberry, a thousand other books about women who stand outside the white middle class are not attempted.

The Biographer's Need to Affirm

Many recent biographies of women, and groups of women, show that the most important criterion of a memorable presentation is the biographer's involvement in the life in its full context. Just as Alice Walker's insistence on recognizing her mother's and Zora Neale Hurston's accomplishments led to her own self-actualization, so did Martha Graham's immense achievement in dance allow her peers—a family that included her biographer—to forgive her self-centered existence. For both women, their reliance on being part of a woman-created community undoubtedly contributed to their achievements.

The biographer's positive depictions are what readers expect. Insofar as there is a logical reason for any biographer's choice of subject, one assumes it is admiration. One assumes that the biographer will attempt to understand the personality—even if the personality is difficult or erratic—and will convey that understanding to the reader. The biographer uses both fact and subjective identification to translate the subject's life for the reader. And in most cases, the biographer has somehow identified with the community that surrounds the subject's life.

Against that set of assumptions comes Carolyn Heilbrun's somewhat harsh review of Carol Brightman's *Writing Dangerously: Mary McCarthy and Her World* (1992). Heilbrun's question is, How did Brightman feel about the subject of her book, and why doesn't she tell the reader what her feelings are? Given Mary McCarthy's legendary nastiness, which the biographer would recognize better than most readers, "it is far from clear how Brightman felt about McCarthy. This biography, like McCarthy's life, seems more concerned with names and places than with steady reflection, becoming almost breathless as it follows her career among the well-known people and the fashionable places of her time." Heilbrun questions whether it is necessary for the reader to learn "that she

[McCarthy] slept with over a hundred men." At issue for Heilbrun is that primary responsibility of any biographer, to let the reader know where she or he stands on the topic in question, the subject's life. Knowing that, the reader will have "a vantage point to develop her or his own views toward her subject."

Heilbrun closes her review with the comment that the possibility of writing a great biography of a woman subject who was successful professionally and fulfilled personally remains slight: the art of writing women's biography is still young. But what good biographies of women have been written in the recent past "suggest that, beyond all else, the biographer must both deeply respect and simply like her subject." She might even, according to Heilbrun, share some sense of family, or community, with her subject.

12

The Best of Them

The year was 1969. A great new audience of women
hungry to know about women was gathering.

Alix Kates Shulman

Judgment. The critic can talk about serious biography or popular,
satisfying or tedious, but finally each reader must decide individu-
ally what biography fulfills his or her need to enjoy—or to understand—a subject. Virginia Woolf said that a biographer had to
make "one seamless whole" out of the separate facts and the "rain-
bow-like intangibility" of the subject's personality. This chapter
talks about biographies that have achieved at least some of the
goals of biography in an exemplary way, but there is no grid or
scheme that will prove definitively that biography A is better than
biography B. If I had space, I would discuss fifty books here rather
than the seven I have included. Of recent books, if I were giving
the Pulitzer Prize for biography, it would go to Blanche Wiesen
Cook's 1992 *Eleanor Roosevelt*, a lucid, energetic, and thoroughly
new telling of that revered woman's story. In the case of each biography discussed here, some kind of new, credible perspective
was presented that made the biography an important narrative
experiment, as well as a fulfilling life story.

Milford's Zelda

Nancy Milford's 1970 *Zelda, A Biography* has become the model for
contemporary women's biography because it changed the way
readers saw Zelda Sayre, wife of F. Scott Fitzgerald. Milford's book

challenged everything people thought they knew about the flamboyant writer and his wife by placing Zelda at the center of the canvas and arranging husband, child, family members, and friends around her in clearly subordinate roles. By charting her life as the youngest child of an affluent Southern family, Milford shows Zelda's development of self-confidence and pride, as well as a not-always-realistic sense of self.

Today, that Zelda Sayre's maternal grandmother committed suicide and her older sister had frequent breakdowns could be considered evidence of a genetic tendency to depression or mania; while she does not interpret the information, Milford at least records this part of her subject's history. Zelda's unpredictable behavior, which Montgomery, Alabama, accepted because she was Judge Sayre's daughter, could also have been the result of mania. Aside from changing her emphasis about these matters, Milford's presentation of the family history and Zelda's childhood and adolescence remains accurate and moving.

What struck readers in 1970 was that Milford's story of Zelda's life with F. Scott Fitzgerald had so often been told inaccurately. By most accounts, Zelda's drinking and bothering of her writer husband had led to his drinking and his inability to get work done: Zelda was a pest, and Scott's friends were relieved when she was institutionalized. In contrast, Milford shows the gradual disintegration of the couple's relationship, placing as much blame on Fitzgerald's insensitivity as on Zelda's aberrant behavior. She describes the situation in 1926 by using a combination of direct authorial statement and illustration: "By the time the Fitzgeralds left Paris for the Riviera in July not only their marriage, but their very identities were in peril. . . . Zelda looked weary and haggard; her complexion, which had always been fresh, was ashen and colorless. Even her speech seemed to have changed. Gerald Murphy remembered her sudden bursts of laughter for no discernible reason. . . . All through that summer Zelda sank more deeply into her private world, becoming increasingly remote from Scott and Scottie."

Milford uses letters from friends (here, Sara Murphy) to buttress her interpretation that Scott was responsible for much of the problem in the marriage: Sara wrote to him, "You don't even know what Zelda or Scottie are like—in spite of your love for them. It seemed to us the other night (Gerald too) that all you thought and felt about them was in terms of *yourself*. . . . I feel obliged in honesty of a friend to write you that the ability to know what another person feels in a given situation will make—or ruin lives."

Milford's extensive use of unpublished correspondence and manuscripts adds much new information to her biography. She also draws on transcribed interviews between Scott and Zelda and with Zelda's therapist to show the cruelty incipient in the marriage—as when Scott forbade Zelda to use any of his material in her writing. (This after he had taken sections of her diaries and letters for use in many of his short stories and novels—as critics often said, Fitzgerald's women characters were usually Zelda.)

Perhaps the most helpful part of Milford's reading of Zelda's character was her attention to the relationship between the woman and her father. Even though her only novel, *Save Me the Waltz*, had made clear the kind of power her father held over her, critics had paid insufficient attention to Zelda's writing to learn about her life from it; discounting her considerable ability as a writer was another way to make her subordinate to Fitzgerald (it was well known that some of the short stories Fitzgerald published during the 1920s were written in part or entirely by Zelda). By establishing that Zelda was a traditional Southern woman, culturally inscribed with the norms of behavior her Alabama town mandated and eager to break out of that coded life, Milford enabled readers to find in her protagonist a woman that nearly everyone could identify with. Zelda's story became its own drama. Married young to a rising literary figure, she excelled at loving, entertaining, and partying. But as she searched for more, rebelling at the prescribed roles beautiful women were made to play, she came in conflict with the male-dominated culture of modernism. In some ways, she was a victim of the literary times as well as of her husband's attitudes— and her own.

Thurman's Dinesen

In 1982, Judith Thurman's *Isak Dinesen, The Life of a Storyteller* did a different kind of re-visioning. Dinesen was comparatively little known in the States, but through this vivid recounting of her exotic, and poignant, life, her biographer was able to create interest not only in her personal hegira but in her writing. A decade after *Zelda*, Thurman's biography drew upon a new feminist consciousness that saw a woman's identity as being shaped more by her own control. Thurman titled the four sections of her narrative by the various names Dinesen chose to use: *Tanne*, her childhood family name; *Tania*, the African version of that, used by Finch Hatton in his conversations with her; *Isak*, her (male) name as writer; and *Pellegrina*, the mystic approaching death. Giving the writer this kind of control of her persona kept the tragic narrative from usurping the story. Divorced from her husband and ill with the syphilis of the spine she had contracted from him, abandoned by her British lover in Africa shortly before his death, Dinesen could have been a pitiful subject. But Thurman instead uses Dinesen's mental and physical pain to show her ability to cope and her monumental will.

Thurman's description of Dinesen's decision to marry the rough sportsman Bror Blixen provided he leave the family's Danish dairy farm for life in East Africa serves as a metaphor for her adventurous temperament. "In this adventure—their marriage and departure for parts unknown—they became partners. A bond of dependence and anticipation grew up around it, heightened by the skepticism of outsiders. . . . It was Tanne, older and cleverer, who logically supplied the form and imaginative energy for their plans, and Bror, fearless and hardy, who supplied the readiness for action." In Thurman's concise writing, the reader receives a great deal of information about each person's complexities.

But Bror's unwise decision to trade the farm they had purchased while still in Denmark for a coffee plantation with unsuitable acidic soil meant they would never prosper. For a time, however, their love for the African life—the country's beauty, its people and animals—united them. As Tania grew more and more pro-native, putting herself at odds with many of the English settlers, she became isolated. Bror found other women; Tania turned to Denys Finch Hatton and lived increasingly in her imagination.

Thurman's biography is the story of a woman in her time and place, the exotic and struggling East Africa, as well as the story of a woman's search for both love and profession. For instance, Thurman describes a recurrent after-dinner scene with Finch Hatton in Dinesen's "sensuous" sitting room,

> filled with small bouquets of roses and long-stemmed white madonna lilies in deep water. There was a leopard skin on the floor; a low divan with Persian pillows; and, concealing the door to the bedroom, an old French wooden screen, painted with fanciful oriental figures. . . . Their friends remember that Denys and Tania liked to experiment with the sensations hashish, opium, or *miraa* could give them. Denys arranged the cushions on the floor before the fire and reclined there, playing his guitar. Tania sat "cross-legged like Scheherazade herself" and told him stories.

The lush world Dinesen created both materially and imaginatively becomes the keystone of her indomitable persona.

While the biography later becomes the narrative of Isak Dinesen as writer, it never relinquishes the dynamic of those African years. Even though she learns to transform her fragility into imaginative power and fictionalizes much about the African years in *Out of Africa* (a book Thurman calls "a sublime repair job"), her re-creation seems a plausible way to maintain control. And maintain control she did. At her death in 1962, Dinesen weighed only seventy pounds. She had died of a willed malnutrition.

Fitch's Bookshop Biography

In 1983 Noel Riley Fitch's *Sylvia Beach and the Lost Generation* attempted to describe a culture as well as a subject: Fitch subtitled the book *A History of Literary Paris in the Twenties and Thirties*. Intrigued with the presence and effect of Beach's Shakespeare and Company as bookstore and publishing house, Fitch wrote about American expatriates in Paris from early in the twentieth century to World War II. Using Beach's various literary undertakings as an index of her personal bravery, Fitch was able to avoid recounting intimate material about Beach's life.

True to her aim, Fitch shaped the book around central events in the bookstore's history—readings and parties, the arguments and patronage of the literary world, and Beach's publication of James Joyce's *Ulysses* in 1922.

> There were light moments of friendship and mutual excitement associated with the birth of *Ulysses*. Joyce would read aloud from *Ulysses* for her, often the Cyclops section. They would burst into peals of laughter at Joyce's rendering of the dog. . . . Subscribers became restless—the October date of the announced publication came and went. Because they had not paid any money yet, Sylvia nervously joked, the subscribers could not sue her for swindling them. . . . By November there were 400 subscribers, but the money had not been collected, because the book was not ready. Funds were low; Joyce had been borrowing advances from both Sylvia and Harriet Weaver.

The picture of Beach that emerges from this book is one of immense generosity and patience, all the sadder in light of the fact that when *Ulysses* was published in America, Joyce took the large publication advance in secret and never attempted to repay Beach.

Fitch's biography kept Beach surrounded with friends throughout, but rarely is there a scene of Adrienne Monnier and Beach alone, despite their thirty-eight-year liaison. Only recently has Fitch commented about the problems of a heterosexual biographer writing about a lesbian. She admitted that while for many subjects, sexuality is a key issue, for others, it may be less significant. Because Beach and Monnier "kept their sexuality private" and were critical of public displays, Fitch chose in this work to underplay the women's relationship. While she agrees with Leon Edel when he complains that readers think sex life is all-important, she acknowledges that attempts to deal with sexuality expose the biographer to the three sins of the genre: "suppression, invention, and sitting in judgment."

Another dilemma facing the biographer of a homosexual subject is whether or not inferences could, or should, be drawn: "A biographer must be careful to distinguish between a truth that is established in fact and a truth that is suggested by circumstantial evidence." Luckily, Fitch assures herself, the biographer can attempt to tell only one version of the subject's life. Therefore, although she knows the life in as much detail as possible, not all details are germane to her project. For Fitch's story of Shakespeare and Company, *all* the people in Sylvia Beach's life were significant, not just her life partner.

Such a rationale might have been more easily accepted in the early 1980s than in the 1990s, when sexuality has become recognized as a valid way into personality configuration. That Fitch, like Deirdre Bair, is currently writing a biography of Anaïs Nin, a most complicated persona where sexuality is concerned, suggests that the very absence of attention to Beach's sexual life might have led her to a subject for which the sexual becomes paramount.

Howard's Mead

Jane Howard's 1984 *Margaret Mead, A Biography* made expert use of a bevy of details, even while omitting the mention of a number of people from Mead's well-traveled life. Like Elisabeth Young-Bruehl's *Hannah Arendt: For Love of the World* two years earlier, this biography drew extensively from the subject's own writing—and other work in her field—so that Howard was able to trace the changes in Mead's professional life as well as in her personal one. Of Mead's three husbands, two were colleagues, and many of her intimate friendships were with other anthropologists, so inclusion of her work was doubly appropriate.

Immersing herself in a field so unfamiliar was difficult; as Howard noted, "Margaret Mead was not my relative, my friend, my employer, or my teacher." While Fitch claimed that the biographer needs some emotional link with the subject, Howard's tactic of denying any association is negated by her economium of the reasons Mead was famous. She implies that Mead's attraction for her is due to her sheer omnipresence, her centrality to so many people's lives. Yet Mead remained a mystery: "The fame she sought and won was on her own terms. She was not only one of the most accomplished and most energetically public women of her time, but one of the most enigmatic."

Acknowledging that, Howard set out to create as whole a Margaret Mead as she could—the real province of the biographer, to discover the personality that escapes everyone else. Calling her "a patron saint of the peripheral," Howard admires the fact that "the world was her field." Mead would not be bound by the perimeters of her academic specialization, and neither would she be bound by the rules of class and race operative in her turn-of-the-century Midwest: "The world was her family. Her sense of kinship began with the people who conceived her and bred her and saw her through childhood. Where it stopped was one of the secrets she kept to herself."

Howard's massive book is written in a dense but amusing style and consequently saves its readers from the boredom common to more academic tomes. It opens, "Lord knows they meant well, thought they didn't believe in the Lord. Margaret Mead's parents were rational, secular agnostics." The kind of people who read Emerson's essays, her family allowed their young "gutsy pragmatist" the privilege and the freedom to find her own directions in marriage, in career, and in personal relationships.

Howard's book recounts all these family matters, as well as Mead's Christmas card list of over five hundred people, several hundred of whom she considered her extended family; it describes the way she went to the weddings, christenings, and holidays of those close families and provided empathetic silence or gaiety, as the occasion demanded. She also, according to Howard,

> made a point of being available when her godchildren needed her. Would you rather talk of the past, she asked one child whose father had suddenly died, or of the present and the future? "Good," said Mead when the child chose the present and future. "That's what I prefer to talk about, too." And when Martha Ullman suffered a youthful heartbreak, her godmother assuaged her grief by canceling her own plans and giving the girl a restorative lunch of egg rolls and vin rosé, along with the journals of Virginia Woolf and Katherine Mansfield.

Less directive or dogmatic than some reminiscences might suggest, Mead's art in human relationships was that of the choreographer. As one of her oldest friends remarked after Mead's death,

"Her greatest forte was getting the right minds together to explain how interdisciplinary ideas could dovetail."

For finally, at the end of Howard's rich plum pudding of anecdote and dialogue, a fitting recovery of Mead's busy life, she summarizes the enigmatic woman:

> Mead's sin, she once told Jean Houston, was greed: greed for new experiences. All her appetites were hearty. By conventional standards she moved around too much, ate and drank too much . . . wrote too much—her bibliography lists 39 books, 1397 other publications, and 43 records, tapes, films, and videotapes. She had 29 honorary degrees and won 40 awards, and seemed genuinely pleased with each one. Some said she hoped for a Nobel Peace Prize, or a post in the Cabinet. For all her laurels, she did not rest, and rejection could hurt her as it hurts anybody. It could make her weep.

After recounting all these kaleidoscopic bits of the woman Mead had become in her seventy-seven years, Howard closed with a good-humored echo of her opening: "Lord knows she meant well. And she did well, too."

A Pulitzer Winner

When in 1985 Elizabeth Frank's *Louise Bogan: A Portrait* was awarded the Pulitzer Prize for biography, it marked an acceptance of the kind of book necessary to tell a woman's story as much as it honored Frank's specific biography. For Bogan's life was full of problematic issues: disastrous sexual and marital liaisons, a tendency to alcoholism, psychiatric treatment, instability, a strangely loyal set of friends, talent that never saved her from the vicissitudes of daily living—all the ingredients for an unpleasant, even macabre, account. In Frank's unyielding control of narrative, she pieced together and sorted through the events of Bogan's life both public and private. Bogan's thirty-eight years as poetry critic for *The New Yorker* helped give her some external stability, but for all that facade, it was an untidy existence.

Frank tells the story flat out. "By the time she was twenty-two, Bogan had been a wife and mother, had left her husband and given her child to her parents' keeping, had become a widow and a betrayed lover within the same year, and had established a solid and growing reputation as a gifted lyric poet." But aside from chronology, Bogan's temperament continued to plague her: "Severe psychic pain was a daily fact of life. It had been so from early childhood and it would continue to be so. Early in 1922 it reached an especially acute point. She needed to get away from New York and live alone. . . . She had a new lover, who had money and later followed her to Europe, but for the time being she wanted to be free of him."

Frank's book does not try to make Bogan a feminist. Thoroughly comfortable with her male-identified life, she often dismissed other women who wanted to be friends and preferred to find her closest friendships with men. This, too, Frank discusses openly: "Bogan's insights into her own sex are often uneasy. Crankily sympathetic with women, she was nevertheless aware, through her own mistakes and her acute observations of others, of the ways in which women seem to perpetuate their own patterns of defeat and failure, and with these she was impatient."

She also insists that Bogan's poetry *is* her narrative, told in her unmistakable voice. Blending discussion of poems with discussion of life is Frank's forte:

> Had Bogan's journals and notebooks from the 1920s survived . . . chances are they might have revealed a good deal about her growing interest in perception. We might well have found brief, richly observed descriptions of natural scenes: colors of earth and hills in various seasons, light at different angles and different times of day. These would have made a good deal more evident her affinities with her American Romantic forebears—Emerson, Thoreau, and Dickinson—with whose imaginations hers most certainly establishes continuity.

Well-received, especially for a book that talked so frequently about Bogan's poems in appreciable detail, this biography stood as an example for the contemporary treatment of the woman as writer, the woman who would not bow to social norms to salvage her personal reputation.

Bair's de Beauvoir

Deirdre Bair's 1990 *Simone de Beauvoir* was a decade in the writing (not an unusual investment of time for a biographer). More importantly, Bair had the privilege of knowing de Beauvoir during the last five years of her life and worked intimately with her on this project. The amount of attention she gives to de Beauvoir's family circumstances, then, is rare, but de Beauvoir made Bair understand that for a woman of good family, after her father had lost his estate and she had no dowry, marriage was impossible.

Bair's emphasis on the innocence of both Simone and her younger sister contrasts sharply with the reputation for immorality that befell the young intellectual woman. Nicknamed "Castor" (the French for *beaver*) because she studied so hard and earned degrees in less time than her classmates, Simone nearly bested Jean-Paul Sartre in their comprehensive examinations. One of their examiners later wrote, "If Sartre already showed great intelligence and a solid, if at times inexact, culture, everybody agreed that, of the two, she was the real philosopher." She was then twenty-one. (Other of her close friends were Merleau-Ponty and Claude Lévi-Strauss.)

The fifty-year relationship with Sartre began as they worked together on their first book, but she would never accept marriage to him. As they worked and lived together, Sartre began the series of affairs that she learned to tolerate and occasionally, as in her liaison with American novelist Nelson Algren, to echo. But de Beauvoir was never quite so intellectual as her pose, and Bair describes her anguish even under the "constant, rigid control" that was her mode.

> She would drink silently and steadily, consuming remarkable quantities of liquor which seemed to have little effect on her sobriety until she started to cry, silent tears at first, then audible

sobs that grew in strength and volume until they racked her body. . . . The first time Sartre witnessed one of her outbursts, her only form of behavior over which he had no control, he reacted in panic with what became his usual response during the next few years—a proposal of marriage. . . . Sartre liked to think of himself as genuinely sensitive and attuned to all her emotional needs, but he was thinking of his own as well. He wanted his "pal" back, and also his alter ego, the one who understood his thoughts and ideas so well that her ideas, suggestions and revisions were often more clearly expressed than his own could have been. Only she shared the wicked jokes they made about their friends; the outrageous descriptions which filled their letters.

Criticized by some because Sartre holds such a prominent place in de Beauvoir's biography, Bair's only comment is that their lives, and their minds, were almost inextricably woven together—and had been since de Beauvoir was barely twenty and Sartre twenty-three. Despite the fact that Bair follows the author's own voluminous memoirs carefully, arguing with their accounts when necessary, she cannot escape the almost dual focus of the book. Neither could de Beauvoir in her own autobiographical writing.

Davis's Nella Larsen

Thadious M. Davis's *Nella Larsen, Novelist of the Harlem Renaissance: A Woman's Life Unveiled* (1994) had a double imperative. The biography had to provide answers to the innumerable questions about Larsen's identity and the reasons for her silence after the novels *Quicksand* and *Passing* were published in the late 1920s. It also had to answer other questions about the way she fit into the black aesthetic movement known as the Harlem Renaissance. Because her second novel dealt with the issue of black women crossing the color line, "passing" in white society, some readers speculated that Larsen herself had passed. Providing a rich historical context for Larsen's complex story, Davis succeeds in telling the story of an immensely talented woman, while also giving the reader new information about a biracial American society in the first half of this century.

The mystery of Nellie Walker, born April 13, 1891, in Chicago's Scandinavian community, is really the mystery of her parents. Davis's attempts to trace the changes in the identity of Nellie's father—does the black man who fathered her also, with the new name of Peter Larson, father her sister, born in 1893; or is her mother married to someone else by that time? Shifts in addresses complement changes in names, but the result of family change is that Nellie has darker skin color than her parents and her sister. Accordingly, Davis surmises, Nellie is sent away to school—and, effectively, sent out of her family. Larsen's journey through life begins, and remains, an isolated one.

Despite all Davis's efforts to supply answers, that journey remains a mysterious one as well. Between 1908 and 1912, no one knows where Larsen was, although she said later that she had spent three years in Denmark, her mother's country. After that period, the record is somewhat clearer, though still fragmented. Larsen attends Fisk Nursing School and continues her training at the Lincoln Training School. She then works as a nurse in Chicago. She becomes head of nursing at Tuskegee Institute. She then takes a position in New York City and there meets Elmer Imes, a black scientist with a Ph.D. in physics from the University of Michigan. About her marriage to him, Davis writes, with the typically tough stance she maintains toward her subject: "Imes appealed to Larsen's desire for social prominence and economic security; moreover, as an older man he satisfied her need for the paternal regard she had lost when Peter Larson/Larsen had positioned himself, his wife, and his daughter Anna entirely within conventional white society. . . . Imes was an engaging man with old-world charm and courtly manners [but] not demonstrative and affectionate."

Marriage helped Larsen rise from the comparatively low social position her nursing career provided, and as Imes's wife, she moved into New York's intellectual life. She worked as a librarian and in publishing as she began to write herself, and once she published fiction, chose in 1927 to use the name Larsen once again, within the *Nella Imes* signature that had been her norm after marriage. Davis traces much of the Harlem life through Larsen's correspondence with Carl Van Vechten and other white patrons of the black arts in the 1920s, but she keeps her attention focused on Larsen's successful campaign to become central to the Renaissance.

Larsen's life during the 1930s, after the publication of her novels had lifted her to heights she had longed to reach, is a dramatic decline—literally, back into nursing and the social level such a return mandated. Her authorship of a story was questioned, her marriage deteriorated (Imes's long-standing affair with a white woman became intolerable to her, and they eventually lived through a public, resentful divorce), and she took her alimony and chose to live abroad for nearly five years. As Davis points out, "Actual or imagined flight had throughout her life been a means of coping with difficulties." The fantasy life Larsen created—in her personal relationships as well as in her fiction—eventually made friends wary of believing anything she said.

Her own disappointing romance with a younger white man, whom she helped to write successfully years after her own publications had ended, provides one focus for the agonizing denouement of Larsen's story. Imes died of cancer, broken and impoverished. Larsen's sister, Anna, living in California, repudiated her existence. The Great Depression came and then ameliorated, seemingly without Larsen's notice. As Davis comments, "Her specific life experiences, rooted in the urban poor and their struggle for survival and achievement and marked by the complexities of female identity, could have provided her with a unique opportunity for meaningful explorations of race, gender, and class in her fiction. Instead, seduced by the glamour of the myth-world of Harlem in the 1920s, she buried much of the material available to her."

Excellent as Davis's contextualizing of Larsen's life as a dark-skinned woman artist in New York and Europe is, expert as her foci on the woman's fragile identity, the narrative of the marriage plot still dominates the biography. The reader finds herself speculating—if Larsen could have stayed Imes's wife, if she could have married the younger man (though he later became so unstable as to require institutionalization), perhaps she would have had some anchor to counter her agoraphobia and her own instability.

As in most biographies of women, here, too, the specter of the couple, the vise of a heterosexual pairing, dominates the telling of women's lives. But such an emphasis is more an accurate reflection of twentieth-century culture than it is a comment on the state of women's biography. For judging the books in themselves, today's reader is reassured that each employs what Heilbrun demanded: a stance on the part of the biographer that is both consistent and definable. When Milford's crisp sympathy for Zelda Fitzgerald changed literary attitudes of half a century, when Thurman's gentle correctives deflated Isak Dinesen's fictionalized memoir, and when Fitch's portrayal of a place and time created a second protagonist (the bookshop) in her biography of Sylvia Beach, readers felt the satisfaction of narratives that delivered on their promise (to tell women's lives—and more). In the same ways, Jane Howard's jaunty understanding of the often contradictory Margaret Mead, Elizabeth Frank's compassionate study of Louise Bogan, Deirdre Bair's warm recounting of the life of Simone de Beauvoir, and Thadious Davis's fully contextualized reading of the enigmatic Nella Larsen intrigued their audiences. These are books that leave the reader hungry in healthy ways—hungry to know more about the lives of women, about the art of women's narratives—fiction, autobiography, and biography—and about themselves. The most effective women's biography does not call attention to its own pyrotechnic descriptions and characterizations so much as it serves as a transparent lens to bring subject and interested reader into contact. The best biography focuses the reader's attention on the subject of the book, not on the biographer.

Women biographers have learned to write women's stories about as well as we can. Nearly every biography that has appeared during the last decade has been credible, interesting, and free of most of the flaws of didacticism and sentimentality that sometimes plague biography. The range of excellence possible during the current season's publication of books shows a kind of culmination of effort and talent: women's biography has come into its own. And its directions for the future are also exciting, even if tempered by Carolyn Heilbrun's recent comment that "feminist books never win awards" and discrimination against them will remain the woman biographer's lot.* As our concept of women's life—its possibility and its challenges—changes with the times, so, too, must the art of biography.

---

*In defending her somewhat negative review of Carol Brightman's biography of Mary McCarthy, Heilbrun pointed out that Brightman's winning the National Book Critics Circle Award was no surprise. *Writing Dangerously* was a compromise; it was hardly feminist. Heilbrun felt that either Blanche Wiesen Cook's *Eleanor Roosevelt* or Ellen Chesler's biography of Margaret Sanger should have won, but she notes that neither even appeared on the list of finalists.

13
Popular Biography

She was like a walking lump of defiance and
low self-esteem.
Lawrence J. Quirk, *Totally Uninhibited*

Most serious biographies are published in press runs of ten thousand hardcover copies; one of these, if it were a best-seller, might reach sales of twenty thousand copies and sell another twenty thousand copies in paperback. The hardcover advance might run to fifteen thousand dollars, but it is often less; the paperback contract might bring ten thousand dollars, but it, too, is usually less— and the original hardcover publisher probably keeps some of the author's share of that payment as a way to recover some of the first advance. Popular biography, however, is more profitable. When publishers contract books like Kitty Kelley's biographies of Nancy Reagan or Elizabeth Taylor or Quirk's *Totally Uninhibited: the Life and Wild Times of Cher*, press runs are at least ten times higher, as are advances. The popular biographer can earn a great deal of money at his or her trade. Serious biographers are often asked why they don't write for this popular market.

One difference is the kind of subject popular biography demands. Names must be instantly recognizable: the subjects are film and television stars, sports figures, women deemed infamous or scandalous (Marla Maples, Eva Peron), victims (Billie Holiday, Edith Piaf), or the wives of famous men (Betty Ford, Princess Diana).

A more significant difference is the way the biographer tells the story. Popular biography seldom contextualizes. It assumes that the reader does not care about detailed historical information and instead concentrates on a strong, and usually simplified,

narrative line. This style of telling also means simplifying character, and the reader may come away with only a sketch of the subject instead of a full picture. There is seldom any attempt to understand why the subject acted as she did, even though, ironically, the
popular biographer takes on the role of a sometimes flamboyant
truth teller, in contrast to the image of the scholarly researcher
who has uncovered every detail of the subject's life. The tone of
popular biography is therefore excited, almost shrill, intent on
persuading the reader that the book is definitive. The allure of the
biography's claim of providing all possible information, and yet
conveying that information in an easily readable form, shows most
obviously in the biographer's language, which is often slangy.

Much popular biography, of course, taps into the heart of
American commercial enterprise: it exists to feed the reader's voy-
euristic appetite, to allow him or her to experience the lives of the
rich and famous. In the case of popular biography of women, it
often plays to a sexual interest.

Lawrence Quirk's 1991 biography of film star Cher (Cherilyn
Sarkisian) is a good illustration of the genre. Beginning with the
intense title, which announces the theme and plot line of the book,
the reader processes the book's jacket photo, which shows Cher in
a see-through sequined gown, as if her partly nude body was another way of illustrating her uninhibited life-style. The jacket also
features the intentionally misleading phrase, "an unauthorized biography" (even though Cher did cooperate with the author). The
title is equally misleading: how can the comparatively conservative woman described in Quirk's book be described as "totally
uninhibited"?

Quirk's study of the woman he calls "the very personification
of Hollywood and the American dream" is an exercise in the
popular biography's tendency to oversimplify. His plot is that Cher
was "no prize" when she was young. Rather than talk about her
adolescence, however, which was traumatic because of learning
disabilities (which the biographer does not mention), Quirk only
looks at her: "The girl who one day became the glamour puss
Cher had a large nose, crooked teeth, and poor posture, not to
mention slightly bowed legs. She had bad skin and wore too much
makeup." There are ways to convey this without the simplifying

inherent in the biographer's word choice; Quirk's chief problem is his tendency to see the outer teenager as the whole person.

From this quick physical description, the biographer moves to a one-sentence sketch of Cher as adolescent: "She affected a harsh fuck-you attitude that was meant to lacerate others before they had a chance to hurt her." The poverty of the biographer's language insults the reader, at least in the context of this nondescript writing. His use of "a harsh fuck-you attitude" is not comic relief but simply the language of a quasi-literate world. Then, his plot line continues, some metamorphosis occurs (the reader is not told what), and Cher is world-famous and "well liked." The sophistry of describing the fact that a millionaire film star has friends—that is, is well liked—as some happy resolution of character escapes this biographer.

As Quirk tells it, Cher's life is primarily the narrative of her taking one young lover after another. The several possible narratives for this book—of a daughter's life with a rejecting father, of her lack of status in school as a complete misfit—are dismissed in three lines: "She seemed to lack any kind of ambition. She'd come from a troubled home, was out on her own at an early age, and was looking for a surrogate father, someone to take care of her." Again, the biographer's narrative is simple. Cher needed someone to take care of her (a man, in this completely heterosexual world): enter Sonny Bono, surrogate father. Later, as Cher's self-confidence grew, she rejected Bono. Quirk traces her growing maturity entirely through descriptions of her liaisons with younger men, people he characterizes only by age.

The sexual and sexualizing approach Quirk uses is a kind of soft pornography. Because he avoids any description of Cher's childhood and adolescence, and because he insists in his simplification that all the reader wants to know is whom the star is having sex with, he forces the reader into seeing the woman as a sex, and a sexed, object. The only narrative in this biography is the sexual one, hardly everything a reader might want to know about a successful film and pop star. In method, Quirk fictionalizes everything by creating scenes, complete with dialogue, that he could not possibly have heard or observed.

In popular biography, this oversimplified reading of famous

women seems to be the norm for all biographers, although men's biographies of women subjects—David Shipman on Judy Garland, Andrew Morton and Anthony Holden on Princess Diana, Donald Spoto on Marilyn Monroe, Christopher Andersen on Madonna—are usually the larger money-makers.

It is one of the ironies of contemporary life that biographies of recent presidents' wives—Nancy Reagan, Barbara Bush, Hillary Clinton—are marketed as popular books, whereas earlier political wives were the subjects of serious biography. In the case of Nancy Reagan, who in 1989 published *My Turn*, her as-told-to autobiography, such publication did not stop Kitty Kelley's 1991 sensationalized version of Reagan's life story. To move from Nancy Reagan's own story, despite its countless references to Ronnie and its posture of apolitical innocence, to the innuendo-filled Kelley narrative is to see the poverty of much popular biography.

The title of Kelley's book is also coded: *Nancy Reagan: The Unauthorized Biography* plays on the illicit tone of *unauthorized*. Rather than being what it literally is—a book written by an independent writer, not someone hired to do the work by the subject or the subject's estate—such a biography rides the coattails of the forbidden. In the case of Kelley's book, she adds to this aura by describing the FBI's questioning her about the project. She enlists the reader's sympathy by discussing what she calls "privileged information" about what the then–First Lady wore on several occasions. But at the center of her presentation is the allure of the "unauthorized" story: what is it that Kelley knows about Nancy Reagan that the reader is going to learn?

Kelley also name-drops about an earlier biography, also unauthorized, of Frank Sinatra. Supposedly, in doing the research for that book, she came across the relationship between Sinatra and Nancy Reagan that was to be one of the threads of this book. But just as Sinatra sued her over her biography of him, so attorney Milton Rudin brought a suit against Kelley in Los Angeles Federal Court because she listed him in her acknowledgments for the Reagan biography. Rudin claimed that Kelley's assistant wrote him saying she was doing research for the Scopus Award given to Reagan by the American Friends of the Hebrew University in 1981. When Rudin refused to be interviewed, the assistant wrote back that his letter would be quoted as his answer. Instead, Kelley listed Rudin as though he had helped with the research for the Reagan biography. Rudin cited these events as evidence that he had been libeled. Making the news in such a way is obviously far different from a biographer's work receiving good reviews.

Kelley's earlier book, *Elizabeth Taylor: The Last Star* (1981), is somewhat more complex than Quirk's book on Cher, although she also creates the dialogue in scenes as if she had observed them. She also uses a sexualized narrative. The preface page, for example, quotes Taylor's remarks on the occasion of each of her weddings. The photos included emphasize her as wife, as one of a couple. There are almost no photographs of the actress on stage or in publicity photos connected with her profession; every part of the book leads the reader to her sexual life.

Titling a biography of a film star to emphasize her professional life (*The Last Star*) only to write her erotic history, and an uncomplimentary one at that, is typical of biography aimed at large sales. The very writing itself is sensationalized, as when Kelley describes the breakup between Taylor and a lover and lists in detail the man's calling a cab for Taylor as he threw her out of her own home and had her driven to an elite hotel. "Then he pulled all her clothes out of the drawers and closets and heaped them in the middle of the living room. He called a second cab, heaved everything inside it, and sent it after the first one." Kelley's narrative exists to tell the gossip she knows, but unless that narrative contributes to characterization, it remains only gossip. Again, the biographer's language is clichéd and elementary.

When Kelley describes Mike Todd, Taylor's third husband, she gives him a rough, idiomatic dialogue, undermining whatever charm he might have had:

> Todd publicized every gift. "This angel-faced baby is three years the senior of my son, Mike Todd, Jr.," he told the press. "But she is a lot of woman. Everything I have is hers—and, brother, that's plenty. . . ."
>
> "I think Mike liked giving her the diamond tiara best of all," recalled a friend. "He told me that when he presented it to her she ran into the bedroom to try it on and came out totally nude to model it for him. He said she jumped around the room and then on top of him wearing nothing but that tiara."

Calculated to be shocking, Kelley's narrative falls flat, largely because her narrative demeans her characters.

She also has the problem of editorializing in ways that aren't helpful, or accurate, as when she notes that "Max Lerner gave Elizabeth the same thing Arthur Miller gave Marilyn Monroe—the feeling of being elevated by the love of an intellectual man whose professional accomplishments and scholarly credentials transcended the tawdry box office. It was the perfect complement of The Brain and The Body, a melding of the cerebral and the sexual." Kelley's use of "The Body" to refer to her subject is as negative a tactic as her comparison to Monroe and Miller is erroneous. This kind of easy platitude warns the reader that there may be little substantial understanding here.

Fortunately, there are levels in popular biography. Phyllis Rose used her considerable skill in writing a study of Josephine Baker, and before writing her biography of Nora Joyce, Brenda Maddox wrote a biography of Elizabeth Taylor. Echoing the title of Edward Albee's play *Who's Afraid of Virginia Woolf?* Maddox called her 1977 book *Who's Afraid of Elizabeth Taylor?* and wrote using a self-conscious form that involved the biographer as well as the subject. *Why I am writing this book* is one of her chief narratives; another is that many of Taylor's most-loved male friends and lovers had died young and unexpectedly. This shift away from sheer sexuality to a consideration of psychological damage for the young woman helps make Taylor into a person. But rather than following this technique and writing a quasi-serious book, Maddox psychoanalyzes everyone, including the moviegoers who loved Taylor in *National Velvet*. (Maddox points out that viewers had fallen in love with the child Elizabeth, whose great passion was her horse, and never forgave her switch to men.)

Maddox's book provides some useful information (about Mike Todd's lack of money, for example), but its effect is spoiled by her bothersome, and frequent, inclusion of herself ("Taylor's image changed from Grieving Widow to Scarlet Woman the week I met the man I was to marry"). There is also downright cynicism: "Elizabeth Taylor has more in common with Elizabeth II than a high voice, an odd shape, and conspicuous handbags. They are growing older in the same way, taking on the sexless look of Oriental potentates, with their geological gems and turbans that hide every shred of hair. And like primitive tribal chieftains, both women carry the royal taboo. The tremendous curiosity that surrounds them is a very thin covering for an intense envy of their privileges and mystical power." These passages, combined with a pervasive tone of condescension, as if no serious writer would write such a book, makes the reader wonder why Maddox wrote the biography.

Again, Carolyn Heilbrun's questions about a biographer's feelings for the subject are valid. Evidently, as an English journalist, Maddox shared the British fascination with Taylor (who was born in England), as most of the world shared the fascination for American film stars, extreme wealth, and fame. She was also intrigued with her own fascination. But to convert that interest into a book aimed at best-seller status did her self-conscious inquiry a disservice, and she ended with a book that was too innovative for its genre and not innovative enough to be considered serious work. By the time she wrote the Nora Barnacle biography, Maddox chose a much more traditional form, keeping herself, as a woman writer, out of the book entirely. Yet if women's biography is to be interesting to the sophisticated readers of contemporary prose, a more interactive model, one that allows some dialogue with the reader, should be used.

Judging from the vapid simplicity of many popular biographies, the evolving form of the "as-told-to" book has a number of strengths. Although still used chiefly with sports stars, most of them male, this kind of biography allows the subject's words at least to be heard. When there is a text to read, it might be characteristically phrased, and it might be about things the subject finds valuable. It might even come close to recording the life as the subject thinks it was lived—no small accomplishment.

When Elizabeth Taylor worked on such a book herself (*Elizabeth Takes Off*, 1987), the information given the reader seems more accurate, and more useful, than most of the stories that had appeared in either the Kelley biography or the Maddox. This is Taylor writing about the maligned Mike Todd:

> He was twenty-five years my senior and eternally young. I could hardly keep up with him. He was the most energetic man I've ever known and he made our short 18 months together one of the most intensely glorious times of my life. . . .

What sweet craziness it was to be married to Mike. Being with him was like appearing in an epic film. He translated the impossible life I had been living on the screen to reality. He had a great gift of showmanship and a great heart as well. On the surface, he seemed to be rough and tough and gruff, but it was an act. He was gentle and honest, with a deeply ingrained integrity that belied his flamboyant exterior.

In this instance, at least, Taylor's words convey her admiration, and without any convincing alternative story in the biographies of either Maddox or Kelley, the reader accepts her version. The same kind of authenticity appears in Susan Strasberg's 1992 *Marilyn and Me: Sisters, Rivals, Friends*, a biography of Marilyn Monroe during her years of involvement in the Strasberg circle, told by the younger daughter of Monroe's teacher, herself an actress. One can only hope there may be a new kind of popular biography in the future, when women biographers will be given the chance to assess famous women's lives from a feminine vantage point and to break out of the conventional and sexualizing ways of telling women's narratives now prevalent in popular books. Anne Edwards's *A Remarkable Woman: A Biography of Katharine Hepburn* and Maria Riva's *Lena: The Life and Times of Marlene Dietrich*, a biography of her mother, are interesting, well-told stories. Perhaps women writers are learning that serious biography can also be written about the famous and the glamorous.

14
Revisionist Biographies of Women

The most curious thing is that the very passages that
once caused me the most anxiety, the moments
when I thought, no, I cannot put this on paper
—are now the passages I'm proud of. That
comforts me out of all I've written.
Doris Lessing to Kate Millet, *Flying*

Every writer makes the kind of choices Doris Lessing describes. Particularly when women writers are faced with the legitimate blurring of genres, as if to force established literary conventions to accept what Barbara Johnson calls "a world of difference," the act of creating becomes uneasy. Any change in accepted literary form implicitly challenges the power of established traditions. Yet to repeat meaningless forms is to go unfulfilled and to find only frustration at the end of the writing process.

After two decades of women's writing good biographies of women, the conventions for biography that once seemed engraved in stone are beginning to shift. Sidonie Smith and Julia Watson discuss changes in the practice of autobiography, and what they describe is true of biography as well: "The more it surrounds us, the more it defies generic stabilization, the more its laws are broken, the more it drifts toward other practices, the more formerly 'out-law' practices drift into its domain." Add to this description of slow change in literary form the belief that women's art often finds more permeable boundaries, that it shies away from rigidity, and we see that stasis is usually negative.

The 1980s and 1990s showed an emerging adventuresomeness on the part of women biographers. Part of their reluctance to

write the same kinds of biographies about the same kinds of subjects was prompted by discussions of questions in critical theory.
First, the practitioners of traditional biography questioned its reliance on "a realist fallacy" that believes in "a coherent, essentially
unchanging and unitary self"; the aim of the good biography was
to "capture" that self. When the reader's concept of a self became
mutable and flexible, the rationale for biography changed.

Second, as Stanley points out, the choice of a subject—the creation of some giant figure, overshadowing the common lives one
knows—is itself a political process. It is also a class-dependent process: few biographies have been written about common women.
Rather, women appear to be notable only when they rise above the
ordinary. In this mode of change, the writing of biography appears to reflect anthropology's interest in what James Clifford
terms "noncelebratory histories."

Efforts are now being made to write biography about ordinary
people. Some of these books grow out of letters or diaries, as did
Susanna K. George's *The Adventures of the Woman Homesteader: Life
and Letters of Elinore Pruitt Stewart* (1992), Laurel Thatcher Ulrich's
*A Midwife's Tale: The Life of Martha Ballard, Based on Her Diary,
1785–1812* (1991), and Nancy F. Cott's *A Woman Making History:
Mary Ritter Beard through Her Letters* (1991). Others follow the tracks
of lost narratives, that of a wife such as *Elizabeth Bacon Custer: And
the Making of a Myth* (1993) by Shirley A. Leckie, or a daughter, as
in Patricia D. Valenti's study of Nathaniel Hawthorne's child, *To
Myself a Stranger: A Biography of Rose Hawthorne Lathrop* (1991). Still
other biographies are about unfamiliar women, such as Joanne
Bentley's *Hallie Flanagan: A Life in the American Theatre* (1988), Susan Ledbetter's *Nellie Cashman, Prospector and Trailblazer* (1993), or
Rachel M. Brownstein's *Tragic Muse: Rachel of the Comédie-Française* (1993).

Other efforts are being made to write unusual, thought-
provoking biography by employing experimental voice, or structure, or even content. Elinor Langer's 1984 biography *Josephine
Herbst* was an experimental narrative that anticipated the current
interest in postmodern method. Part of the time Langer's own
voice describes her writing the book; her staccato prose is reminiscent of Josie Herbst's, and the reader has some trouble deciding
whether the story is about Herbst or about Langer. Quotations

from Herbst form a pastiche of language that tells the story. When the unmarried Josie and John Herrmann are living together and are in conflict with his conservative parents over their life-style, Langer creates a montage of imagined voices:

> Because when: *The Father*: Mr. Herrmann gets that letter he turns to his wife and says "What shall we do next?" and: *The Mother*: Mrs. Herrmann says "Ask for the license" and: *The Son*: when John gets that letter he types on the bottom "My wife and myself do not wish to be futher insulted. . . ." And: *Josie*: Josie is afraid John's parents will disown him and he will blame her for it and: *John*: John is afraid Josie will think he doesn't love her and: *Josie*: Josie is afraid he doesn't love her and: *John*: he does love her and: *Josie*: she loves him and: *Josie and John*: they conclude "if we love, why not marry?" . . . *The Biographer*: I think it is too bad because they hadn't ever decided to get married.

Again, as Langer begins the chapters on Herbst's involvement in the Spanish Civil War, she stops to draw the reader into the process of writing the book. She tells of writing two earlier versions of this section, one theatrical and the other focused on a photo of a pale, unsmiling Josie. Neither version worked. Somehow she had to reveal Herbst's personal passion—the self in relation to the experience. Langer also relies heavily on textualizing Herbst's own writing. Subtitled *The Story She Could Never Tell*, Langer's book fits method to story by means of a fluid voice that does not pretend to be Herbst's.

A more typical study is Miranda Seymour's 1993 *Ottoline Morrell: Life on the Grand Scale*, which tells a revisionist story in a fairly conventional way. Trying to rid the six-foot-tall art patron and socialite of the tone of grotesque caricature her biography had become is not easy. Though friends with members of the Bloomsbury group, Ottoline found herself ridiculed in their letters and fictions. Seymour's access to Lady Ottoline's diaries and correspondence, however, as well as new letters from her longtime lover Bertrand Russell, allow her to narrate a different story—that of a proud, talented woman burdened by her husband's instability and her own illness and passion.

Biography: Moving toward Fiction?

This aim, of revising history—or at least women's personal history—is shared by all biographers of women subjects. Frequently, biographers admit the role of fictionality in their work, as when Carol Felsenthal titles her 1993 biography of Katharine Graham *Power, Privilege and the "Post": The Katharine Graham Story* or Jerry Aline Fleiger chooses the title *Colette and the Fantom Subject of Autobiography* (1990) to suggest the fused identities of subject/writer/biographer/autobiographer.

One of the most interesting recent biographies, which pushes the art of biography very near fiction, is Claire Tomalin's *The Invisible Woman: The Story of Nelly Ternan and Charles Dickens* (1991). Winner of Britian's NCR Book Award, the quasi-fictional account of the young actress Dickens (as "Charles Tringham") lived with during the last thirteen years of his life is also fascinating revisioning. Tomalin uses Dickens's coded messages and his lost diary for 1867, which was found at a 1922 auction; but she relies mostly on her considerable ability to see the story from Nelly Ternan's point of view.

This is a departure from the customary perspective about Dickens's affair. When Phyllis Rose, for example, tells the story in "Catherine Hogarth and Charles Dickens" in *Parallel Lives*, she focuses on the breakup of the writer's marriage and the resulting arrangements for his custody of the children. Rose then connects the dissolution of the home in 1858 to the conflicted male characters in Dickens's later novels *Our Mutual Friend* and *Edwin Drood*, men who hide their secret passions. That Rose left Dickens's own secret passion a mystery makes Tomalin's biography even more intriguing. Here is that unspeakable yet common world of Wilkie Collins, who often had a wife and two mistresses in three separate households and took his holidays in adjacent seaside resorts where he came and went among the three families without detection, and the artists George Cruikshank and William Frith, both with two households filled with children—in Frith's case, twelve with his wife and seven with his mistress—living just a few minutes from each other.

Dickens, who was fifty-five when he began the liaison with the twenty-eight-year-old Ternan, did better by her, but he could not marry her so long as his wife lived. While Ternan's family accepted the vivacious actress's choice, she was forced to lead a reclusive life that, Tomalin concludes, was "mostly rather grim." She gave up her career, went through several pregnancies only to lose the babies, and moved household often. As Tomalin acknowledges, "Inevitably it is through Dickens that Nelly's story has to be traced during these hidden years; but it is precisely at this point that his own record also grows more obscure." In 1860 he burned much of his correspondence, for example, and at the same time asked friends to destroy his letters to them. He also had several addresses and an office, as well as constant lecture tours in progress: he was purposely elusive.

As Dickens became more invisible, so did Nelly Ternan. Consequently, Tomalin's title emphasizes the difficulty of trying to get at the unwritten story, the narrative of a subject without language or voice.

The same lack of information is the basis for art historian Eunice Lipton's *Alias Olympia* (1993). The supposed biography of Edouard Manet's most famous model, Victorine Meurent, the subject of his great paintings *Olympia* and *Déjeuner sur l'Herbe*, Lipton's narrative is subtitled *A Woman's Search for Manet's Notorious Model & Her Own Desire*, signaling the reader that the narrative is both autobiography and biography. The story is, in fact, a literal search, with what suspense there is deriving from the literary sleuthing. When Lipton goes to Paris and discovers that Meurent was also a painter who exhibited and was a member of the prestigious *Société des Artistes Français*, that she was probably lesbian, and that she lived perhaps thirty-five years longer than had been previously documented, the reader is satisfied. (The book is particularly interesting read in tandem with Otto Friedrich's conventional *Olympia: Paris in the Age of Manet*.) But in *Alias Olympia*, Lipton's subjective text, her own story, is perhaps more important. For a traditionally trained art historian to write such a book, creating facts where few existed in order to tell her story, is a great departure from the conventions of the field.

Both the Tomalin and the Lipton biographies point to the difficulty of writing about subjects forced to be voiceless. Ellen

Ternan could not have left an account of her life, so hidden was her role as Dickens's lover. Victorine Meurent left behind the image of her body rather than her voice, and because that image was so elusively sexual, so flamboyant in its womanliness, even a hint that it was off-limits to the male gaze would have destroyed the impact of its vaunted nudity. Yet even as she modeled for Manet, Meurent was inscribing a far different story from the one in which she appeared to be cast.

The practical difficulties of writing biography of a Ternan or a Meurent are many. No one saves the letters of semiliterate women. No one comments in print on illicit affairs, either heterosexual or lesbian: the whole structure of language is in collusion to erase such entanglements, to preserve the power of the patriarchy. So Manet was never known in conjunction with his model's fortunes, even though she, too, was a painter, just as Dickens was not known by his liaisons with his actress, even though the stage was his world, too, for much of his lifetime. Both biographers recognize the difficulties and try through their choices of titles to prepare readers for their unorthodox, but effective, works.

Fiction: Moving toward Biography?

From these books, it is only a small step to fiction based on biography but identified as fiction.* Rosemary Lively's 1987 *Moon Tiger,* Alison Lurie's 1988 *The Truth About Lorin Jones,* and Brenda Gittelson's 1991 *Biography* prepared a readership for Frances Sherwood's 1993 *Vindication,* a fictional biography of Mary Wollstonecraft, and Michelle Cliff's *Free Enterprise,* the narrative of Mary Ellen Pleasant, the civil rights activist who used her chain of hotels

---

*This is not the point of discussion prompted by Joe McGinniss's *The Last Brother,* his book about Edward Kennedy that claims to be biography. More a part of the stream of heightened and increasingly fictionalized journalism, of which Truman Capote's 1965 *In Cold Blood* is a prototype, the McGinniss book purposely insults all the conventions of biography, while yet being marketed as that genre. Aside from issues of outright plagiarism, *The Last Brother* is an unfortunate example of negative reviews, and critical questions, actually increasing a book's sales.

as hiding places for runaway slaves. Susan Fromberg Schaeffer's *First Nights* is a more complex narrating of two women's autobiographies (told, by an author, or several authors, as biographies). Anna Asta, the Greta Garbo–like character, a naive Swedish starlet when the book opens, has the more compelling story, but it is intertwined with the narrative of Ivy Cook, her West Indian maid, whose memories of her homeplace, Green Island, are ironically peaceful. Kidnapped as a child by her father, Ivy has led her long life one day at a time, doing the best she can. Her stolid practicality counterpoints the aging of the fearful, reclusive Asta, and much of the book concerns their later lives—when ostensible glamour is gone.

The macabre presence of a strangely familiar man, who had eagerly photographed Anna throughout her career, forces the reader—and the women—to redefine what is present and what is past in this ultra-self-conscious text. The book begins with a prologue spoken by Anders Estersen, a filmmaker who has been Anna's friend throughout her career and Ivy's as well, a section that helps the reader identify the worlds about to be juxtaposed. And in the book's early segments, Schaeffer writes a cavalierly postmodern story, calling the reader's attention to the way the story is phrased, structured, and voiced.

Schaeffer places an early voiced (and characteristically abstract) memory of Anna's—"I know: I have to argue about everything. When I tell myself something, then I argue with myself. . . . This bores me, you see. I'll explain why later, how stupid it is to try and find something interesting in the life of an individual"—close to a more concrete voicing of Ivy's—"I don't know why I wasn't more unhappy when I was a young child, but I think it had something to do with the porches and the front steps. Every night, we would sit, either on our own steps or someone else's, and people would tell stories. They told stories about the little unbaptized children who died and came back as mischievous spirits, their feet on backwards. That was how you recognized them." Characterization, too, occurs through these memories of stories, as when Anna recalls, "I used to love to listen to my mother talk. In an instant, she could summon up the farm of her childhood, its gray painted buildings with their black roofs rising up out of the snow-covered fields, the trees black like dancing women the witch froze and left to stand on the horizon." But the fragmented narrative is also the story of the women's love for each other, set as they are on the difficult task of defining themselves and their existences: "Now I am in Miss Anna's room, sitting on the edge of her bed, my back stiff, reading her what I have written down, and she says, No, no, Ivy, that won't do. A story isn't a broken mirror, pieces of glass all over the place. A story is a whole thing, it has a beginning and an end, like a bolt of cloth." Wrong as Anna is, the question poised at the edge of the reader's consciousness throughout the novel is Ivy's question to her friend, "Who is going to make sense of us?"

Estersen's memoir of these "beautiful ladies in snow" recounted his urgings that both Anna and Ivy record their stories—by voice and in writing. "We cannot live without words," he persuaded them. And in this introduction, they each told a favorite fairy tale—"One story per life"—to center their memoirs. In this tactic, the reader recognizes, as Schaeffer wrote recently, "It is the conception of biography as used by the analyst (first causes, later developments) that has influenced me most profoundly." And analystlike, Estersen must then put the fragments together to find, and memorialize, the women's lives: "I leave myself out, you see: out of the picture. But I am there. I am the one telling you everything. I am the story teller."

Further Definitions

Whatever the image of the narrator in fiction or in biography has come to be, Estersen's comment strikes home in a number of ways. As readers know, the way the voice of the biographer appears is one of the most contested conventions of the genre. Women's biography is mature enough now that its practitioners are willing to experiment and perhaps demand that conventions change so that they can narrate the stories they find interesting in voices that enable, enhance, or even challenge those narratives.

Just as they have ideas about what the process of biography should be, readers have an image of what the biographer does in relation to facts. All of us like the notion that the biographer becomes the subject, that writing biography is a process of metamorphosis, but in most cases, the transfer is not quite that simple. Sometimes biographers find that they do not even like their subjects. Usually, as Dee Garrison describes, a "peculiarly reciprocal relationship" evolves:

> The biographer is visible in the selection of documents and testimony, in the intuitive choice of a quote or incident to move along the story, and, above all, in the choice to write this particular life and not another. Surely all scholars to some degree choose their topics in order to enact the main themes of their own lives. The unique nature of the biographer's task simply magnifies that affinity. The elusive link between biographer and subject is a source of analytical and literary power.

Garrison does not, however, worry that such a bond will lead to flaws in the narrative, although she admits, "The biographer must contend with the impulse to tell one's own life story in the process of writing someone else's." Her point is echoed by Emily Toth's comment that biographers "inevitably . . . do play god, shaping others' lives to our own agendas."

For biographer Phyllis Rose, the process is less identification than "appropriation." Rose describes the way the biographer appropriates her subject's life, taking from it psychic qualities that may be personally useful. Arnold Rampersad calls the immersion that writing biography requires "approximation." The biographer has to accept that simply identifying with a subject is not enough; rather, the whole recovery process is an immense amount of different kinds of work. Finally, according to Rampersad, the biographer must face the inevitable frustration of learning that the "self cannot be recovered, the truth cannot be recovered, the truth cannot even be identified—not the truth of life, only certain facts." The satisfactions of writing biography are more modest and more in keeping with a text that grows out of the author's playing Boswell.

Once a biographer has chosen a subject and dedicated herself to investigating and researching the life in question and interviewing those who had contact with that life, she does merge in some ways with the subject. Her ultimate goal is to understand the subject's motivation, a task that rests to a great extent on some psychological compatibility. This is not to say that biographers can write only about subjects like themselves but that there must be some inherent empathy within the biographer for the subject (and this would be true, of course, regardless of gender differences).

From my own perspective, writing the life of Sylvia Plath was in some ways easy because I, too, had grown up in those American 1950s. As one of the "lucky" college women, I married at twenty, while still an undergraduate, and so was spared Plath's desperation about ever finding a husband. Her panic when she turned twenty-three, a Fulbright student in England, and her conviction that she would surely be an "old maid," was one of the comic moments in what is a largely somber story of a woman driven to excel, a prototype of what we were later to call the "superwoman." The panic, however, was all too real, and when her marriage to Ted Hughes seemed—in her eyes—to have failed, she could not face another search for an appropriate mate. The strain of depression in her father's family surfaced twice in her life, and the second time she succeeded in dying.

While writing the Plath biography allowed me to rely in some ways on my own cultural experiences, working on the biography of the Daniel Stein family meant intensive research into Austrian-Jewish immigrant lives from the mid-1800s to the 1940s, when Gertrude and her brother Leo were the last of the five siblings to die. I spent years studying Jewish culture, Radcliffe and Harvard in the 1890s, medical schools at the turn of the century, the European art and literary worlds, and lesbianism. These were not parts of my experience, but the character and spirit of Gertrude Stein as diligent and brilliant woman writer soon became a part of my psyche. Much as I admired both Plath and Stein, my love went to the latter—because of her humor and her indomitability. My relationship with each subject came close to what Phyllis Rose called "appropriation," and I felt personally enriched as a result of my five years of immersion in the Steins' family story.

The biographer may never be completely satisfied with the re-creation of her subject's life, but at least she has made a courageous attempt to find material, compile a factual base, and shape a meaningful narrative for the reader. In this aim, the biographer of the

1990s does not differ from the biographer of the 1890s. What has changed in these hundred years is the value contemporary readers are willing to give to reading about the lives of women. It is their interest that has encouraged the many varieties of narratives categorized as women's biography, one of the most interesting genres in book publishing today.

As Emily Toth recently said, "There is no last word on feminist biography, just as there is no limit on the interpretations that can be made of women's lives." But as we think of Beryl Markham's insistence that a woman's story be a way of creating "remembrance" that will open "corridors familiar in the heart," the reader can hope that the new biographies of women will provide satisfying ways of exploring, and of telling and retelling, some of the oldest stories of humankind.

. . . and though we listen only
haphazardly, with one ear,
we will begin our story
with the word *and*

Lisel Mueller,
"Why We Tell Stories"

Notes

(x) "feminist women . . . passion"
 Blanche Wiesen Cook, "Books: The Womanly Art of Biography," 60.
(21) "within conflicting . . . sister, lover)"
 Shari Benstock, *The Private Self*, 5.
(29) "four-page formula"
 Susan Willis, *Specifying*, 14–15.
(30) "Women's writings . . . resist easy classification"
 Shari Benstock, Introduction to *Private Self*, 4.
(30) "the woman who . . . name or definition"
 Carolyn Heilbrun, *Writing a Woman's Life*, 96.
(33) "Cara and Sara . . . world of thought"
 Leslie Stephen, *George Eliot*, 24.
(34) "I have not, and . . . Eliot's conduct"
 Ibid., 47.
(34) "an industrious student"
 Ibid., 197.
(35) "declared that he . . . as impossible"
 Gordon S. Haight, *George Eliot, A Biography*, 528.
(35) "extraordinary attraction . . . for women"
 Ibid., 493.
(35-36) "He was prepared . . . could not write"
 Phyllis Rose, *Parallel Lives*, 224.
(36) "gnawed by rats"
 Ibid., 229.
(36) "To the end . . . on the piano"
 Ina Taylor, *George Eliot, Woman of Contradictions*, 210.
(37) "threw himself from . . . allowed to drown"
 Ibid., 219.
(38) "Is the story . . . happening to you?"
 Victoria Glendinning, "Lies and Silences," 51.
(41) "I have seen . . . in health"
 Quoted in Maureen Peters, *An Enigma of Brontës*, 168–169.
(41) "In addition to being . . . kind of utterance"
 Katherine Frank, *A Chainless Soul*, 98–99.
(42) "hostage at home"
 Ibid., 213.
(42) "The light-headed . . . attention as well"
 Ibid., 257.

(45) "a tall young woman . . . proud stride"
Richard Ellmann, *James Joyce*, 162.
(46) "To any other writer . . . seemed ordinary"
Ibid., 163.
(46) "You made me a man"
Quoted in ibid., 163.
(47) "tonguelash his sons . . . fancied ingratitude"
Ibid., 41.
(48) "surely the complex . . . himself responsible"
Hélène Cixous, *Exile of James Joyce*, 15.
(48) "one of the most . . . the century"
Richard Ellmann, *James Joyce*, 1982, 159.
(48) "important because she . . . he upon her"
Brenda Maddox, *Nora*, 492.
(49) "tasteless intrusion"
Alice Hunt Sokoloff, *The First Mrs. Hemingway*, 40.
(49) "as in a trap"
Gioia Diliberto, *Hadley*, 91.
(51) "her republican simplicity of manners"
Elizabeth F. Ellet, *Queens of American Society*, 103.
(53-54) "He seriously considered . . . his freedom"
Kenneth S. Davis, *FDR, New York Years*, 10.
(55) "hysterical"
Ibid., 329–330.
(55) "the turmoil in my heart . . . the prospect"
Eleanor Roosevelt, *Autobiography*, 163.
(58) "His coat doesn't . . . his wrist"
Anne Morrow Lindbergh, *Bring Me a Unicorn*, 201.
(60) "I went through it . . . again"
Anne Morrow Lindbergh, *Locked Rooms*, 13.
(60) "There is a difference . . . inside of me"
Ibid., 13.
(60) "Bad night. C home at 2"
Ibid., 6.
(60) "Bad night . . . morning light"
Ibid., 7.
(60-61) "Terrible night . . . make it unhappen"
Ibid., 12.
(61) "Down in the subway . . . my boy?"
Ibid., 4.
(61) "When someone dies . . . ever suffered"
Ibid., 5.
(62) "one of the . . . his time"
Dorothy Herrmann, *Anne Morrow Lindbergh*, 1.
(63) "Harmony comes gradually . . . her character"
Beryl Markham, *West with the Night*, 248.

(66) "most transporting pleasure . . . arms of space"
Isak Dinesen, *Out of Africa*, 229.
(66) "Denys had . . . story told"
Ibid., 217.
(66) "Denys and I . . . with lions"
Ibid., 219.
(66) "Denys taught me . . . Greek poets"
Ibid., 218.
(69-70) "How is it possible . . . in the heart"
Beryl Markham, *West with the Night*, 3.
(71) "Like rock strata . . . alter"
Joyce Carol Oates, Introduction to *Best American Essays, 1991*, xviii.
(75) "much more than . . . engenders"
Virginia Woolf, "The New Biography," 197.
(75) "The true length . . . matter of dispute"
Virginia Woolf, *Orlando*, 306–307.
(77-78) "These days, there . . . to Colorado"
William Pritchard, "Writers Shouldn't Be Married," 11.
(79) "*pathography*"
Joyce Carol Oates, "Adventures in Abandonment," 3.
(79) "So many biographies . . . the subject"
Arnold Rampersad, Interview in Gail Porter Mandell, ed., *Life into Art*, 54.
(80) "really, really deep . . . assumptions"
Phyllis Rose, Interview in Gail Porter Mandell, ed., *Life into Art*, 104.
(80) "What I'm interested . . . they have"
Ibid.
(80) "narration can be . . . fictional event"
Paul Michael Lutzeler, "Fictionality in Historiography and the Novel," 30.
(80-81) "no sequence of events . . . story"
Hayden White, *Metahistory*, quoted in ibid.
(86) "Is everything a story? . . . she talked"
Rayna Green, "High Cotton," 119.
(89) "It is very seldom . . . to do"
Charlotte Perkins Gilman, "The Yellow Wallpaper," 761–762.
(90) "today's children . . . their lives"
Margaret Mead, *Blackberry Winter*, 11–12.
(90) "There were treasures . . . rush of memories"
Ibid.
(90-91) "The Angel of . . . dentist"
Maya Angelou, *I Know Why the Caged Bird Sings*, 180.
(91) "old coffee-brown . . . telling stories"
Isak Dinesen, "The Blank Page," 1418.
(92) "No one says . . . *crooked*"
Minnie Bruce Pratt, "Crime Against Nature."

(93) "Maybe . . . tell the story"
Ibid.
(95) "part biography and part autobiography"
Tim O'Brien, Review of *The Duke of Deception*, 46.
(95) "a first-rate autobiography"
John Irving, Review of *The Duke of Deception*, 1.
(96) "by his own admission . . . more rewarding"
Joel Conarroe, Review of *This Boy's Life*, 1.
(96) "a book about fathers . . . treat them"
Peter S. Prescott, Review of *Patrimony*, 53.
(96) "What the narrator . . . her generation"
Mona Simpson, Review of *Fierce Attachments*, 7.
(97) "fixed forever in . . . existence"
Wendy Gimbel, Review of *Fierce Attachments*, 549.
(98) "energetic, fun-loving, book-loving woman"
Gloria Steinem, "Ruth's Song," 131.
(98) "That's why our . . . alone together"
Ibid., 133.
(98) "My ultimate protection . . . mother at all"
Ibid., 135.
(98) "Pity takes distance . . . of surviving"
Ibid.
(98) "functioning was not . . . the world"
Ibid., 133.
(99) "I miss her . . . in life"
Ibid., 146.
(99) "her death forced . . . different life"
Letty Pogrebin, *Deborah, Golda, and Me*, 19.
(99) "I can bemoan . . . unassimilated family"
Ibid., 28.
(100) "She invented . . . daughters deserved"
Ibid.
(100) "I don't like . . . to say"
Ibid., 32.
(101) "had no right to do so"
Mary Catherine Bateson, *With a Daughter's Eye*, 30.
(101) "In my family . . . our lives"
Ibid., 20.
(101) "Margaret always had . . . her arrangements"
Ibid., 97.
(101) "Thinking back to . . . Aunt Marie"
Margaret Mead, *Blackberry Winter*, 273.
(102) "let the nurse . . . whole weekend"
Bateson, *With a Daughter's Eye*, 25.
(102) "This book cannot . . . reconstruction"
Ibid., 227.

(103) "We talk in . . . tossed bouquet"
Ibid., 222.

(103n) "motherhood changed Mead's life"
Rosalind Rosenberg, "Margaret Mead," 541.

(104) "About this time . . . to believe"
Sissela Bok, *Alva Myrdal*, 77.

(104) "Alva, meanwhile . . . her own"
Ibid., 79.

(106) "I am here . . . the principal?"
Kim Chernin, *In My Mother's House*, 44.

(106) "I'll tell you . . . no longer victims"
Ibid., 93.

(107) "It is late . . . than life"
Ibid., 307.

(107) "Personal involvement is central"
Blanche Wiesen Cook, "Biographer and Subject," 400.

(109) "As the only . . . my own"
Carole Ione, *Pride of Family*, 212.

(109) "By 1943, scarcely . . . over again"
Monica Sone, *Nisei Daughter*, 216.

(112) "Capper is the first . . . her mother"
Susan Belasco Smith, Review of Capper's *Margaret Fuller*, 23.

(113) "an eccentric . . . bridge player"
Emily Toth, "The Shadow of the First Biographer," 288.

(113) "When she named . . . of men"
Emily Toth, *Kate Chopin*, 333.

(114) "not a villain . . . of women"
Toth, "Shadow," 288.

(114) "love-motherhood-loneliness paradigm"
Ibid., 292.

(115) "paranoia"
R.W.B. Lewis, *Edith Wharton, A Biography*, 88.

(115-116) "It was a stretched-out . . . of it"
Ibid., 105; also see 76.

(116) "Don't I know . . . wordless existence"
Quoted in Shari Benstock, manuscript of *No Gifts from Chance*,
unpaged.

(116) "long and often-interrupted literary apprenticeship"
Ibid.

(117) "life and work . . . inseparable"
John Middleton Murry, *Katherine Mansfield and Other Literary
Portraits*, 71.

(118) "made capital out of her death"
Quoted in Claire Tomalin, *Katherine Mansfield*, 240.

(118) "boiling Katherine's bones to make soup"
Quoted in ibid., 241.

(118) "the Greatest of Women . . . someone holy"
Samuel Cron Cronwright-Schreiner, *The Life of Olive Schreiner*, 382; see also
vii, 195, 246.
(121) "Who Alice James . . . have been"
Jean Strouse, "Alice James: A Family Romance," 71.
(121) "her dialogue with the future"
Jean Strouse, *Alice James, A Biography*, 275.
(122) "And what would . . . reminded her"
Ibid., 160.
(122) "hideous . . . ghastly"
Quoted in R.W.B. Lewis, *The Jameses*, 404.
(122-123) "I am being . . . the mind"
Quoted in Burr, ed., *Alice James, Her Brothers, Her Journal*, 252.
(123) "The past [to H.] . . . contrary viewpoint?"
Liz Stanley, *The auto/biographical I*, 7.
(125) "This interwoven story . . . written about"
Mary Anne Caws, *Women of Bloomsbury*, 4.
(125) "I have stated . . . to life"
Ibid.
(126) "Just before her sixtieth . . . have been"
Ibid., 31.
(126-127) "Much of what . . . Vorse's life"
Dee Garrison, "Two Roads Taken," 72
(127) "friendship biography"
Liz Stanley, *The auto/biographical I*, 215.
(127) "a need to conceptualize . . . textual product"
Ibid., 234.
(128) "and myself, her first . . . contemporary"
Margaret Mead, *An Anthropologist at Work*, xvi.
(128-129) "Martha cast her . . . proved life"
Agnes DeMille, *Martha*, 14.
(129) "the tours . . . and life"
Ibid., 271.
(129) "she was old . . . and held"
Ibid., 411.
(129-130) "I became aware . . . existed"
Alice Walker, *In Search of Our Mothers' Gardens*, 83.
(130) "racial health . . . human beings"
Ibid., 85.
(131) "A legacy is . . . dimension"
Melva Joyce Boyd, manuscript of *Discarded Legacy*, unpaged.
(131) "merges from the . . . her work"
Ibid.
(132) "Not to write . . . to open"
Arlyn Diamond, "She Too Had a Dream," 4.

(133) "it is far from . . . her time"
Carolyn Heilbrun, "A Man's Woman," 17.
(134) "a vantage point . . . her subject"
Ibid., 17–18.
(134) "suggest that, beyond . . . her subject"
Ibid., 18.
(135) "one seamless whole"
Virginia Woolf, "The Art of Biography," 229.
(136) "By the time . . . and Scottie"
Nancy Milford, *Zelda*, 154.
(136-137) "You don't even . . . ruin lives"
Quoted in ibid., 155.
(138) "In this adventure . . . for action"
Judith Thurman, *Isak Dinesen*, 106.
(139) "sensuous . . . filled with . . . stories"
Ibid., 186.
(139) "a sublime repair job"
Ibid., 283.
(140) "There were light . . . Harriet Weaver"
Noel Riley Fitch, *Sylvia Beach*, 107.
(140) "kept their sexuality private"
Noel Riley Fitch, "The Elusive 'Seamless Whole,'" 61.
(140) "suppression, invention, and sitting in judgment"
Ibid., 60.
(140-141) "A biographer must . . . circumstantial evidence"
Ibid., 63.
(141) "Margaret Mead was not . . . my teacher"
Jane Howard, *Margaret Mead*, 11.
(141) "The fame she sought . . . most enigmatic"
Ibid., 12.
(142) "a patron saint of the peripheral"
Ibid., 13.
(142) "the world was her field . . . kept to herself"
Ibid., 15.
(142) "Lord knows . . . secular agnostics"
Ibid., 21.
(142) "made a point . . . Mansfield"
Ibid., 317.
(143) "Her greatest forte . . . dovetail"
Ibid., 429.
(143) "Mead's sin, she . . . weep"
Ibid., 439.
(143) "Lord knows she . . . did well, too"
Ibid., 441.
(144) "By the time . . . lyric poet"
Elizabeth Frank, *Louise Bogan*, 45.

(144) "Severe psychic pain . . . free of him"
   Ibid., 51.
(144) "Bogan's insights into . . . impatient"
   Ibid., 650.
(144) "Had Bogan's journal . . . continuity"
   Ibid., 111.
(145) "If Sartre already . . . real philosopher"
   Quoted in Deirdre Bair, *Simone de Beauvoir*, 145.
(145) "constant, rigid control"
   Ibid., 169.
(145-146) "She would drink . . . their letters"
   Ibid.
(147) "Imes appealed to . . . and affectionate"
   Thadious M. Davis, *Nella Larsen*, unpaged galley proof.
(149-150) "feminist books never win awards"
   Carolyn Heilbrun, Letter, 4.
(152) "the very personification . . . dream"
   Lawrence J. Quirk, *Totally Uninhibited*, 13.
(152) "The girl who . . . makeup"
   Ibid., 17.
(154) "privileged information"
   Kitty Kelley, *Nancy Reagan*, 4.
(155) "Then he pulled . . . first one"
   Kitty Kelley, *Elizabeth Taylor*, 257.
(155) "Todd publicized . . . that tiara"
   Ibid., 94.
(156) "Max Lerner gave . . . the sexual"
   Ibid., 141.
(156) "Taylor's image changed . . . to marry"
   Brenda Maddox, *Who's Afraid of Elizabeth Taylor?* 139.
(156-157) "Elizabeth Taylor has . . . mystical power"
   Ibid., 237.
(157-158) "He was twenty-five . . . flamboyant exterior"
   Elizabeth Taylor, *Elizabeth Takes Off*, 71–72.
(159) "a world of difference"
   Barbara Johnson, *A World of Difference*, 2–4.
(159) "The more it . . . its domain"
   Sidonie Smith and Julia Watson, *De/Colonizing the Subject*, xviii.
(160) "noncelebratory histories"
   James Clifford and George E. Marcus, eds., *Writing Culture*, 11.
(161) "Because when . . . get married"
   Elinor Langer, *Josephine Herbst*, 86.
(163) "mostly rather grim."
   Claire Tomalin, *Invisible Woman*, 190.
(163) "Inevitably it is . . . more obscure"
   Ibid., 129.

(165) "I know: I . . . an individual"
Susan Fromberg Schaeffer, *First Nights*, 58.
(165) "I don't know . . . you recognized them"
Ibid., 53.
(165-166) "I used to love . . . horizon"
Ibid., 75.
(166) "Now I am . . . bolt of cloth"
Ibid., 500.
(166) "We cannot live without words"
Ibid., 10.
(166) "It is the conception . . . most profoundly"
Susan Fromberg Schaeffer to author, June 23, 1993.
(166) "I leave myself out . . . story teller"
Susan Fromberg Schaeffer, *First Nights*, 50.
(167) "peculiarly reciprocal relationship . . . The biographer . . . literary power "
Dee Garrison, "Two Roads Taken," 68.
(167) "inevitably . . . do play . . . our own agendas"
Emily Toth, "The Shadow of the First Biographer," 292.
(167) "appropriation"
Interview with Phyllis Rose in Gail Porter Mandell, ed., *Life into Art*, 113.
(167) "approximation . . . self . . . certain facts"
Interview with Arnold Rampersad in Gail Porter Mandell, ed., *Life into Art*, 63.
(169) "There is no . . . women's lives"
Emily Toth, "The Shadow of the First Biographer," 292.
(169) "remembrance . . . heart"
Beryl Markham, *West with the Night*, 3.

Bibliography

Alexander, Meena. *Women in Romanticism: Mary Wollstonecraft, Dorothy Words-worth and Mary Shelley*. London: Macmillan, 1989.

Alpern, Sara, Joyce Antler, Elisabeth Israels Perry, and Ingrid Winther Sco-bie, eds. *The Challenge of Feminist Biography: Writing the Lives of Modern Ameri-can Women*. Urbana: U of Illinois P, 1992.

Anderson, Linda. *Remembered Futures: Women and Autobiography in the Twentieth Century*. New York: St. Martin's, 1993.

Angelou, Maya. *I Know Why the Caged Bird Sings*. New York: Random House, 1969.

Ascher, Carol, Louise DeSalvo, and Sara Ruddick, eds. *Between Women: Biog-raphers, Novelists, Critics, Teachers and Artists Write about Their Work on Women*. Boston: Beacon, 1984.

Atlas, James. "Choosing a Life." *New York Times Book Review*, January 13, 1991, 1, 22–23.

Bair, Deirdre. *Simone de Beauvoir*. New York: Summit, 1990.

Bateson, Mary Catherine. *With a Daughter's Eye: A Memoir of Margaret Mead and Gregory Bateson*. New York: Morrow, 1984.

Bell, Susan Groag, and Marilyn Yalom, eds. *Revealing Lives: Autobiography, Biography, and Gender*. Albany: State U of New York P, 1993.

Benstock, Shari. *No Gifts From Chance: A Biography of Edith Wharton*. New York: Scribner's, 1994.

———. *Women of the Left Bank: Paris, 1900–1940*. Austin: U of Texas P, 1986.

——— ed. *The Private Self*. Chapel Hill: U of North Carolina P, 1988.

Bentley, Joanne. *Hallie Flanagan: A Life in the American Theatre*. New York: Knopf, 1988.

Bok, Sissela. *Alva Myrdal: A Daughter's Memoir*. Reading, Mass: Addison-Wesley, 1991.

Boyd, Melva Joyce. *Discarded Legacy: Politics and Poetics in the Life of Frances E. W. Harper, 1825–1911*. Detroit: Wayne State UP, 1994.

Braxton, Joanne M. *Black Women Writing Autobiography: A Tradition Within a Tradition*. Philadelphia: Temple UP, 1989.

Brightman, Carol. *Writing Dangerously: Mary McCarthy and Her World*. New York: Clarkson Potter, 1992.

Brodzki, Bella, and Celeste Schenck. *Life/Lines: Theorizing Women's Autobiog-raphy*. Ithaca, N.Y.: Cornell UP, 1988.

Brownstein, Rachel M. *Tragic Muse: Rachel of the Comédie-Française*. New York: Knopf, 1993.

Burr, Anna Robeson, ed. *Alice James, Her Brothers, Her Journal.* New York: Dodd, Mead, 1934.

Caws, Mary Ann. *Women of Bloomsbury: Virginia, Vanessa, and Carrington.* New York: Routledge, 1990.

Chernin, Kim. *In My Mother's House: A Daughter's Story.* New York: Ticknor and Fields, 1983.

Chesler, Ellen. *Woman of Valor: Margaret Sanger and the Birth Control Movement in America.* New York: Simon and Schuster, 1992.

Chesler, Phyllis. *Women and Madness.* Garden City, N.Y.: Doubleday, 1972.

Child, Lydia Maria. *Good Wives.* 1833. Reprint. New York: C. F. Francis, 1859.

Chodorow, Nancy. *Reproduction of Mothering: Psychoanalysis and the Sociology of Gender.* Berkeley: U of California P, 1978.

Cixous, Hélène. *The Exile of James Joyce.* Trans. Sally A. J. Purcell. London: Calder, 1976.

Cliff, Michelle. *Free Enterprise.* New York: Dutton, 1993.

Clifford, James L. *From Puzzles to Portraits: Problems of a Literary Biographer.* Chapel Hill: U of North Carolina P, 1970.

Clifford, James, and George E. Marcus, eds. *Writing Culture: The Poetics and Politics of Ethnography.* Berkeley: U of California P, 1986.

Cohn, Dorrit. "Fictional versus Historical Lives: Borderlines and Borderline Cases." *Journal of Narrative Technique* 19 (1989): 3–24.

Conarroe, Joel. Review of *This Boy's Life. New York Times Book Review,* January 15, 1989, 1.

Cook, Blanche Wiesen. "Biographer and Subject: A Critical Connection." In *Between Women,* ed. Carol Ascher, Louise DeSalvo, and Sara Ruddick, 397–411. Boston: Beacon, 1984.

———. "Books: The Womanly Art of Biography." *Ms.* (January-February 1991): 60–62.

———. *Eleanor Roosevelt, Vol. I, 1884–1933.* New York: Viking, 1992.

Cott, Nancy F. *A Woman Making History: Mary Ritter Beard through Her Letters.* New Haven: Yale UP, 1991.

Cranston, Sylvia. *H.P.B.: The Extraordinary Life and Influence of Helena Blavatsky.* New York: G. P. Putnam's Sons, 1993.

Cronwright-Schreiner, Samuel Cron. *The Life of Olive Schreiner.* London: Unwin, 1924.

Culley, Margo. *Fea[s]ts of Memory: The Autobiographical Writings of American Women.* Madison: U of Wisconsin P, 1992.

Curie, Eve. *Madame Curie, A Biography.* Trans. Vincent Sheean. Garden City, N.Y: Doubleday, Doran, 1937.

Daly, Mary. *Gyn-Ecology: The Metaethics of Radical Feminism.* Boston: Beacon, 1978.

———. *Webster's First New Intergalactic Wickedary of the English Language.* Boston: Beacon, 1982.

Davidson, Cathy N., and E. M. Broner, eds. *The Lost Tradition: Mothers and Daughters in Literature.* New York: Ungar, 1980.

Davis, Kenneth S. *FDR: The New York Years, 1928–1933*. New York: Random House, 1985.

Davis, Thadious M. *Nella Larsen, Novelist of the Harlem Renaissance: A Woman's Life Unveiled*. Baton Rouge: Louisiana State UP, 1994.

DeMille, Agnes. *Martha, The Life and Work of Martha Graham*. New York: Random House, 1991.

DeSalvo, Louise A. *Virginia Woolf: The Impact of Childhood Sexual Abuse on Her Life and Work*. Boston: Beacon, 1989.

Diamond, Arlyn. "She Too Had a Dream." *Women's Review of Books* (April 1993): 1, 3–4.

Diliberto, Gioia. *Hadley*. New York: Ticknor and Fields, 1992.

Dillon, Millicent. *After Egypt: Isadora Duncan and Mary Cassatt*. New York: Dutton, 1990.

Dinesen, Isak. "The Blank Page." In *The Norton Anthology of Literature by Women*, ed. Sandra Gilbert and Susan Gubar, 1418–1423. New York: Norton, 1985.

———. *Out of Africa and Shadows on the Grass*. 1937. Reprint. New York: Vintage, 1989.

Dodd, Valerie A. *George Eliot: An Intellectual Life*. London: Macmillan, 1990.

Drabble, Margaret. *Virginia Woolf: A Personal Debt; An Essay*. New York: Aloe, 1973.

Edel, Leon. "Biography and the Science of Man." In *New Directions in Biography*, ed. Anthony M. Friedson, 1–11. A Biography Monograph. Honolulu: UP of Hawaii, 1981.

———. *Writing Lives: Principia Biographica*. New York: Norton, 1984.

Ehrenreich, Barbara, and Deirdre English. *For Her Own Good: 150 Years of the Experts' Advice to Women*. Garden City, N.Y.: Doubleday, 1978.

Ellet, Elizabeth F. *The Queens of American Society*. New York: Scribner, 1867.

Ellmann, Richard. *James Joyce*. New York: Oxford UP, 1959.

———. *James Joyce*. Rev. ed. New York: Oxford UP, 1982.

Faludi, Susan. *Backlash: The Undeclared War against American Women*. New York: Crown, 1991.

Felski, Rita. *Beyond Feminist Aesthetics: Feminist Literature and Social Change*. Cambridge: Harvard UP, 1989.

First, Ruth, and Ann Scott. *Olive Schreiner*. New York: Schocken, 1980.

Fitch, Noel Riley. "The Elusive 'Seamless Whole': A Biographer Treats (or Fails to Treat) Lesbianism." In *Lesbian Texts and Contexts: Radical Revisions*, ed. Karla Jay and Joanne Glasgow, 59–69. New York: New York UP, 1990.

———. *Sylvia Beach and the Lost Generation*. New York: Norton, 1983.

Forster, Margaret. *Significant Sisters: The Grassroots of Active Feminism 1839–1939*. New York: Knopf, 1985.

Foster, Frances Smith. *Written by Herself: Literary Production of African American Women, 1746–1892*. Bloomington: Indiana UP, 1993.

Frank, Elizabeth. *Louise Bogan: A Portrait*. New York: Knopf, 1985.

Frank, Katherine. *A Chainless Soul: A Life of Emily Brontë*. Boston: Houghton Mifflin, 1990.

Fraser, Rebecca. *The Brontës: Charlotte Brontë and Her Family*. New York: Crown, 1988.

Friday, Nancy. *My Mother/My Self: The Daughter's Search for Identity*. New York: Delacorte, 1977.

Garrison, Dee. *Mary Heaton Vorse*. Philadelphia: Temple UP, 1989.

———. "Two Roads Taken: Writing the Biography of Mary Heaton Vorse." In *The Challenge of Feminist Biography*, ed. Sara Alpern, Joyce Antler, Elizabeth Israels Perry, and Ingrid Winther Scobie, 65–78. Urbana: U of Illinois P, 1992.

Gelles, Edith B. *Portia: The World of Abigail Adams*. Bloomington: Indiana UP, 1992.

George, Susanna K. *The Adventures of the Woman Homesteader: Life and Letters of Elinore Pruitt Stewart*. Lincoln: U of Nebraska P, 1992.

Gilbert, Sandra M., and Susan Gubar. *The Madwoman in the Attic*. New Haven: Yale UP, 1979.

Gilligan, Carol. *In a Different Voice: Psychological Theory and Women's Development*. Cambridge: Harvard UP, 1982.

Gilman, Charlotte Perkins. "The Yellow Wallpaper." In *The Heath Anthology of American Literature*, vol. 2, 761–773. Lexington, Mass.: Heath, 1990.

Gimbel, Wendy. Review of *Fierce Attachments*. *The Nation* 224 (April 25, 1987): 549.

Gittelson, Brenda. *Biography*. New York: Knopf, 1991.

Givner, Joan. *Katherine Ann Porter: A Life*. New York: Simon and Schuster, 1982.

———. *The Self-Portrait of a Literary Biographer*. Athens: U of Georgia P, 1994.

Glasgow, Ellen. *The Woman Within*. New York: Harcourt, Brace, 1954.

Glendinning, Victoria. "Lies and Silences." In *The Troubled Face of Biography*, ed. Eric Homberger and John Charmley, 49–62. New York: St. Martin's, 1988.

———. *Vita: The Life of V. Sackville-West*. London: Weidenfeld and Nicolson, 1983.

Gornick, Vivian. *Fierce Attachments, A Memoir*. New York: Farrar, Straus, 1987.

Grattan, Clinton Hartley. *The Three Jameses, A Family of Minds: Henry James, Sr., William James, Henry James*. 1932. Reprint. New York: New York UP, 1962.

Green, Rayna. "High Cotton." In *That's What She Said: Contemporary Poetry and Fiction by Native American Women*, ed. Rayna Green, 119–124. Bloomington: Indiana UP, 1984.

Greer, Germaine. *Daddy, We Hardly Knew You*. London: Hamish Hamilton, 1989.

Griffin, Susan. *Woman and Nature*. New York: Harper and Row, 1978.

Haberman, Ruth. *Modernizing Lives: Experiments in English Biography, 1918–1939*. Carbondale: Southern Illinois UP, 1987.

Haight, Gordon S. *George Eliot, A Biography*. New York: Oxford UP, 1968.

Heilbrun, Carolyn G. "A Man's Woman." *Women's Review of Books* (January 1993): 17–18.

————. "Letter." *Women's Review of Books* (April 1993): 4.

————. *Writing a Woman's Life*. New York: Norton, 1988.

Hellman, Lillian. *Maybe*. Boston: Little, Brown, 1980.

————. *Pentimento*. Boston: Little, Brown, 1973.

Herrmann, Dorothy. *Anne Morrow Lindbergh: A Gift for Life*. New York: Ticknor and Fields, 1993.

Hiatt, Mary. *The Way Women Write*. New York: Teachers College P, 1977.

Hirsch, Marianne. *The Mother/Daughter Plot: Narrative, Psychoanalysis, Feminism*. Bloomington: Indiana UP, 1989.

Homberger, Eric, and John Charmley, eds. *The Troubled Face of Biography*. New York: St. Martin's, 1988.

Honan, Park. *Authors' Lives*. New York: St. Martin's, 1990.

Howard, Jane. *Margaret Mead, A Life*. New York: Simon and Schuster, 1984.

Howe, Julia Ward. *Margaret Fuller*. London: W. H. Allen, 1889.

Hunt, Violet. *The Wife of Rossetti: Her Life and Death (Elizabeth Eleanor Siddal)*. New York: Dutton, 1932.

Hurlbert, Ann. *The Interior Castle: The Art and Life of Jean Stafford*. New York: Knopf, 1992.

Iles, Teresa, ed. *All Sides of the Subject: Women and Biography*. New York: Teachers College P, 1992.

Ione, Carole. *Pride of Family: Four Generations of American Women of Color*. New York: Summit, 1991.

Irigaray, Luce. *Speculum of the Other Woman*. Trans. Gillian C. Gill. Ithaca, N.Y.: Cornell UP, 1985.

Irving, John. Review of *The Duke of Deception*. *New York Times Book Review*, August 12, 1979, 1.

Jardine, Alice. *Gynesis: Configurations of Women and Modernity*. Ithaca, N.Y.: Cornell UP, 1985.

Jelinek, Estelle C. *The Tradition of Women's Autobiography: From Antiquity to the Present*. Boston: Twayne, 1986.

————, ed. *Women's Autobiography: Essays in Criticism*. Bloomington: Indiana UP, 1980.

Johnson, Barbara. *A World of Difference*. Baltimore: Johns Hopkins UP, 1987.

Jones, Kathleen. *Learning Not To Be First: The Life of Christina Rossetti*. Moreton-in-Marsh, Gloucestershire: Windrush P, 1991.

Kakutani, Michiko. "Fiction? Nonfiction? And Why Doesn't Anybody Care?" *New York Times*, July 27, 1993, Bl, 8.

Kelley, Kitty. *Elizabeth Taylor: The Last Star*. London: Michael Joseph, 1981.

————. *Nancy Reagan: The Unauthorized Biography*. New York: Simon and Schuster, 1991.

Kolodny, Annette. "A Map for Rereading: Or, Gender and the Interpretation of Literary Texts." *New Literary History* 11 (1980): 451–467.

Kristeva, Julia. *Desire in Language: A Semiotic Approach to Literature and Art*. Trans. Leon S. Roudiez, Alice Jardine, and Thomas Gora. New York: Columbia UP, 1980.

Langer, Elinor. *Josephine Herbst*. Boston: Little, Brown, 1984.

Lash, Joseph P. *Eleanor and Franklin*. New York: Norton, 1971.
———. *A World of Love: Eleanor Roosevelt and Her Friends, 1943–1962*. Garden City, N.Y.: Doubleday, 1984.
Leckie, Shirley A. *Elizabeth Bacon Custer: And the Making of a Myth*. Norman: U of Oklahoma P, 1993.
Ledbetter, Susan. *Nellie Cashman, Prospector and Trailblazer*. College Station: Texas A&M UP, 1993.
Leonardi, Susan J. *Dangerous by Degrees: Women at Oxford and the Somerville College Novelists*. New Brunswick, N.J.: Rutgers UP, 1989.
Levin, Phyllis Lee. *Abigail Adams*. New York: St. Martin's, 1987.
Lewis, R.W.B. *Edith Wharton, A Biography*. New York: Harper and Row, 1975.
———. *The Jameses: A Family Narrative*. New York: Farrar, Straus, 1991.
Lindbergh, Anne Morrow. *Bring Me a Unicorn: Diaries and Letters, 1922–1928*. New York: Harcourt, Brace, Jovanovich, 1972.
———. *Hour of Gold, Hour of Lead: Diaries and Letters, 1929–1932*. New York: Harcourt, Brace, Jovanovich, 1973.
———. *Locked Rooms and Open Doors: Diaries and Letters, 1933–1935*. New York: Harcourt, Brace, Jovanovich, 1974.
Linde, Charlotte. *Life Stories: The Creation of Coherence*. New York: Oxford UP, 1993.
Lionnet, Françoise. *Autobiographical Voices: Race, Gender, Self-Portraiture*. Ithaca, N.Y.: Cornell UP, 1989.
Lipton, Eunice. *Alias Olympia*. New York: Scribner's, 1993.
Lomask, Milton. *The Biographer's Craft*. New York: Harper and Row, 1986.
Lovell, Mary S. *Straight on Till Morning: The Biography of Beryl Markham*. London: Hutchinson, 1987.
Lutzeler, Paul Michael. "Fictionality in Historiography and the Novel." In *Neverending Stories, Toward a Critical Narratology*, ed. Ann Fehn, Ingeborg Hoesterey, and Maria Tatar, 29–44. Princeton, N.J.: Princeton UP, 1992.
Maddox, Brenda. *Nora: A Biography of Nora Joyce*. London: Hamish Hamilton, 1988.
———. *Who's Afraid of Elizabeth Taylor?* New York: M. Evans, 1977.
Malcolm, Janet. "Annals of Biography: Sylvia Plath, The Silent Woman." *The New Yorker* (August 23/30, 1993): 84–159.
Mandell, Gail Porter, ed. *Life Into Art: Conversations with Seven Contemporary Biographers*. Fayetteville: U of Arkansas P, 1991.
Markham, Beryl. *West with the Night*. 1942. Reprint. San Francisco: North Point P, 1983.
Matthiessen, F. O. *The James Family*. New York: Knopf, 1947.
Mead, Margaret. *Blackberry Winter: My Earlier Years*. New York: Morrow, 1972.
———, ed. *An Anthropologist at Work: Writings of Ruth Benedict*. New York: Atherton, 1966.
Meyers, Jeffrey. *Katherine Mansfield, A Biography*. New York: New Directions, 1978.
Middlebrook, Diane Wood. *Anne Sexton, A Biography*. New York: Harper and Row, 1990.

Milford, Nancy. *Zelda, A Biography*. New York: Harper and Row, 1970.

Miller, Jean Baker. *Toward a New Psychology of Women*. Boston: Beacon, 1976.

Miller, Nancy K. *Getting Personal*. New York: Routledge, Chapman and Hall, 1991.

————, ed. *The Poetics of Gender*. New York: Columbia UP, 1986.

Mills, Kay. *This Little Light of Mine*. New York: Dutton, 1993.

Milton, Joyce. *Loss of Eden: A Biography of Charles and Anne Morrow Lindbergh*. New York: HarperCollins, 1993.

Mitchell, Juliet. *Psychoanalysis and Feminism*. New York: Vintage, 1974.

Moers, Ellen. *Literary Women: The Great Writers*. Garden City, N.Y.: Doubleday, 1976.

Murry, John Middleton. *Katherine Mansfield and Other Literary Portraits*. London: Constable, 1959.

Nadel, Ira Bruce. *Biography, Fiction, Fact and Form*. London: Macmillan, 1984.

Novarr, David. *The Lines of Life: Theories of Biography, 1880–1970*. West Lafayette, Ind.: Purdue UP, 1986.

Oates, Joyce Carol. "Adventures in Abandonment." *New York Times Book Review*, August 28, 1988, 3, 33.

————. Introduction to *The Best American Essays, 1991*, ed. Joyce Carol Oates. New York: Ticknor and Fields, 1991.

O'Brien, Sharon. *Willa Cather: The Emerging Voice*. New York: Oxford UP, 1987.

O'Brien, Tim. Review of *The Duke of Deception*. *Saturday Review*, September 29, 1979, 46.

O'Connor, Ulick. *Biographers and the Art of Biography*. London: Quartet, 1993.

Owen, Ursula, ed. *Fathers: Reflections by Daughters*. London: Virago, 1983.

Pachter, Marc. *Telling Lives: The Biographer's Art*. Washington, D.C.: New Republic Books, 1979.

Pascal, Roy. *Design and Truth in Autobiography*. Cambridge: Harvard UP, 1960.

Personal Narratives Group. *Interpreting Women's Lives: Feminist Theory and Personal Narratives*. Bloomington: Indiana UP, 1989.

Peters, Maureen. *An Enigma of Brontës*. New York: St. Martin's, 1974.

Petrie, Dennis W. *Ultimately Fiction: Design in Modern American Literary Biography*. West Lafayette, Ind.: Purdue UP, 1981.

Pflaum, Rosalynd. *Grand Obsession: Madame Curie and Her World*. Garden City, N.Y.: Doubleday, 1989.

Pogrebin, Letty Cottin. *Deborah, Golda, and Me: Being Female and Jewish in America*. New York: Crown, 1991.

Pratt, Mary Louise. "Fieldwork in Common Places." In *Writing Culture*, ed. James Clifford and George E. Marcus, 27–50. Berkeley: U of California Press, 1986.

Prescott, Peter S. Review of *Patrimony*. *Newsweek*, January 14, 1991, 53.

Pritchard, William H. "'Writers Shouldn't Be Married.'" *New York Times Book Review*, June 21, 1992, 11.

Pratt, Minnie Bruce. "Crime Against Nature." *Crime Against Nature*, 111–120. Ithaca, N.Y.: Firebrand Books, 1990.

Quirk, Lawrence J. *Totally Uninhibited: The Life and Wild Times of Cher.* New York: Morrow, 1991.

Rankin, Daniel. *Kate Chopin and Her Creole Stories.* Philadelphia: U of Pennsylvania P, 1932.

Reagan, Nancy, with William North. *My Turn: The Memoirs of Nancy Reagan.* New York: Random House, 1989.

Rich, Adrienne. *Of Woman Born: Motherhood as Experience and Institution.* New York: Norton, 1976.

———. "Vesuvius at Home: The Power of Emily Dickinson." *On Lies, Secrets, and Silence.* New York: Knopf, 1978.

———. "When We Dead Awaken: Writing as Re-Vision (1971)." *On Lies, Secrets, and Silence.* New York: Knopf, 1978.

Richards, Laura E., and Maude Howe Elliott. *Julia Ward Howe, 1819–1910.* 1916. Reprint. Boston: Houghton Mifflin, 1925.

Roosevelt, Eleanor. *The Autobiography of Eleanor Roosevelt.* New York: Harper and Brothers, 1958.

Rose, Phyllis. *Parallel Lives: Five Victorian Marriages.* New York: Knopf, 1983.

———. "Writing Our Own Lives." *Ms.* (September-October 1993): 76–77.

Rosenberg, Rosalind. "Margaret Mead." In *Portraits of American Women: From Settlement to the Present*, ed. G. J. Barber-Benfield and Catherine Clinton, 527–546. New York: St. Martin's, 1991.

Roth, Philip. *Patrimony, A True Story.* New York: Simon and Schuster, 1991.

Schaeffer, Susan Fromberg. *First Nights.* New York: Knopf, 1993.

Schellinger, Paul, ed. *St. James Guide to Biography.* Chicago: St. James Press, 1991.

Seyersted, Per. *Kate Chopin: A Critical Biography.* Baton Rouge: Louisiana State UP, 1969.

Seymour, Miranda. *Ottoline Morrell: Life on the Grand Scale.* New York: Farrar, Straus, 1993.

Sherwood, Frances. *Vindication.* New York: Farrar, Straus, 1993.

Showalter, Elaine. *The Female Malady: Women, Madness, and English Culture, 1830–1980.* New York: Oxford UP, 1985.

Simpson, Mona. Review of *Fierce Attachments. New York Times Book Review*, April 26, 1987, 7.

Skidelsky, Robert. "Only Connect: Biography and Truth." In *The Troubled Face of Biography*, ed. Eric Homberger and John Charmley, 1–16. New York: St. Martin's, 1988.

Smith, Sidonie. *A Poetics of Women's Autobiography: Marginality and the Fictions of Self-Representation.* Bloomington: Indiana UP, 1987.

———. *Subjectivity, Identity, and the Body.* Bloomington: Indiana UP, 1993.

———, and Julia Watson, eds. *De/Colonizing the Subject: The Politics of Gender in Women's Autobiography.* Minneapolis: U of Minnesota P, 1992.

Smith, Susan Belasco. Review of Capper's *Margaret Fuller. Women's Review of Books* (June 1993): 23.

Smith-Rosenberg, Carroll. *Disorderly Conduct: Visions of Gender in Victorian America.* New York: Oxford UP, 1985.

————. "The Female World of Love and Ritual: Relations between Women in Nineteenth-Century America." *Signs: Journal of Women in Culture and Society* 1 (1975): 1–29.

Sokoloff, Alice Hunt. *Hadley: The First Mrs. Hemingway*. New York: Dodd, Mead, 1973.

Sone, Monica. *Nisei Daughter*. 1953. Reprint. Seattle: U of Washington P, 1979.

Sprague, Rosemary. *George Eliot, A Biography*. Philadelphia: Chilton, 1968.

Spurling, Hilary. *Secrets of a Woman's Heart (Ivy Compton-Burnett)*. New York: Knopf, 1984.

Stanley, Liz. *The auto/biographical I: the theory and practice of feminist auto/biography*. Manchester, England: Manchester UP, 1992.

Stein, Gertrude. *The Autobiography of Alice B. Toklas*. New York: Harcourt, Brace, 1933.

Steinem, Gloria. "Ruth's Song (Because She Could Not Sing It)." *Outrageous Acts and Everyday Rebellions*, 129–146. New York: Holt, Rinehart & Winston, 1983.

Stephen, Leslie. *George Eliot*. London: Macmillan, 1902.

Stetson, Erlene. *Glorying in Tribulation, A Biography of Sojourner Truth*. East Lansing: Michigan State UP, 1994.

Strasberg, Susan. *Marilyn and Me: Sisters, Rivals, Friends*. New York: Warner, 1992.

Strouse, Jean. *Alice James, A Biography*. Boston: Houghton Mifflin, 1980.

————. "Alice James: A Family Romance." In *Psychoanalytic Studies of Biography*, ed. George Moraitis and George H. Pollack, 63–84. Madison, Conn.: International UP, 1987.

Taylor, Anne. *Annie Besant, A Biography*. New York: Oxford UP, 1992.

Taylor, Elizabeth. *Elizabeth Takes Off*. New York: Putnam, 1987.

Taylor, Ina. *George Eliot: Woman of Contradictions*. London: Weidenfeld and Nicolson, 1989.

Thurman, Judith. *Isak Dinesen: The Life of a Storyteller*. New York: St. Martin's, 1982.

Tomalin, Claire. *The Invisible Woman: The Story of Nelly Ternan and Charles Dickens*. New York: Knopf, 1991.

————. *Katherine Mansfield, A Secret Life*. New York: Knopf, 1988.

Toth, Emily. *Kate Chopin, A Life of the Author of "The Awakening."* New York: Morrow, 1990.

————. "The Shadow of the First Biographer." *Southern Review* 26 (April 1990): 285–292.

Trzebinski, Errol. *The Lives of Beryl Markham*. New York: Norton, 1993.

————. *Silence Will Speak*. London: Heinemann, 1977.

Ulrich, Laurel Thatcher. *A Midwife's Tale: The Life of Martha Ballard, Based on Her Diary, 1785–1812*. New York: Knopf, 1991.

Valenti, Patricia D. *To Myself a Stranger: A Biography of Rose Hawthorne Lathrop*. Baton Rouge: Louisiana State UP, 1991.

Wagner-Martin, Linda. *Sylvia Plath, A Biography*. New York: Simon and Schuster, 1987.

Walker, Alice. "Zora Neale Hurston: A Cautionary Tale and a Partisan View" and "Looking for Zora." *In Search of Our Mothers' Gardens: Womanist Prose*, 83–116. New York: Harcourt, Brace, Jovanovich, 1983.

Weinberg, Steve. *Telling the Untold Story: How Investigative Reporters Are Changing the Craft of Biography*. Columbia: U of Missouri P, 1992.

Weintraub, Stanley. *The Four Rossettis: A Victorian Biography*. London: Weybright and Talley, 1977.

Welty, Eudora. *One Writer's Beginnings*. Cambridge: Harvard UP, 1984.

Wharton, Edith. *A Backward Glance*. New York: Scribner's, 1934.

White, Hayden V. *Metahistory: The Historical Imagination in Nineteenth Century Europe*. Baltimore: Johns Hopkins UP, 1973.

Willis, Susan. *Specifying: Black Women Writing the American Experience*. Madison: U of Wisconsin P, 1987.

Wolff, Geoffrey. *The Duke of Deception: Memories of My Father*. New York: Random House, 1979.

Wolff, Tobias. *This Boy's Life, A Memoir*. New York: Atlantic Monthly Press, 1989.

Woolf, Virginia. "The Art of Biography." *The Death of the Moth and Other Essays*, 187–197. New York: Harcourt, Brace & Co., 1942.

———. *Flush*. New York: Harcourt, Brace, 1933.

———. "The New Biography." *Collected Essays*, 229–335. New York: Harcourt, Brace, Jovanovich, 1967.

———. *Orlando, A Biography*. New York: Harcourt, Brace, 1928.

———. *A Room of One's Own*. New York: Harcourt, Brace, and World, 1957.

———. *Three Guineas*. London: Hogarth, 1952.

Yellin, Jean Fagan. *Women and Sisters: The Antislavery Feminists in American Culture*. New Haven: Yale UP, 1989.

Young-Bruehl, Elisabeth. *Hannah Arendt: For Love of the World*. New Haven: Yale UP, 1982.

Zinsser, William, ed. *Extraordinary Lives: The Art and Craft of American Biography*. Boston: Houghton Mifflin, 1986.

———. *Inventing the Truth: The Art and Craft of Memoir*. Boston: Houghton Mifflin, 1987.

Journals

a/b Auto/Biography Studies. U of Kansas Press.

Biography. U of Hawaii Press.

Granta 41, ed. Bill Bruford. *Biography*. New York: Penguin, 1993.

Women's Studies (1991), special issue, Women's Autobiographies.

Index

Ackroyd, Peter, 19
Adams, Abigail, 44, 50–51, 56
Adams, Henry, 5–6, 52
Adams, John, 50–51
Adams, Léonie, 128
Adams, Marion (Clover) Hooper, 5–6, 52, 122
Albee, Edward, *Who's Afraid of Virginia Woolf?*, 156
Alcott, Bronson, 23
Alcott, Louisa May, 2, 23
Alexander, Meena, *Women in Romanticism*, 124
Algren, Nelson, 145
Allen, Paula Gunn, 28, 85
Alvarez, Julia, 28
American literature, 1, 5, 82n
Andersen, Christopher, 154
Anderson, Margaret, 125
Angelou, Maya, 88–91; *I Know Why the Caged Bird Sings*, 90–91
Anthony, Katharine, 2
Anthony, Susan B., 3, 20
Antigone, 22
Antin, Mary, 76
Anzaldúa, Gloria, 85
Arendt, Hannah, 31, 141
Arnow, Harriette, 88–89
Atwood, Margaret, 26, 28
Auerback, Nina, 28
Augur, Helen, 3
Austin, Mary, 76
autobiography, x, 1, 54–57, 60–68, 69–77, 89–91, 95–97, 159, 163

Bair, Deirdre, 141, 145–146, 149
Baker, Josephine, 156
Ballard, Martha, 160
Bambara, Toni Cade, 23
Barnacle, Nora, *see* Joyce, Nora Barnacle
Barnes, Djuna, 89, 125

Barney, Natalie, 125
Bateson, Mary Catherine, 97; *With a Daughter's Eye*, 101–103
Batten, Jean, 63
Beach, Sylvia, 31, 125, 139–141, 149
Beard, Mary Ritter, 160
Beckett, Samuel, *Endgame*, 97
Bell, Vanessa, 125–126
Benedict, Ruth, 124, 127–128; *The Chrysanthemum and The Sword*, 128; *Patterns of Culture*, 128
Benstock, Shari, 21, 115–116; *The Private Self*, 30; *Women of the Left Bank, Paris, 1910–1940*, 125
Bentley, Joanne, *Hallie Flanagan*, 160
Berryman, John, 7
Besant, Annie, 21
Betts, Doris, 26
biography, ix–x, 1–4, 5–10, 38, 78–83, 95–97, 133–134, 149–150, 159–169; "as-told-to," 157; defined, 1, 38, 95–96, 164n; fact in, 9–10, 75; as fiction, 8–9, 162–169; gender differences in, 5–6, 11–19, 69–84, 149–150; history of, 1–6; identity and, 8–9; marginalized subjects of, 130–133; as moral instruction, 1, 5, 10; performance and, 8; popular, 151–158; and public-private controversy, 5–6; as "realist fallacy," 160; role of, x; as success story, 5–6; traditions of, 5–10, 73–75, 111–123, 159–169. *See also* body in biography; ethics of biography; exotic in biography; family biography; feminist biography; friendship biography; sexuality in biography; voice
Blackwell, Alice S., *Lucy Stone*, 3

193

Ternan, Nelly (Ellen), 162–164
Thoreau, Henry David, 144; *Walden*, 82n
Thurman, Judith, 149; *Isak Dinesen, The Life of a Storyteller*, 67, 137–139
Todd, Mike, 155–158
Toklas, Alice B., 12, 73–74, 76, 125
Tomalin, Claire: *The Invisible Woman: The Story of Nelly Ternan and Charles Dickens*, 162–163; *Katherine Mansfield, A Secret Life*, 117, 118
Toth, Emily, 31, 112–114, 167, 169; *Kate Chopin*, 31, 113–114
travel narrative, 1
Truman, Harry, 20, 21
Trump, Donald, 6
Truth, Sojourner, 132
Trzebinski, Errol, 64–65, 67; *The Lives of Beryl Markham*, 64; *Silence Will Speak*, 67
Tucker, Susan, *Telling Memories among Southern Women*, 91
Tyler, Anne, 23, 26

Ulrich, Laurel Thatcher, *A Midwife's Tale: The Life of Martha Ballard*, 160
utopian narratives, 29

Valenti, Patricia D., *To Myself a Stranger: A Biography of Rose Hawthorne Lathrop*, 160
Viramontes, Helene María, 28
voice, 30, 111–123, 126–127, 166–169
Vorse, Mary Heaton, 126–127

Wagenknecht, Edward C., *Jenny Lind*, 2
Walker, Alice, x, 26, 127, 129–130, 133; *The Color Purple*, 28; *In Search of Our Mothers' Gardens*, 130; *Possessing the Secret of Joy*, 28
Walton, Izaak, *Life of John Donne*, 1
Watson, Julia, 159
Weinberg, Sydney Stahl, *The World of Our Mothers*, 91

Weintraub, Stanley, *The Four Rossettis*, 120
Welty, Eudora, 85, 88–89
Wharton, Edith, x, 26, 75–76, 77, 87–88, 114–116, 125; *A Backward Glance*, 75–76; "Her Son," 26; "The Journey," 116; "Joy in the House," 26; "The Lamp of Psyche," 116; *A Mother's Recompense*, 26; *The Valley of Decision*, 116
White, Edmund, 20
White, Hayden, *Metahistory*, 80–81
Whitman, Walt, *Leaves of Grass*, 82n
Wilde, Oscar, 20
Wilkerson, Margaret, 132
Willis, Susan, 29
Wilson, Edmund, 23
Wivel, Ole, *Romance for Valdhorn*, 67
wives as biographical subjects, 27, 43, 44–62, 151
Wolfe, Thomas, 20
Wolff, Geoffrey, 95–97; *The Duke of Deception*, 95
Wolff, Tobias, 95–97; *This Boy's Life*, 95
Wollstonecraft, Mary, 38, 124, 128, 164
"women's sentence," 88
Woolf, Leonard, 22, 126
Woolf, Virginia, x, 7, 11, 12, 31, 33, 74–75, 80–81, 94, 109, 125–126, 127, 135, 142; "The Art of Biography," 75; *Flush*, 74–75; *Jacob's Room*, 88; *Journal of Mistress Joan Martyn*, 75; *Mrs. Dalloway*, 88; *Orlando*, 75; *A Room of One's Own*, 22, 27; *Three Guineas*, 22; *To the Lighthouse*, 88
Wordsworth, Dorothy, 121, 124
writing by women, x, xi, 82–84. *See also* stories

Yamamoto, Hisaye, 28
Yellin, Jean Fagan, *Women and Sisters*, 125
Yezierska, Anzia, 22–23, 76, 101
Young-Bruehl, Elisabeth, *Hannah Arendt*, 31, 141

About the Author

Linda Wagner-Martin (formerly Wagner) is Hanes Professor of English and Comparative Literature at the University of North Carolina, Chapel Hill. The author or editor of many books in modern American literature, she has been a president of the Society for the Study of Narrative Technique and currently serves as president of the Ernest Hemingway Foundation. She has been a Bunting Institute fellow, a Guggenheim fellow, and the recipient of grants from the National Endowment for the Humanities, the Rockefeller Foundation, the American Philosophical Society, and ACLS, as well as institutional and state awards for teaching and leadership. A former editor of *The Centennial Review*, Wagner-Martin serves on the editorial boards of *Studies in American Fiction, American Poetry, Modern Fiction Studies, Narrative, Resources for American Literary Study, Papers in Language and Literature, The Hemingway Review*, and other journals. A member of the *D. C. Heath American Literature Anthology* team, she is coeditor of *The Oxford Companion to Women's Writing in the United States* (1994) and its accompanying anthology of women's writing. Her biographies include books on Ellen Glasgow, Sylvia Plath, and most recently Gertrude Stein.

(continued from front flap)

as partial invention, she weighs the possibilities of ever achieving a true depiction of a life and outlines the responsibility of the biographer and the art of biographical writing.

As an accomplished biographer herself, Wagner-Martin weaves comments about her experiences writing about Sylvia Plath, Ellen Glasgow, John Dos Passos, and, most recently, Gertrude Stein throughout her discussion. Her point of view is always illuminating, lively, and readable.

Telling Women's Lives is the first overview of the writing and the history of biographies about women. It is a significant contribution to the reassessment of the work of the hundreds of women writers who have made a difference in our conception of what women's stories—and women's lives—have been, and are becoming. The book is a must-read for anyone who loves reading biographies, particularly biographies of women.